EVA HESSE

Lucy R. Lippard

New York ● New York University Press ● 1976

To Eva Hesse and the friends who supported her,
and to Robert Smithson, who was one of them.

Library of Congress Catalog Card Number: 76-17380

ISBN: 0-8147-4971-2 (cloth)
       0-8147-4972-0 (paper)

Manufactured by Imprimeries Reunies, Switzerland

.39

CONTENTS

ACKNOWLEDGEMENTS

I have a great many people to thank for cooperation in the writing of this book, first among them the artist's family, especially her sister, Helen Hesse Charash; her friend and dealer—Donald Droll; and the designers of the book—Sol LeWitt and Pat Steir. Others who gave generously of time, encouragement and critical comment are Tom Doyle, Linda Shearer, Gioia Timpanelli, Ethelyn Honig, Naomi Spector, Nancy Graves, Angela Westwater, Xavier Fourcade, and Carole Gallagher. Cindy Nemser's extensive interview with Eva Hesse has been, with Hesse's own writings, a major source, and I am especially grateful for her permission to use it.

The following people talked to me about Hesse and her work, or lent materials and/or memories which were immensely helpful: Nancy Holt and the late Robert Smithson, Ruth Vollmer, Mel Bochner, Grace Bakst Wapner, Rosie and Norman Goldman, Bill Barrette, Douglas Johns, Martha Schieve, David Magasis, Irving Petlin, Camille Norman, Ellen Leelike Becker, Sylvia Stone, Dorothy James, Dr. and Mrs. Samuel Dunkell, Marilyn Fischbach, Robert Ryman, Richard Serra, Ellis Haizlip, Robert Slutzky, Regina Trapp, Dr. William Schapiro, and Rick Finnegan of M. Knoedler & Co.

I also want to thank Susan Ginsburg for her exhaustive chronology, catalogue, and bibliography; Joan Simon for her kind but expert editing; Poppy Johnson and Karen Smith for typing the resulting mess; Sara Slavin for assisting the designer; and Charles Simonds for constant criticism and support.

Because this is not a full-scale biography, but a book about art, it has been impossible to mention Hesse's many personal and/or professional friends in and out of the art world; nor has any attempt been made to reproduce or catalogue all existing paintings and drawings since the focus here is on the sculpture. Owners of the sculpture are listed in the sculpture catalogue at the back of the book, rather than in the captions.

L.R.L.

Contingent, 1968–69, fiberglass and latex on cheesecloth, 8 units, each 9½–11′ x 3–4′.

Between the fall of 1965 and her death at thirty-four in May 1970, Eva Hesse made some 70 sculptures and many more drawings which have assured her place as a major artist. This was what she wanted: to be a major artist and to be acknowledged as such. She knew she was "good" even before her work had matured. By the time she died she had had the satisfaction of knowing that others shared that knowledge. She would have been gratified by the exhibition of her work at the Guggenheim Museum in New York in 1972, which traveled to other museums throughout the United States; by the reviews (at least by those which treated her as an artist rather than a tragic female stereotype), and by the homage paid that show by her fellow artists. The full range of work was even more impressive than many of her friends had realized.

I have a confidence in my understanding of formal esthetics and I don't want to be aware of it or make that my problem. That is not the problem. Those things are solvable. I solved them beautifully. What makes a tight circle or a tight little square box more of an intellectual statement than something done emotionally, I don't know. Art is an essence, a center. I am interested in solving an unknown factor of art and an unknown factor of life. My life and art have not been separated. They have been together.[1]

The sheer density of Hesse's confrontation with the materials of her life and her art seems to have invested that art with an extra-esthetic force—almost a nervous tremor that manifested itself formally as well as emotionally. Thus a formal reading of her work may be useful on one level, but it is necessarily dependent on a psychological reading, which in turn is dependent on the effect made by that form on the viewer, who must always remember that it tends to be one's *own* reading, not the artist's. This poses a particular problem with Hesse's work, since she herself was much given to psychological self-insight and self-discussion. In psychoanalysis most of her adult life, obsessed with the bizarre events of her childhood, she was aware of the implications of all her actions as part of her internal history. While she herself could joke, for instance, about the sexual images in some of her earlier work, and could enjoy relaxed and honest associational readings from a friend, she was wary of being publicly categorized as some sort of Surrealist or psychic abstractionist, as she would have been, had she lived longer, of being some sort of woman artist. In fact, her life and her art were so close that she did not concentrate on any specific content while she was making a piece: "First, when I work, it's only the abstract qualities I'm working with, which is the material, the form it's going to take, the size, the scale, the positioning, where it comes from—the ceiling or the floor," she explained to Cindy Nemser early in 1970. "However, I don't value the totality of the image on these abstract or esthetic points. For me it's a total image that has to do with me and life. It can't be divorced because I don't believe art can be based on an idea of composition or form. In fact, my idea is to counteract everything I've ever learned or been taught about those things, to find something else, so it is inevitable that it is my life, my feeling, my thoughts. . . . I'm not a simple person. The content is greatest on that level—the total absurdity of life in that sense—and it's probably increased because I've been so sick for this year. . . . If something is absurd, it's much more exaggerated, more absurd if it's repeated. . . . Repetition does enlarge or increase or exaggerate an idea or purpose in a statement."

The absurdity Hesse talked about so often could absorb pathos but was never sentimental; this characterized the artist as well as her work. I described her sculpture in 1966 as "both strong and vulnerable, tentative and expansive." Her stepmother said it sounded like a description of Eva herself. I did not then, nor will I in this book, hesitate to "read into" Hesse's work my knowledge of Hesse herself. She was a close friend for many years, and it would be a futile exercise, as well as something of a rejection, to attempt to ignore that knowledge. At the same time, it is clear that others, friends as well as those who know only the work, whose subjective reactions to Hesse differ from mine, will disagree. Rather than impose my personal view so consistently, I will quote, perhaps more than seems necessary, from her own and other people's reactions, so that the reader can construct his or her own image. To make this book personal at all was a difficult decision; since her death Hesse's memory has been exploited even by those writers who purported to be seriously discussing her art. In view of this, I began with a hyper-awareness that the only way to write about Hesse was to tread a fine and dangerous line between the art and the life—to emulate, in other words, the "edge" she spoke of walking herself.

Eva's work was very rational, but a struggle, with irrational forces threading through it. I think I was most interested in her perception of the world, her outlook. There was an understanding of the more troubled areas, a kind of natural comprehension–not sentimental—but sort of facing them. She had no external notion of a world outside of hers. I saw her as a very interior person making psychic models (Robert Smithson).[2]

1936–1959

Hesse was born in Hamburg, Germany on January 11, 1936. To escape Nazi pogrom on November 10, 1938, she and her older sister Helen were sent on a children's train to Holland, where they remained in a Catholic children's home for a few months until their parents were able to come for them. From there they went to relatives in London, and then with the aid of other relatives, to New York, arriving June 23, 1939. Eva's childhood, until she was about 12 years old, was documented by her father in a series of journals he kept for both children, which included photographs, narratives, newspaper clippings, memorabilia, and day-to-day accounts. These were to have a great effect on the artist, who began keeping diaries of her own in her early teens in which she often referred to herself in the third person. They may also have established her near-obsession with autobiography, or with the past. "Her emotional soil was not of the present," one friend recalls, while another never went to Hesse's house "without a memento from the past being brought out. . . . She fed off that material; its physical presence maybe filled some of the voids in her life."

In New York the family stayed at first with Ernst Englander, one of their sponsors and later a collector of Hesse's work, then moved to 639 West 170th Street, in Washington Heights. Wilhelm Hesse, educated as a criminal lawyer, could not continue his profession here and had to begin his training all over again as an insurance broker. The events of the war years severely depressed Ruth Marcus Hesse, and six years later, after a separation and divorce, she took her own life. Hesse's father had remarried in the meantime, and the family continued to live on West 170th Street. Both children did well in local public schools, Hesse receiving "honor awards" all through Junior High, although her lowest grades were in art and

1. Eva Hesse as a school girl.

sewing. Her teen-age diaries, however, reflect frequent misery and anxiety, which as an adult she tended to emphasize as a formative factor on both her art and her personality. Helen, whom the artist called her "healthy sister," was to recall their childhood in far less traumatic terms.

Hesse decided to be an artist early in life. In June 1952, she graduated from the (high) School of Industrial Arts (after being elected the "Most Beautiful Girl in the Senior Class"). In September, following the example of her friend Walter Erlebacher, she entered Pratt Institute to take an "advertising design course." She didn't like it. "The only painting I knew, and that was very little, was Abstract Expressionism, and at Pratt they didn't stress painting at all. . . . I was also very much younger, at least emotionally, than everybody else, as well as chronologically—there were many GI's. . . . I waited until I was getting A's instead of C's and declared I was quitting. I had to know that it wasn't because I wasn't doing well. I quit in the middle of the year [December 1953]. I had lived away from home but now I had to go back and as soon as I got there they said get a job. Where do you go for a job at sixteen and a half knowing very little, but having an interest in Art? So I took myself to *Seventeen Magazine,* and for some strange reason, they hired me. I think it was just because of the 'gall' of coming up there." The job was part-time; three afternoons a week she studied figure drawing from the model at the Art Students League in a class without a teacher. "The days I didn't do that I went to the Museum of Modern Art and went to the movies." She also took the entrance examination for Cooper Union, was accepted, and began the program in September 1954.

The same month a color-illustrated article was published on her in *Seventeen's* "All Yours" section. The prints, watercolors, and gouaches which appear there are skillful if prosaic, ranging from straight representation to semi-abstract to semi-Cubist works displaying several different touches and styles, the most interesting in view of her later work being a glowering lithograph called *Subway* (fig. 2) in which highlighted faces are brought out of a heavy black wash of gloom. (It was her first lithograph.) The statements accompanying the work are touchingly naive: "The 'Tree' stood alone, straight and firm like so many, and I tried to compare it to human beings. I did it at camp between basketball and swimming . . . 'Mother and Child' has a light tone. I used circular movement and shapes to portray the bond of love." She is quoted as saying that she feels "growing up with people who went through the ordeal of those Nazi years makes [her] look very closely—very seriously —beneath the surface of things . . . 'For me being an artist means to see, to observe, to investigate . . . I paint what I see and feel to express life in all its reality and movement.' "

It was around this time, still in her mid teens, that Hesse wrote a letter to her father in which she told him that she had chosen to be an artist: "Daddy, I want to do more than just exist, to live happily and contented with a home, children, to do the same chores everyday." She was already intensely ambitious, seeking in art a means to escape her own immaturity and the emotional turmoil of her life. And she already inspired in her friends and family an intense admiration, devotion, and protectiveness. Very pretty, capable of great charm, but always a little sad and unsure of herself, with difficulties relating to her peers, Hesse's need to be loved was logically exaggerated. From art school until her death, the search for interwoven emotional and intellectual maturity became a repeated theme in her diaries. Her romantic or existential view of the artist as a socially isolated misfit with a spiritual duty to integrate his or her art into society was modified but never wholly erased by real experience of the art world after school.

While in school she wrote: "the degree to which I become a 'painter' is synonymous with what I make of myself as a person. . . . In effect the person I am is a result of what I encounter, perceive and learn. Further insight gained will result in positive attitudes enabling one to become a productive person not isolated from outside influence."

At Cooper Union, Hesse received a stipend from a Jewish agency. She lived first on East 6th Street, and in her second year moved to the Judson Student House, working summers at the Educational Alliance and Camp Lebanon, where she had earlier been a camper. In retrospect, she remembered "loving Cooper from the start," but her diaries show certain dissatisfactions. In March 1955, she wrote, "I felt this week I really wanted to leave art school as I discovered we don't really learn here. Here we have just to work. . . . Just to paint and discuss the painting is not enough." She studied with Nicholas Marsicano, Victor Candell, Will Barnet, Robert Gwathmey and Neil Welliver, though "they had absolutely nothing to do with her development except for Welliver, who taught an Albers-oriented color course and really *jarred* all of us," Camille Reubin Norman recalls. Another classmate remembers Cooper then as "a little Cézanne school." A good deal of work from Hesse's school years has been kept, but for the most part it is undated and not of great interest except for the premonitions it provides of her mature work, perceptible only with hindsight. There are conventional figure drawings and still lifes from Pratt and the Art Students League. There are drawings from Cooper, "a combination of academic figure drawing and abstract expressionism." There are very few landscapes, some Picassoid drawings, Cézannesque lithographs, undistinguished etchings, some lovely collages and photoprints—circles and tree branches emerging from black grounds (fig. 3). Hesse was an accomplished draughtsman from the beginning and "had instinctively a 'beautiful' color sense" (C. R. Norman). The most interesting aspect of her student work as a whole is what seems to have been a predilection for "painting out" around shapes, and for a wandering, tentative, string-like line. A Cooper drawing of ladders, pipes, and a washbowl could, purely coincidentally, be a sketch for the 1966 sculpture *Laocoon*. All of these characteristics found their first major outlet in the wash and ink drawings of 1960–61.

2. Subway, 1954, lithograph, reproduced in *Seventeen Magazine*, September 1954.

3. Photogram, c. 1957, 13⅞ x 11", Fourcade, Droll, Inc., New York.

3a. Untitled, c. 1954, charcoal, 12 x 15″, Dr. Helene Papanek, New York.
4. Italy No. 5, 1956, oil on canvas, 34 x 48″, whereabouts unknown.

At the end of three years at Cooper Union, Hesse received a scholarship to Yale's summer art school at Norfolk, Connecticut and entered the Yale School of Art and Architecture in the fall of 1957, leaving with a Bachelor of Fine Arts in 1959. "I didn't like it very well, but I stayed—a combination of being afraid to get out of school because that was frightening, and of being defeated. . . . I did well there but the schools depend both on faculty and students and the faculty really was very poor. . . . I don't know that the students were bad but they immediately responded to the tension and friction and uninterest. Albers was past Yale's retirement age but was allowed to remain because they had no one to replace him, and Rico LeBrun and Bernard Chait fought each other through us. The result was that the work wasn't very good." She took Josef Albers' color course and was his favorite student, but she had already taken it with Welliver at Cooper, and she found Albers' "style-minded position limited . . . paradoxically weak and strong." She loved his course, but didn't do the problems "out of need or necessity. He couldn't stand my painting and of course I was much more serious about the paintings. . . ." Irving Petlin, who was at Yale for a year with Hesse, remembers how Albers and his assistants tried to "drive the expressionist out of all the New Yorkers, who came with a certain manner of abstraction. Albers' validity worried Eva, but his art just didn't make sense to her. It was a very restrictive and guilt-ridden environment based on public praise. Eva managed to straddle the two camps, but didn't really fit in either. She was really encumbered by personal ambivalences. She would work very hard and then dissolve in pain and frustration, then pull herself together and work very hard again. Her work wasn't up to the level of either her mind *or* her anxiety. . . . With hindsight I could say she was headed for sculpture because she really liked the sense of something *concrete*. Painting can only go so far to supply that logic of realness. Her painting wasn't 'real' enough for her."

5. Untitled, 1956–57, oil on canvas, 16 x 20″, whereabouts unknown.
6. Untitled, 1956–57, oil on canvas, 34 x 36″, whereabouts unknown.

7. Untitled, c. 1958, pen and ink, 9 x 12", whereabouts unknown.

Hesse's first-year roommate, Ellen Leelike Becker, who had also been at Cooper, recalls that she was "a very good collagist, a great *arranger*; she could take anything and arrange it. I remember one day she and Victor[3] had gotten some long-stemmed reeds from a swamp and placed them all through the room in bottles; it was like walking through a fantasy forest, like those things at the Guggenheim, hanging. That show was really very consistent with Eva's Yale and Cooper work."

There seems to have been no drastic change in Hesse's "abstract figurative" painting from Cooper (fig. 4) to Yale (figs. 5, 6), although each year the color intensified, and her canvases became less dependent on drawing, somewhat flatter, with hints of geometric figure references and a more solid and painterly treatment, probably as much the result of hard work on her part as the influence of any particular teacher. She was also very skillful at the typical "Yale school" drawing, dominated by scratchy cross-hatched line and eccentric, semi-abstract contour (fig. 7). One wash and pencil drawing (fig. 8) suggests her later work in its technical ease combined with clear underlying structure and a couple of hanging, jutting forms. The transparencies taken at Yale show her color to have been uniformly warm, running from hot reds, yellows, and pinks to browns and duller earth tones crossing over ambiguous images. The paintings have a contained turbulence, not successfully resolved; the result is a tentative quality, a reluctance to be as free as she was able to be in the drawings. In her mature work, of course, Hesse used the natural color and light of her materials most effectively.

Hesse was already wrestling at this time with the problems of thought versus feeling. In her diary she asked herself, "Does sentiment interfere with intellectual thought? What is arbitrary, what essential?" In an excellent paper for a Philosophy of Art class in May 1959, titled "An Abstract and Concrete Consideration of Form in Painting," she wrote about Abstract Expressionism in a manner indicating how

8. Untitled, c. 1958, wash and pencil, 9 x 12", whereabouts unknown.

11

9. Self Portrait, 1960–61, oil on canvas, 36 x 36″, Dr. and Mrs. Samuel Dunkell, New York.

strongly she identified with its goals: "The Abstract Expressionist attempts to define a deeply-rooted bond between himself and nature and to evoke this kind of union between himself and his painting. He does this by suggesting the forces that shape things, equating an objective experience of nature into a subjective expression of his feeling toward nature. . . . The introduction of a new element can suggest a totally new image and necessitate destroying form in order to rebuild." But she also concluded that "this attitude . . . denies for painting the notion of evolution." She worried that her art was confused by her life, and after working on a painting for two weeks, reassured herself: "I feel deeply engrossed and it really is a painter's concern and not a substitution for the repressed problems. . . . The need to be successful makes it impossible to feel that [any] effort will be enough satisfaction. . . . If my whole security is based on myself, then I have to be perfect. Therefore I can't be dependent on another person's opinion." She had a constant need to analyze any involvement with the emotional, comparing it, often unfavorably, with the "intellectual" side which she felt she lacked. She was driven by the complications and extremes of her life, and felt that these frustrations kept her from achieving what she was capable of.

At Yale, Hesse began to read a great deal; Gide, Nabokov, Joyce, Dostoevsky, Austen, Ortega, and McCullers are mentioned. ("I have become a reader—the thing I've wanted most, but was in too great a conflict with myself to do.") She began to make a list of word definitions, a habit continued and later intensified by friends involved with linguistics and by searches for sculpture titles. The diaries, however, contain few references to her own work. A rare entry noted that she was making a "series of drawings in ink with my main tool a crudely shaped wrong side of small brush. The drawings can best be described as imagined organic and natural

12

10. Eva Hesse with Josef Albers at the Yale School of Art and Architecture, c. 1958.

forms of 'growth.' They are essentially quite free in feeling and handling of medium 'ultra alive.' " Class notes posed the question: "Do artists' materials consist of mind or matter? *Materials have resistance, are stimuli;* materials—two points of view: a) materials lifeless till given shape by creator b) materials by their own potential created the end."[4]

Altogether Yale was not an easy time for Hesse, though at the end of two years there she said they had been the most eventful of her life, "most traumatic—with the greatest changes inside myself." She was still in therapy and felt she needed it "more and more." On the advice of her first doctor, Helene Papanek, who remained a lifelong friend, she changed to a male psychiatrist, Dr. Samuel Dunkell, with whom she continued to the end of her life with some respites. Her diaries contain constant notations for sessions with him—self-analyses and insights gained from thinking, reading, or from classes in psychology, and she gave him a self-portrait showing a cloud around the right side of her head, supposedly indicating a "schizophrenic syndrome" (fig. 9). She always had friends and lovers but worried incessantly about her "deeprooted insecurity" which made "relationships impossible." She wrote of looking forward to having children, but then, "I sympathize with women who are weary of their mates, bored by their relationship and are yet bound by it." On leaving Yale she listed her goals: "That of being a real person, painter—of getting to Europe, of having a happy love relationship, a family, children." But in particular she was "determined to *fight* to be a painter, fight to be healthy. No mediocrity for me."

13

After Yale, Hesse applied to graduate school at UCLA, but it did not work out. She returned to New York City, where she supported herself by working in Margaret Moore's jewelry store on West 4th Street. The apartment at 82 Jane Street she had inherited from Camille Norman was too small to work in, and she found studio space in a garage in the neighborhood; later she shared a space at 3 Ninth Avenue with artist Phyllis Yampolsky. The "art world" had been very important to Hesse even when she was a student. While still at Yale, she had made an attempt to be included in the Museum of Modern Art's "Sixteen Americans" exhibition; her friend Ellis Haizlip recalls accompanying her when she took paintings and drawings there to be viewed, and her profound disappointment when she was turned down. An artist who was seeing her in New York during 1959–60 remembers her making a conscious effort to become more professional and to enter the art world at that time. Among the artists she met in the summer of 1960, through Yale friends Ellen and Harvey Becker, was Sol LeWitt, who became a good friend and was later to be extremely influential in her life; at that point, however, he had not yet found his mature style either.

On November 2, 1960, Hesse began a new diary on a high note. "Again, a beginning, a new chapter. I have moved so rapidly. I feel so alive. I am almost too anxious for every moment, and every future moment. Optimism and hope—even confidence. It cannot be defined as happiness, very rarely am I actually happy. But that bugs me less. Maybe I care not whether or not I am happy." Her painting, which had become more abstract and much looser since leaving Yale, was developing slowly and her intentions far outreached her accomplishments. "I will strip me of superficial dishonesties," she wrote determinedly that fall. "I will paint *against* every rule I or others have invisibly placed." The conflict between structure and spontaneity raised at Yale still worried her: "I should like to achieve free, spontaneous painting delineating a powerful strong structured image. One must be possible with the other. A difficult problem in itself, but one which I shall achieve." Soon after she added, "One thing has changed of late, or developed—I want to feel I can and should sell paintings. What I am doing now might not be a peak of matured painting; but they are good, follow an idea, and they are work of a young, active

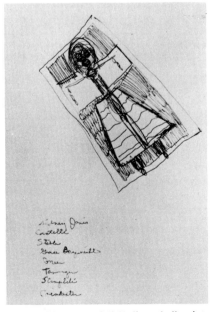

11. Untitled sketch inside cover of 1961 diary, ball-point pen, 7⅝ x 4⅜".

developing painter . . . . Only painting can now see me through and I must see it through. It is totally interdependent with my ambitions and frustrations. It is what I have found through which I can express myself, my growth—and channel my development. . . . Within its scope I can develop strength and conviction." In late January 1961 she could write "I am beginning to sell and show my work, in that order. One gave me the confidence to proceed."

Yet aside from such earnest declarations, there is still little in her diary about her work or about the experiences of her first year as a professional artist in New York. The only notes relating to specific art or artists this year are the following: "Dubuffet is really good. I enjoy his drawings, mainly for his humor—his esthetic is there and is there with ease: He makes no obvious contention with that aspect alone; . . . Bob Slutzky's work is to my eyes really fine! . . ." and in response to Lee Bontecou's show at Leo Castelli—"very fine!" In the spring, she asked herself "Why do I write so little regarding painting?"

One reason was probably fear of her own inadequacy. Another, her respect for the written word, which may have kept her from committing ideas she mistrusted as naive or "not intellectual" to paper. At the beginning of the 1961 notebook there is a curious stylized doodle of a doll-like female figure with round head, round eyes, and mouth giving it a horrified expression (fig. 11). A T-shaped dress forms a cross with oval legs and tiny feet dangling below it. Within the dress shape is what appears to be a crucifixion with blood dripping from the arms. The doctor had called her an "asexual child" and though she acknowledged to herself that she was "pretty and popular," and her friends assured her of her femininity, she kept on worrying about it. The winter of early 1961 she was in the hospital with a "cold" and felt guilty because she wasn't really sick but only "being a child" so that she would be taken care of. When in February she moved into a "great loft" at Park Avenue South and 19th Street, she worried about her tendency to compete with Eila Kokkinen, with whom she shared the space. A rather desperate childishness based on need for affection continued to be a major part of Hesse's character though it was always mitigated by an intensity that made her very likeable, and was increasingly combined with a great inner strength and determination. These elements formed her art as much as any esthetic components or art world experiences and I emphasize them, along with her concern with humanism (as seen in her figurative style of the 1950's and early 1960's) because they are responsible for the depth of her mature abstraction.

The drawings from 1960–61 are among the most beautiful in Hesse's oeuvre, and in retrospect it seems that, had circumstances been different, they might well have led her directly into the mature sculpture which they so often resemble. She could always draw, even when she was having trouble with painting, and the drawings expressed her deepest feelings. They were mostly ink, brush, wash; mostly grays, blacks, and browns, with heavy but eccentric and often whimsical shapes. Though Hesse had yet to make her first sculpture and had not considered the possibility of a "girl being a sculpture" [sic],[5] she seemed to be forming a vocabulary of shapes that longed to be independent of the page. The origins of her own sculpture are, again with hindsight, easily discovered. There are irregular rectangles, parabolas, trailing linear ends, circles bound or bulged out of symmetry, sometimes tangled balls (figs. 12–22). There are shapes painted out with black, the white forms negative and contained; there is an eye-like form framed twice in rectangles on a dense gray wash ground which could have been one of the 1969–70 Woodstock series (fig. 17); there are tangled cores and hanging shapes and one of a "soft" shape hanging from a box (fig. 18) which could have been a sketch for some variation of the 1969 sculpture *Contingent* (fig. 209). The images are ominous in character, almost gothic in their gloom, though frequently leavened by a particular humor.

12. Untitled, 1960, brown and black ink, brush, pen, 13⅝ x 10⅞″, Fourcade, Droll, Inc., New York.
13. Untitled, 1961, brown and black ink wash, 10⅜ x 9¼″, Fourcade, Droll, Inc., New York.

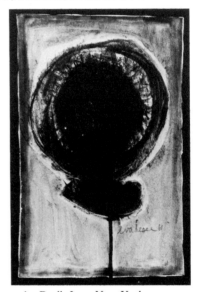

14. Untitled, 1961, pencil, brown and black ink, 9 x 6″, Fourcade, Droll, Inc., New York.
15. Untitled, 1960–61, brown and black ink, 9 x 6″, Fourcade, Droll, Inc., New York.

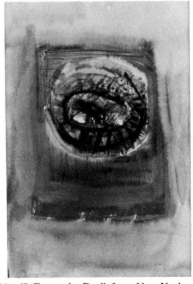

16. Untitled, 1960–61, brown and black ink, gray gouache, 4½ x 6″, Fourcade, Droll, Inc., New York.
17. Untitled, 1960–61, ink wash, 8½ x 5¾″, Fourcade, Droll, Inc., New York.

18. Untitled, 1961, brown ink and pencil, 9½ x 6″, Lucy R. Lippard, New York.

A small painting dated January 1961 (fig. 19) is one of the few canvases I know from this period in which the quality of the drawings is to some extent retained in paint. The colors are subdued, a little muddy, the forms reduced to a rather limp phallic shape hovering in the shadowed margin at the left, and a wistful lost balloon-like form moving with a mixture of gaiety and menace to the top right of the canvas. The weight of the medium and color is contradicted by the lightness of that upsurge.

It is impossible not to write about these works in anthropomorphic, sometimes surrealizing terms; they are inherent in the work as well as in my sense of the character of their maker. Because of Hesse's total absorption of herself in her work, one reads the work as one read the person, not in a gossipy or personally associative so much as in an archetypal manner; in that sense this interpretation could be arrived at by someone who did not know the artist at all. In fact, those who had no personal contact with Hesse know more about her than they realize, for to reach out to her work or to be reached by it is to be in touch with her most profound aspirations.

19. Untitled, 1961, oil on canvas, 16 x 16″, private collection, New York.

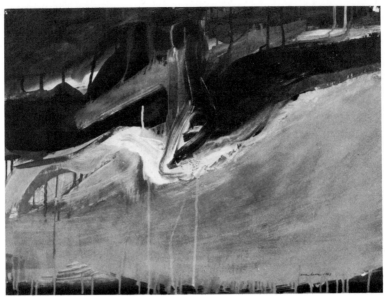

20. Ashokan, 1961, casein on paper, 17⅝ x 24″, Fourcade, Droll, Inc., New York.

In April 1961, Hesse had her first show and met the man she was to marry. The show was titled "Drawings: Three Young Americans." It was held at the John Heller (later Amel) Gallery, and also included works by Donald Berry and Harold Jacobs. The brochure reproduced Hesse's semiotic drawing of four vertical black *personnage* shapes, the two left ones tall and thin with tiny "heads," the two on the right boldly brushed as big circles with heavy stem "bodies" and a circled scrawl over one; they were surrounded by a washed rectangular "frame" (fig. 22). It is a powerful drawing, quite surpassing any of Hesse's paintings at the time, and completely overshadowing the reproduced works of the other two artists. Don Judd reviewed the show in *Arts* (April 1961) and said "Eva Hesse is the most contemporary and proficient" of the three. "Her small and capersome ink-and-wash drawings are a combination of the stroke (used as both sign and association) and of encompassing rectangles." Brian O'Doherty in the *New York Times* (April 18, 1961) spelled her name wrong, but said she had a "gnomic capacity." (Both reviewers were later to become her friends.) At the same time she had a drawing in the Brooklyn Museum International Watercolor Exhibition. In her diaries, however, she wrote nothing about her reactions to these events, or anyone else's, noting simply the opening of "her show" was "last eve." Just below: "I have been with Tom Doyle the last three days"; and "this is the beginning of being fully in the midst of the art world."

She had met Doyle—a lively and charming Pennsylvania and Ohio Irishman, several years older than she, a dedicated sculptor, good talker, Civil War buff, and Joyce addict—at the opening of his first show at the Allan Stone Gallery. Hesse was seriously attracted to him from the beginning, although she told her diary that the relationship would "not be easy," and she was discussing with her friend Rosie Goldman[6] "woman's role, feminine"—with husband and wife "both artists." She was "very happy," but her work was difficult: "In painting I get so close, then change, destroy, alter—whether it is just a particular painting—or a whole idea. It is never quite seen through to the end and I get distrustful of myself and reneg, cancel out. To be able to finish one, a serious one, stand ground . . . Tom is reluctant about my wanting to paint. Competitiveness. . ." They spent the summer together in Woodstock, and she was "too happy" to write in her diary. In fact, there are no diary entries for the rest of 1961 or most of 1962. Doyle remembers the first two years as "idyllic," but by the next summer there were already problems, and he was aware of Hesse's having "the kind of anxiety that keeps happiness from happening."

18

21. Untitled, 1961, ink and gouache, 12 x 9", Marc S. Moller, New York.

They were married on November 21, 1961, and moved into a big loft on Fifth Avenue between 15th and 16th Streets. To help pay the rent, they sublet portions of it to Grace Bakst Wapner, an artist they had met in Woodstock, and to her former college roommate Ethelyn Honig. Both became close friends of Hesse and Doyle through the years, but sharing the studio at that point was not an easy proposition for any of them. Honig kept a diary in which she described her surroundings: "To the left in this huge place is Tom's studio. Very dark, filled with wood and stone with mysterious tools and shapes. Chaotic really. Tom seems gay and charming—not frightening at all. Eva has explained that he is staining his wood pieces. They seem like awkward trees. . . . Eva's studio is in the front and is less womb-like. The glass window from ceiling to floor is vast. It overlooks office buildings and cafeterias. . . . Eva's paintings [figs 24, 26, 28] are stacked along the walls. There is more order here. I don't care much for them though they seem bold. They have the look of de Kooning with signs and symbols. The colors are harsh against white grounds. The brush strokes are thick. The symbols do not seem married to the background. I find them awkward. Perhaps I prefer more finesse. They are full of energy. . . . Grace and I work in the center of this place, between Eva's and Tom's studio. . . . When I arrived this morning . . . I spoke with Eva and Tom about the show of Pop Art at Janis'. . . . I said that I thought the Abstract Expressionists were about to be turned over. Eva, and particularly Tom, didn't care for the show. They felt disturbed by it. . . . Eva is always looking at what I am doing . . . very critically or competitively. . . . Eva seems to be compulsive . . . She seems to be setting standards for herself; finding qualities in other people that she will not tolerate in herself. I find her interesting but this critical quality touches off my own defensiveness." Later Honig recalled: "We were all aware that ideas about art were being shaken. . . . We saw that the precepts of our teachers were being questioned. Each seemed to be searching for a new structure and a new image. . . . A book very much looked at in that studio was by Stuart Davis. It was as if a generation was trying to take a look at its own environment and was then looking at and reviewing past masters to draw upon. In the following year Eva abandoned the softness of the acrylic [or Magna] paint and the images became harder and seemed to hold together in a consistent way . . . We were all extremely aware of Bob Rauschenberg, Roy Lichtenstein [who had been a teacher of Doyle's in Ohio], Claes Oldenburg and Jasper Johns. I remember discussing Warhol's ideas with Eva and Tom concerning having other people doing the work and creating art in a factory, assembly-line manner. It was threatening to say the least to artists

22. Untitled, 1961, from brochure for John Heller Gallery, "Three Young Americans," 1961.

who were involved with the physicality of work; the need to touch and shape with one's own hands. The very scale of such an idea was frightening. There was a loss of intimacy. . . . Of this group, Kaprow, Oldenburg and Johns held most appeal."

"I think there was a time," Hesse herself recalled in 1970, "when I met the man that I married . . . I shouldn't say I went backwards, but I did because he was a more mature artist and was developed and I would unconsciously be somewhat influenced and he would push me in his direction. When I met him I already had a drawing show that was much more me." While it is unfair to say that Doyle consciously pushed her in his direction (it was more likely that his own energy and assurance at that time were impossible to combat and that she was directly affected by Pop art's vitality) Hesse's 1962 drawings (figs. 27, 29) were much more "up-to-date," much less personal and expressionist than those of 1960–61. The major change was in the bright color and the dislocated space that related directly to that in the contemporary sculpture of Doyle, George Sugarman and David Weinrib, although the exaggeratedly tenuous ties between forms was typically hers. While she continued to use her own formal vocabulary, she began (perhaps under the influence of Al Held or Öyvind Fahlstrom, with whom she was very impressed at the time) to add X's, words, collaged additions (cut from other drawings, not from ready-made materials), and funky sexual images reminiscent of an abstract Oldenburg. ("Anna Eleanor Roosevelt" is written twice across one 1962 drawing; Hesse would certainly have identified with her life.) One of her few notes from this year reads: "Reckless throughout, looking, searching, then giving up, but all much too soon. The painting that is of importance is never the one where the esthetic stands alone and is both the form and content. The esthetic is a means to an end."

From 1962 through 1964 Hesse's work (figs. 25–35) became less and less skillfully beautiful, using more chaotic space, comic strip format, more mechanical line, and harsher color. The most personal elements of her art—the ragged line and almost pathetic funny rounded and oval anthropomorphic shapes were now subordinated to a hectic composition which made them lose their ponderous beauty.

23. Eva Hesse and Tom Doyle, c. 1963.

Many of these are good drawings, but the work as a whole from this period reflects a confusion perhaps rooted in a conflict between loyalty to the inner imagery of Gorky and de Kooning and the brash newness of Pop Art. Grace Wapner remembers Hesse working very sporadically and with great difficulty during the time at Fifth Avenue. She recalls two strange de Kooningesque portraits, and Doyle recalls that "Eva got into a kind of figurative thing, almost Dubuffetish, all floppy." Hesse also subscribed to the Abstract-Expressionist life-style mystique—to the notion that an artist's life necessarily involved poverty and sacrifice; an artist did not have money, children, a "normal life." She was also aware that their friends, though very fond of her, rarely asked to see her work; they in turn remember that she rarely asked them to look at it. She was considered more a wife than an artist by the men she knew, but Sylvia Stone recalls that she "never considered Eva just a wife after the first months. She was so intense and passionate; I thought she'd make a name for herself even though the work wasn't that good then."

The Doyles returned to Woodstock in the summer of 1962 and here, accidentally, Hesse seems to have made her first sculpture, although not yet considering it in any way a serious artistic possibility. A group of artists, later to join the original "Park Place Group" (Ginnever, Magar, Forakis, Myers, Weinrib)[7] with Kaprow, de Maria and others, organized (to use the word loosely) the Ergo Suits Travelling Carnival, a mélange of happenings and events that was supposed to entertain "the art capitals of the world." It was great fun for the participants, and baffling as well as infuriating to then staid Woodstock. One of the highlights was a chaotic "Sculpture Dance," in which the artists danced around inside of the sculptures they had made. "Eva made a really floppy one," Doyle recalls. "It was a beautiful piece, a tube of soft jersey and chicken wire and it just sort of flopped around, a soft, kind of funny piece with something hanging off of it. The whole thing was the material, and it was very much like what happened later. She didn't dance in it herself. Bill Giles and Tony Magar both got in it."

One of the few diary entries for 1963 reads: "I guess I am doing well but I am not happy in how I feel. . . . There is a tenseness and anxiousness that never leave me. . . . I am constantly dissatisfied with myself and testing myself. I have so much

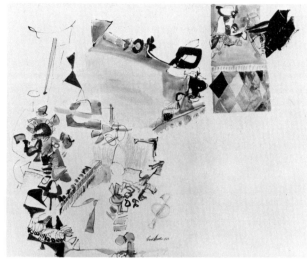

24. Untitled, c. 1962, magna on canvas, whereabouts unknown.
25. Untitled, 1963, ink and watercolor, 22½ x 28½″, Fourcade, Droll, Inc., New York.

anger and resentment within me. Why still now? . . . It is as difficult as it is said to be to be an artist's wife and an artist also.'' Another says: ''Art is contradictory and all that. It is to take [a] stand alone.'' And another: ''One needs a point of view. Can that be one of chaos? Can be simple idea (limited)—obvious strength of intent —clear and or many embracing one idea—interest, flexibility, change?'' Yet despite her frustration with her work, and without having any clear idea of where it was headed, Hesse doubted neither its potential strength nor her own drive and ambition. She already allowed herself the fantasy of making great art that every major artist entertains, a fantasy which opens up endless possibilities and allows them, in turn, to become ''realities.'' In March 1963 she had her first one-woman show, a small group of drawings at the Allan Stone Gallery (fig. 30). They were virtuoso collage, color, pen-and-ink works which showed how completely she had been able to assimilate the influence of the painters and sculptors around her, while maintaining an individual ''touch.'' They were not going to change the world, but they were highly accomplished and far more individual than the paintings of that period. Valerie Petersen's review in *Art News* (May 1963) said Hesse was a student of Marsicano and Albers: ''She smashes down on little cut-out shapes, half-erased ideas, repetitive linear strikings, and sets up new relationships. She invents dimension and position with changes of kinds of stroke, levels of intensity, starting and breaking momentum and by redefining a sense of place from forces which are visible coefficients of energy.''

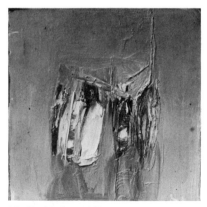
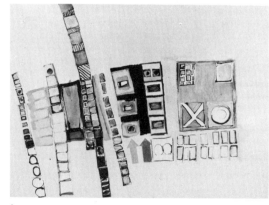

26. Untitled, c. 1962, magna on canvas, whereabouts unknown.
27. Untitled, c. 1962, collage, gouache, ink, 22 x 30″, Fourcade, Droll, Inc., New York.

28. Untitled, c. 1963, magna on canvas, whereabouts unknown.
29. Untitled, 1962, collage, gouache, chalk, pencil, ink, 21¾ x 30″, Fourcade, Droll, Inc., New York.

That winter the rent on the Doyles' Fifth Avenue loft was raised beyond their means and they moved to the Bowery, taking two lofts directly opposite each other between Broome and Grand Streets. His studio was on the east side of the street and hers was above their living quarters on the west side. Both new places had to be made over from scratch, always hard to deal with since any art work is effectively halted for the duration, and doubly so in this case since they had barely finished remodeling their previous home. It was at this point that I met them; I lived with my husband, painter Robert Ryman, a block up the Bowery. My first impression of Eva was that of a beautiful, fashionable, but spoiled little girl. She was in a state of total anxiety due to the living conditions (not recommended for a compulsive house-keeper), to tensions within the marriage, and certainly to her own work, although at the time I too considered her "Tom's wife" rather than a serious artist. Her drawings were beautiful but not unique, and her paintings were much too murky for my tastes; her personal manner contradicted the strength and depth I perceived only later. Around this time she wrote in her diary, "I still want to be a little girl, and yet I resent when then I do not feel I get respect as an adult." On the other hand, one could not help but like her; when she was cheerful, she was delightful and intelligent company. I was not to know Eva as a close friend until the fall of 1965, though we saw a good deal of each other that year of 1963–64 as part of a neighborhood group which included Sol LeWitt, Robert and Sylvia Mangold, Frank Viner, and Ray and Mary Lou Donarski.

The Doyles had barely gotten settled this time (the places were still not fully set up, though they were both working, Hesse sporadically) when the chance for what

30. Untitled, 1963, from brochure for first one-woman show,
Allan Stone Gallery, New York, 1963.

she called "an unusual kind of Renaissance patronage" came up. The German industrialist and collector Arnhard Scheidt, who, through Al Held and the Basel curator Nolde Rüdlinger, had seen Doyle's stone sculptures and wanted to buy some, decided it would be easier to transport the Doyles than the work. He offered them a year to work in his abandoned factory buildings in Kettwig-am-Ruhr with support and materials, in exchange for a certain amount of sculpture. Hesse, of course, was thrown in as lagniappe; Herr Scheidt now owns some of her first sculptures.

This was an unparalleled chance to work, without interruption by jobs, money problems, or the art world. Yet for Hesse, the prospect of a trip to Europe, her first since her childhood escape, was mitigated by the fact that she was to return to the "fatherland" that had murdered many members of her family. She was apprehensive on many counts, not the least of which were the lonely confrontation of her marriage and her still embryonic work. The spring before they left, she made a large series of drawings with elements of collage on a white ground, sharp acid colors, black ink delineating the softer ink washes, arrows and squares or "windows" (figs. 25, 35). Honig remembers being shocked at "the placement of the forms on the paper. They were completely off-balance and therefore irritating. A drawing that Eva gave me has all of the forms off the right side. The left side is completely blank, which leaves one with an uneasy feeling. . . .When she got back from Germany, I said I didn't see the connection between the large space drawings like the one she'd given me and the new work, and she said they were both 'impossible space,' 'impossible machines.' " At the time, however, Hesse felt that none of her work was "impossible" enough. She wanted to break all the rules but didn't know where to start. She complained to Sylvia Stone that there just didn't seem to be anything to do; she'd have to stop making art. Early in 1964 she wrote in her diary, with both doubt and envy, of artists who had a clear vision of what they were doing. "It is an idea, point of view; the work is quite secondary. However, it is true that with the making you do see things which you would not otherwise." In another notebook on January 4, 1964, she wrote the classic female complaint: "I cannot be so many things. I cannot be something for everyone. . . . Woman, beautiful, artist, wife, housekeeper, cook, saleslady all these things. I cannot even

31. Untitled, 1964, oil on canvas, whereabouts unknown.
32. Untitled, 1964, oil on canvas, whereabouts unknown.

be myself, nor know what I am. I must find something clear, stable and peaceful within myself within which I can feel and find some comfort and satisfaction." She felt she was wasting precious time, time in which she should be making great art, because she had yet to discover that vision. Grace Wapner recalls her feeling "so desperately that if she could *only* find the truth, only *understand*, she would be released."

Hesse and Doyle arrived in Luxembourg by Icelandic Airlines on June 7, and by the middle of the month they were settled in Kettwig, where their studios were the whole top floor of a factory, "a football field long," overlooking the Ruhr and near Düsseldorf and Cologne. Hesse worked, voluntarily, in a tiny room built specially for her. During the first two weeks in Germany, she had "terrible gruesome nightmares" which gradually lessened and turned into "day dreaming, phantasizing. . ." She had already done "many drawings. Coming along, sometimes. I feel these good tho I get discouraged. Staying at studio gets a little easier and more pleasant." She had also completed two "tiny very expressionistic" oils. "Feel rather enthused since I enjoyed them and they seemed real to me. Somehow I think that counts. What counts most is involvement and for that to happen one must be able to give lots. Just like with a person. It just seems to me that the 'personal' in art if really pushed is the most valued quality and what I want so much is to find it in and for myself. 'Idea' painting is great if it truly belongs to a person. However fails if externally acquired." On July 1 she wrote that she realized "it is good to be what one is. In fact, the more I'm me, the better I would paint as then it can only be mine as no one else is me. . . . I still agonize about my painting but at least now the agony is in and about work. And if I work that will probably change into another kind of feeling. And if it remains it is better placed there than back into myself."

At the end of June they had gone to Documenta, the huge international exhibition at Kassel, and she spent many hours at the show: "Went through both painting shows again. Looked more carefully than I ever have before. Somehow I felt everyone's involvement in art more genuine. The interest of those I spoke with was very real. I liked Alechinsky and Jorn particularly. Also Alan Davies." When she returned she began to worry about her color. "I can't stand the color I use and yet it mostly develops in the same way. This I should change. Since I decided I liked it not. It is amazing how this happens again and again. The Picassos at Documenta had an interesting use of color. I end up with red, yellow, blue, green and I hate it. It is dumb and uninteresting and I know better. I guess I am so involved in creating my own forms that I can't at time be involved that much. But ironically they scream in color and then I am defeated by my own lack of concern." This passage seems to be a better explanation of Hesse's later self-restriction to monochrome than the influence of other artists on her work.

The rest of the summer and fall was a fragmented time. They worked in isolation and traveled to see people or sightsee (see chronology). In July, Hesse began suffering from pains in her legs, later diagnosed as anemia, but she wondered then if she were "setting up one last block" to working. "I'm still not working right, as I know in my mind one should, but I have been more consistently at work than ever before. There will never be a more adequate situation for work than now. Tom feels this also." She felt her problems were more overwhelming than his because he knew what he wanted. "Very basic and conceptual aims are still unclear to me. I must work them out. I have actually painted very few paintings. It is hardly any wonder that such difficulties arise." Such rationalizations always sank to doubt again: "Am wondering if not my reasons for working are all wrong. The need for recognition, praise, acceptance is so excessive a need it causes an impossible pressure to live with, my feelings of inadequacy are so great that I oppose them with equally extreme need for outside recognition to establish some equilibrium. I think

33. Untitled, 1964, oil on canvas, 34¼ x 41″, Mr. and Mrs. F. Arnhard Scheidt, Kettwig.

it is so in everything but greatest in art.'' Yet in August she wrote her friend Rosie Goldman that she had hung all her drawings on the wall of her huge studio and ''as a group I think I should be pleased with them.'' She also finished her first painting, having ''cut the first two up.''

The next two months were spent traveling, alone to Mallorca to visit Ethelyn Honig, and then with Doyle to Paris, Italy and Switzerland. They returned October 4, and she found it hard to get back to work ''after so long a period of doing nothing.'' Things were going badly with their marriage, due at least in part to the fact that they were taking a lot of short, social trips which Hesse rarely enjoyed. She noted in her diary that the ''fear and anxiety'' were not so bad in Kettwig as in New York, but admitted to a feeling of ''utter helplessness.'' Yet she finished a painting in two days ''in contrast to one month of first two.'' In November she read Simone de Beauvoir's *The Second Sex*, which made a strong impression on her. ''Simone de Beauvoir writes woman is object—had been made to feel this from first experience of awareness. She has always been made for this role. It must be a conscious determined act to change this. Mine is not as much the acceptance of object role as it was insecurities from a broken, sick, unsupportive home. I survived not happily but with determination, goals, and an idea of a better way.'' November 21: ''I really feel I keep blocking my growth. Why? What does being adult entail? . . . I still doubt myself in both myself and my work. In competing with Tom I must unconsciously be competing with my alter ego. In his achievements I see my failures. . . . Resentments enter most precisely if I need be cooking, washing, or doing dishes while he sits King of the Roost reading.'' In a December entry, she quotes from *The Second Sex*: ''What woman essentially lacks today for doing great things is forgetfulness of herself; but to forget oneself it is first of all necessary to be

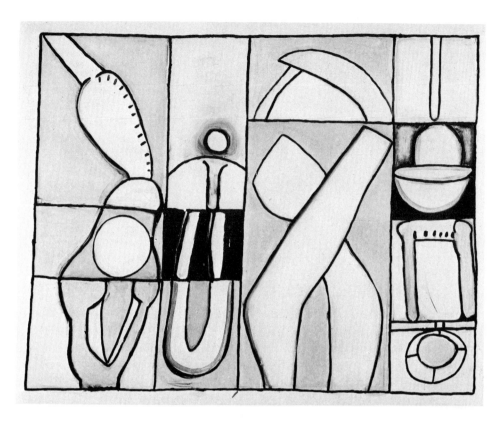

34. Untitled, 1964, oil on canvas, 31 x 39¾", Mr. and Mrs. F. Arnhard Scheidt, Kettwig.

firmly assured that now and for the future one has found oneself.''

This process for Hesse seems to have begun almost simultaneously with these notes. The drawings she had been making up to this time resembled those from 1962–64; at times they bordered on fussiness, including too many elements, and too worked-over. In Germany they became increasingly simple, cruder, brighter, less involved with draughtsman's technique, and much flatter. Spatially, they are even more "disturbing" than the earlier ones. Some are vignettes, compartmented hearts, arrows, writing ("And he sat in a box"); others are more volumetric, like drawings of sculptures in space; in a few, the painting is blurry and layered as in the 1961 and 1969 drawings. Gradually one kind of image began to dominate—a flat but fundamentally organic "machine" element (figs. 36–43). It seems to have been around November 1964 that this figure emerged as a central focus. Hesse made some colorful "drawings for children in studio. . . . Red blue yellow green in squares and one on letters of the alphabet. Today made one with numbers 1–10. They are clear, direct, powerful. It set me off again because they are different, just enough to make me wonder where I am going. Why and is there an idea or too many different ones? . . . Why is it that I cannot see *objectively* what I am about? My vision of myself and of my work is unclear, clouded. It is covered with many layers of misty images. . . . I do want to simplify my turmoil." A sketchbook contains a drawing by one of the Scheidt children, Karl, and then an "imitation" by Hesse with some attributes of the machine images but a conscious attempt to make an "adult's children's drawing." Her first use of the grid may have been a conscious reference to Jasper Johns' number and alphabet paintings or may simply have arisen from the children's play. Whatever the reason, she was making some kind of breakthrough.

27

35. Boxes, 1964, ink, gouache, collage, 20½ x 23½", Dr. and Mrs. Samuel Dunkell, New York.
36. Try to Fly, 1964, ink wash, 19⅝ x 25⅝", Manfred and Erika Tischer, Düsseldorf.

"The drawings sustained her all that time," Doyle recalls. "Her drawings were always fantastic. She could draw like a sonofabitch. But she wasn't really doing anything, just floundering around, doing things she could do and do too well and had been done before. I was trying to get her to get the *drawings* onto the canvas. And some of them were like that, but it never really worked. Her drawings were in a way more like sculpture than paintings—the way they related in space—that's maybe why she couldn't transfer them to painting, It's a matter of finding your own *material*." Early in December Hesse was complaining that she couldn't work, and Doyle recalls, "I told her why don't you try some of the shit lying around here. They were tearing up the old weaving things in the factory. . . . We could use anything we wanted. The workers all brought us stuff they thought we'd like—they were breaking up machines. There were miles of that string there. The string was really what got her going." Hesse's diary entry for December 4: "Started sculpture, lead wire through a huge screen. Shortage of wire forced change to plaster." December 10: "Plaster! I have always loved the material. It is flexible, pliable, easy to handle in that it is light, fast-working. Its whiteness is right. I will take those screens. Finish one I began in lead. Then get cloth cut in strips and dip in plaster and bring through screen. I needed a structure that is perfect."

Thus two of the things that were to characterize most succinctly her mature work were come upon accidentally: the grid and the process of compulsive winding or bandaging or poking-through. On December 14 she wrote more precisely to Rosie Goldman: "I want to explain what I have been doing. And *although I already question validity, worth, meaning, antecedent etc. I have been enjoying the newness and the work. In the abandoned factory where we work there is lots of junk around.*

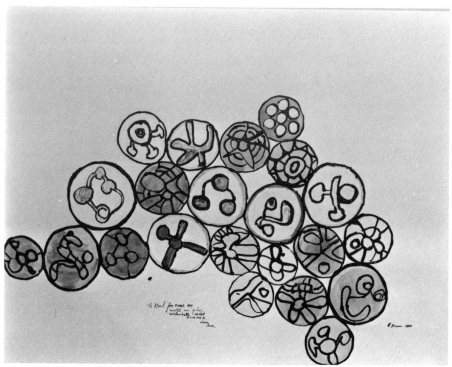

37. "For Karl. . . .", 1964, ink, watercolor, 17 x 22", Karl Scheidt, Kettwig.

Tom has used much steel and odds and ends for his sculpture. I have all these months looked over and at much of the junk. *I finally took a screen, heavy mesh which is stretched on a frame like so and taken cord which I cut into smaller pieces. I soak them in plaster and knot each piece through a hole and around wire. It is compulsive work which I enjoy.* If it were really a new idea it would be terrific. But it is not. However I have plans with other structures and working more with plaster. It might work its way to something special. I will try to draw what it looks like [fig. 44].On other side it's the *knots* that are seen. It is all white."

This piece, which resembled Hesse's mature work more than any of the other German pieces, was not finished, or was destroyed or lost. It is not among the fourteen construction-reliefs completed, shown, and photographed at the end of the year. Doyle recalls that it was based on a green screen-like machine guard that "stood by itself like sculpture, was three-dimensional but also a two-dimensional surface, which was familiar to her and easier to begin with." He remembers thinking to himself "this is it, all that tying and everything, it's really *her*." He thinks this first piece may have seemed too radical a departure, since it didn't survive. The first completed relief, some months later, was *Ringaround Arosie*, which was much closer to the paintings and drawings (fig. 46). In fact, she had not yet seriously considered making sculpture. She wrote in her diaries that for her, painting had become simply fantasizing, "Making art. 'painting a painting.' The Art, the history, the tradition, is too much there. I want to be surprised, to find something new. I don't want to know the answer before but want an answer that can surprise." On December 15 she quoted from Fitzgerald's *Save Me the Waltz* a passage about Zelda's frustration with dancing; "Just substitute painting," she added.

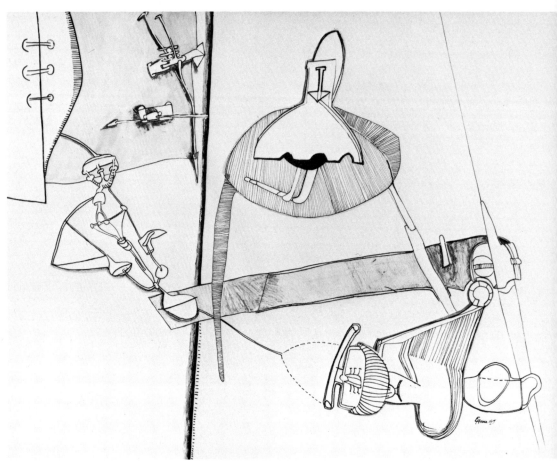

38. Untitled, 1965, pen and ink, 19¾ x 25½″, Fourcade, Droll, Inc., New York.

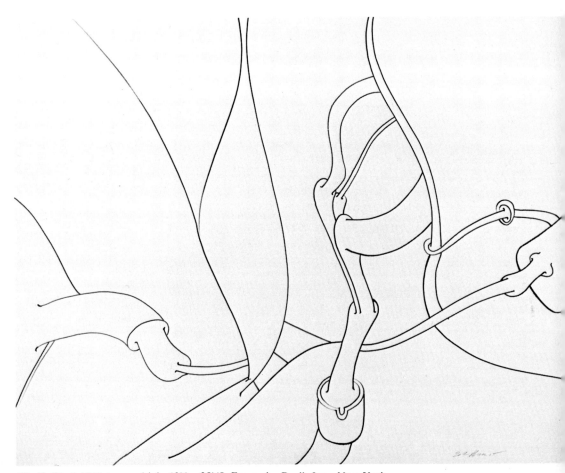

39. Untitled, 1965, pen and ink, 19½ x 25½″, Fourcade, Droll, Inc., New York.

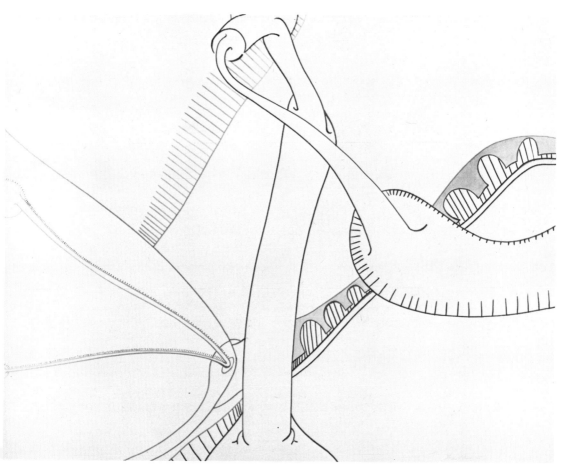

40. Untitled, 1965, pen and ink, whereabouts unknown.

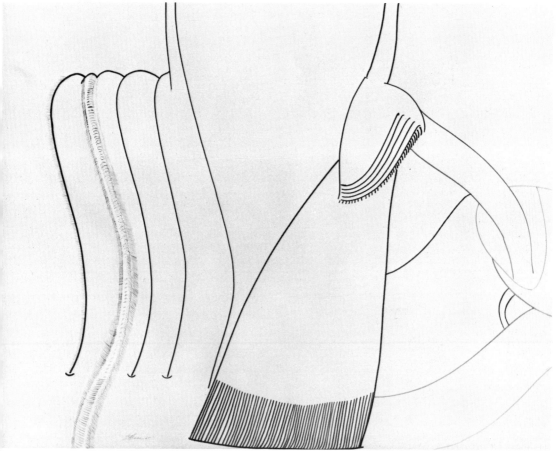

41. Untitled, 1965, pen and ink, whereabouts unknown.

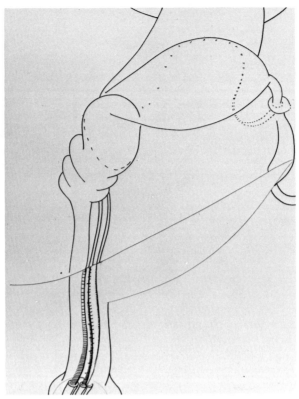

42. Untitled, 1964, pen and ink, whereabouts unknown.

And unfortunately just at this exciting and fertile moment she left on a Christmas trip to Berlin. There she saw, among other things, the Laocoon at the Pergamon Museum, the title of which she was to borrow the next year for her first large freestanding sculpture. When they returned in January she learned that her father was hospitalized with pneumonia in Florida. On February 5, she was still telling herself "If painting is too much for you now, fuck it. Quit. If drawing gives some pleasure—some satisfaction—do it. Go ahead. It also might lead to a way other than painting, or at least painting in oil. First feel sure of idea, then the execution will be easier.

"Same eve., later. I did a drawing, I really like now at the moment. Will eagerly await tomorrow, with hope that it will still mean something to me then. . . . I will continue drawing, push the individuality of them even though they go against every 'major trend.' Fuck that. So did everyone I admire at the time they started to go against."

It seems to have been at this point that she began isolating her "machine" images so that in their singleness they began to suggest sculpture and to inspire more interest and confidence in the possibility of making reliefs. A large number of small pen drawings exist in which Hesse, with a sure and even hand, outlined image after image of great variety and imagination. These were followed, or accompanied, by many larger drawings, executed on good paper in pen and ink, sometimes with different colored inks on one drawing and even on one single contour line, sometimes a striped or patterned area, less frequently a light wash over one or another delineated area (figs. 38–43). The grounds were almost always white, with all the energy concentrated in the image itself. The shapes are organic in source, humorously combined with machine appurtenances, joints, nozzles, rims, cords. They demonstrate an impressive combination of loose and fluid, obviously automatic or free forms with a line that is absolutely straightforward and devoid of modulations. It is the line that is mechanical rather than the image, but the punning play between the two, and between hard and soft, is at the core of the drawings. In the early ones there are images that recall mouths, chairs, lamps, shoes, a vacuum cleaner; there is

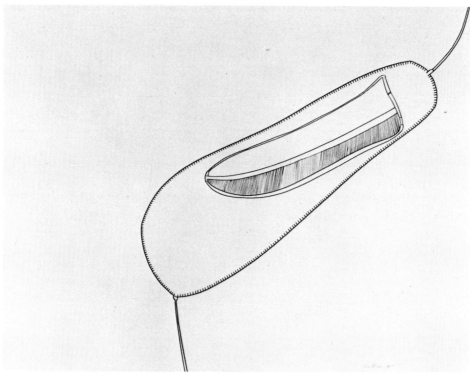

43. Untitled, 1965, pen and ink, 18⅛ x 24⅛", Fourcade, Droll, Inc., New York.

an "orange squeezer" that recalls Oldenburg and ambiguous blobs recalling Peter Forakis' abstract comic books. There are penis-like jut-outs that recall the shapes in Doyle's sculpture, but softened into another substance. Many of the organic shapes appear to be "bound" by line into "sausage" forms, anticipating the next year's sculpture. Other images also suggest later work: a "ball and chain," pendulums, balloons, an undisguised penis with thorns, tendrils drawn off other shapes, a ubiquitous dotted line. The loops and stems and gangling tentacles suggest growth, as did her earlier drawings, but there is a new element which incorporates the crudity she had been searching for and a formal element that is determinedly neutral, as well as a volume freed from ties in space and association with other forms. Although the forms are single, and vignetted, they are highly active. Things are coming out of things, pushing and nudging their other parts. One drawing looks like a detailed study from some fantastic pipe joint. Others are teethed gears, fingers reaching out as though trying to emerge into three dimensions. "If crazy forms do them outright, strong clear," she wrote. "No more haze . . . . If playacting—eventually I'll feel it. Without trying I'll never know."

"Of course she always dug the funky stuff. It was always in her drawings," says Doyle. "It was just getting into something else. That was the whole thing. When she started to see them like in *real,* they took off. I think there were connections to Hans Haacke, and the fetish part of Günther Uecker, and Joseph Beuys; his ideas—the felt and the 'fat corners' intrigued her. I think there was also a lot of connection to the people we were around in New York—Weinrib, di Suvero, those guys—who were working with things that were around—that whole kind of junk, pick-up, find-em-on-the-street sculpture thing. I think that had a definite influence on the kind of *idea* she was working on. . . . I was very happy she was getting into something. She got plaster from the workers—some sort of spackle they used. She was also messing around with papier-mâché. It really suited her, her whole image. The reliefs started out sort of landscapey and complex. The first ones were more like painting, less jumping off the surface, more building up. Right away though she got much more adventurous about the whole thing and got into the wire and then filling them up with rope. You could date them by the way the color became less and less important. They started out like paintings and ended up like drawings. From the painter-sculptor idea and back to the drawing idea . . . Once she took a little piece from my sculpture I wasn't using and used it in hers. In a way I felt we were very close then, in spite of all the shit. . . . She really helped me more than anyone else with my color. . . . The German experience really focused both of us."

In February, Scheidt invited a group of professors and art historians to come to Doyle's and Hesse's studios. It was a let-down for both of them. "I am ultimately convinced that people must first be told that so and so is great and then after a period of given time they come to believe it for themselves," she noted bitterly, and correctly, in her diary. The fact remains, however, that both artists were well received and given shows later in the year. Their connections with German artists were few, due to Kettwig's relative isolation, but Hans Haacke happened to be teaching at the high school there and through him and his American wife Linda they met others. Doyle, more outgoing than Hesse, saw more German artists and art events than his wife, but together they had a few close friends, among them Thomas Lenk and the Düsseldorf photographer Manfred Tischer, of whose wife, Erika, Hesse was particularly fond.

March was a generally depressing month. ("Everything looks bleak to me.") Hesse seems to have thought a good deal about her position as a woman, probably because she and Doyle were leading almost separate lives by then. Some time before, a German factory worker had found her attractive and questioned her about why she couldn't just be Tom's beautiful wife, why she had to be an artist. She had "overreacted" to his comment and had been upset by it for days, perhaps feeling threatened in the light of her deteriorating marriage. "Do I have a right to womanliness?" she asked her diary. "Can I achieve an artistic endeavour and can they coincide?"

Yet the week of March 18: "I produced four drawings which I like—at this moment." She turned to Sol LeWitt in a long letter about the work, saying that he understood her because they were opposites. "What drives us to work. It seems to me some kind of recognition which maybe we cannot give ourselves. Mine seems to be disproportionate . . . . One should be content with the process as well as the result. I'm not!" Describing her drawings, she listed several stages. "First kind of like what was in past—free, crazy forms—well done and so on. They had wild space, but constant, fluctuating and variety of forms, etc. Paintings were enlarged versions attempts at similar space, etc.

"Second State—contained forms somewhat harder often in boxes and forms become machine-like, real like, and as if to tell a story in that they are contained. Paintings follow similarly.

"Third state. drawings clean, clear but crazy like machines. forms larger, bolder articulately described so it is weird they become real nonsense.

"So I sit now after two days of working on a dumb thing which is three-dimensional. Supposed to be continuing with last drawing. All borders on pop at least to the European eye. That is anything not pure or abstract expressionist is pop like the 3-d one now actually looks like breast and penis—but that's ok and I should go on with it maybe. . . but I don't know where I belong so I give up again. All the time it is like that. . . . Have really been discovering my weird humor and making sick or maybe cool but I can only see things that way—experience them also but I can't feel cool—that is my hopelessness. Like it all is based on fear and cannot be cool when one constantly feels fear. . . . Everything for me personally is glossed with anxiety. . . . How do you believe in something deeply? How is it one can pinpoint beliefs into a singular purpose?"

On April 14 LeWitt answered this letter in no uncertain terms and with the best possible advice: "You seem the same as always, and being you, hate every minute of it. Don't! Learn to say 'Fuck You' to the world once in a while. You have every right to. Just stop thinking, worrying, looking over your shoulder, wondering, doubting, fearing, hurting, hoping for some easy way out, struggling, gasping, confusing, itching, scratching, mumbling, bumbling, grumbling, humbling, stumbling, rumbling, rambling, gambling, tumbling, scumbling, scrambling, hitching, hatching, bitching, moaning, groaning, honing, boning, horse-shitting, hair-splitting, nit-picking, piss-trickling, nose-sticking, ass-gouging, eyeball-poking, finger-pointing, alleyway-sneaking, long waiting, small stepping, evil-eying, back-scratching, searching, perching, besmirching, grinding grinding grinding away at yourself. Stop it and just DO.

"From your description, and from what I know of your previous work and your ability, the work you are doing sounds very good. 'Drawings—clean-clear but crazy like machines, larger, bolder, real *nonsense.*' That sounds wonderful—real nonsense. Do more. More nonsensical more crazy more machines, more breasts, penises, cunts, whatever—make them abound with nonsense. Try and tickle something inside you, your 'weird humor.' You belong in the most secret part of you. Don't worry about cool, make your own uncool. Make your own, your own world. If you fear, make it work for you—draw and paint your fear and anxiety. And stop worrying about big, deep things such as 'to decide on a purpose and way of life, a consistent approach to even some impossible end or even an imagined end.' You must practice being stupid, dumb, unthinking, empty. Then you will be able to DO! [The DO's are drawn and decorated and very large.] I have much confidence in *you* and even though you are tormenting yourself, the work you do is very good. Try to do some BAD work. The worst you can think of and see what happens but mainly relax and let everything go to hell. You are not responsible for the world— you are only responsible for your work, so do it. And don't think that your work has to conform to any idea or flavor. It can be anything you want it to be. But if life would be easier for you if you stopped working then stop. Don't punish yourself. However, I think that it is so deeply engrained in you that it would be easier to DO." (Continuing in this vein, he also mentions his work, which has "much changed since you left and it is much better.")

Hesse's diary entry for April 14, the day LeWitt was writing the above, says: "I am working steadily. I will give much effort now, as I might well soon be on my own." A supplies list scribbled on a 1965 machine drawing includes "liquitex varnish, pipe or rod, rubber hose, stove pipe, sand, and test cord." In letters to Rosie Goldman she said her "machine drawings" were "like outer space networks" and on April 1 she was working on a "three-dimensional contraption. Not finished yet but it is weird not machine-like but weird." On April 16 she "worked all day and night, had fun"; and on April 27, she finished *An Ear in a Pond* (fig. 49). This seems to have been the time when she buckled down to work and began to realize that the three-dimensional "contraptions" were really leading her somewhere. On May 4 she wrote Rosie that she was "working like crazy. First we cannot take home our work I don't think. Transporting would be very expensive. . . . My things might be transported but also will see. If really good can have gallery take them here—will see. Have one completed. I will describe. Am working on masonite which is pressed wood fibers. On this I build forms (glue and paper) on some forms I have glued cord. On one I have a heavy twisted cord which comes out of a form and hangs loose. On another there are two metal forms which can be moved." At the bottom of the page she drew sketches of the first four pieces. In another letter she wrote, "My drawings are very HARD. That is they are forms I

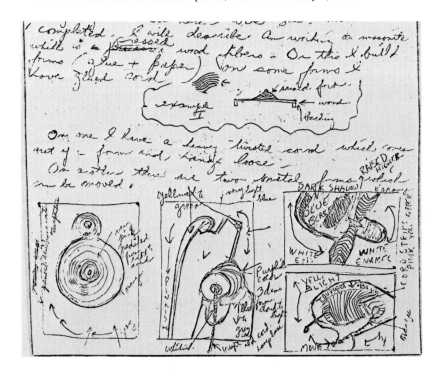

44. Sketch of first three-dimensional piece (destroyed)
    from letter of Dec. 14, 1964, to Rosie Goldman;
    sketch of next three-dimensional pieces, from letter of May 4, 1965.

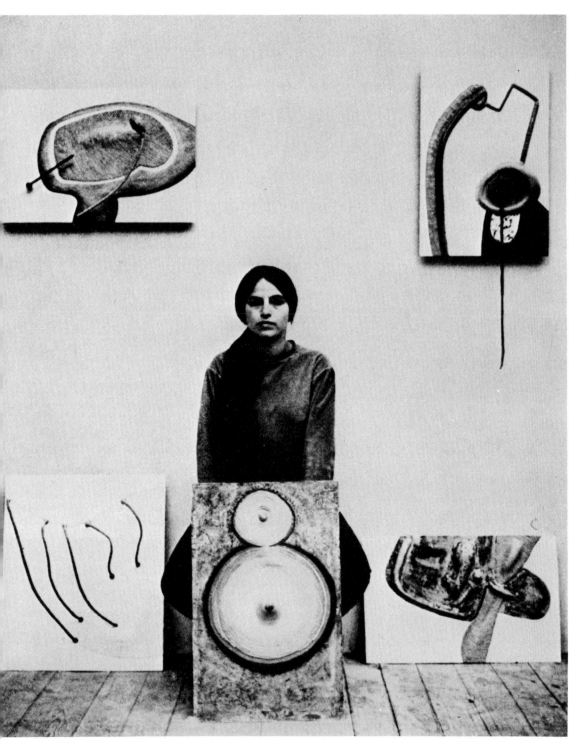

Cover of brochure for one-woman show at the Kunstverein für die Rheinlande und Westfalen, Düsseldorf, August 1965.

have always used but enlarged and very clearly defined. Thus they look like *machines,* however they are not functional and are nonsense."[8]

Though all are similar in style, only a few of the drawings from this period are directly related to the reliefs (e.g. those close to *Two Handled Orangekeyed Utensil* (fig. 48), and *Legs of a Walking Ball* (fig. 51). As time went on, the deadpan images found a drawing style consistent with their "hardness," though repeated circles, concentric circles, coiled forms like rolls of fat, sometimes made to look hard, sometimes soft, continued to inject a strongly organic image. One group drawn in a heavy black line cut out and mounted like "patterns" for sculpture. One has notes on it "Must go out further," "build this—purple light-dark" "draw this in exactly—paint." Eventually these drawings became so sensuous and sleek, even elegant, that they approached slickness, and Hesse stopped making them.

The first of the four constructions sketched in the letter to Rosie is the one eventually titled *Ringaround Arosie* (fig. 46); she described its execution in the same letter: raised forms built up from papier-mâché then cord glued concentrically. She notes that another piece has a "heavy twisted cord which comes out of a form and hangs loose" *(An Ear in a Pond),* and on another there are "two metal forms which can be moved," *(Legs of a Walking Ball,* in which the "legs" move). The fourth piece is *Two Handled Orangekeyed Utensil.* A list of titles dated by month in Hesse's diary indicates rapid production once she was committed to working in three dimensions.[9] She probably worked on more than one at a time: "March 1. Ringaround Arosie. April 2. Two Handled Orangekeyed Utensil. April 3. An Ear in a Pond. May 4. Legs of a Walking Ball. May 5. [blank; later named Oomamaboomba.] June 6. Tomorrow's Apples. June 7. 2 in 1. June 8. H + H. July 9. Cool Zone. July 10. Pink." A separate note documents "July. C-Clamp Blues," leaving the three last pieces to be made during the rest of July, as her show opened August 6. The catalogue photograph (fig. 45) presumably shows the five earliest pieces.

Ringaround Arosie: This is the one Hesse said reminded her of a "breast and penis," though in fact both rosy-nippled circles look like breasts—a little one on top of a big one, forming a sort of doubly female figure. The ground is a crusty gray from which the brilliant circles project abruptly. Both are carefully wound in cord, the larger one a kind of breast-within-a-breast, graded from an orange border to a dark pink to a progressively lighter pink and then darker pink again for the raised portion. Except for the color and the difference in size between the circles, this piece resembles reliefs made in 1966–67.

46. Ringaround Arosie, 1965, pencil, acetone varnish, enamel, ink, glued cloth-covered electrical wire on papier-mâché and masonite, 26⅜ x 16½".

 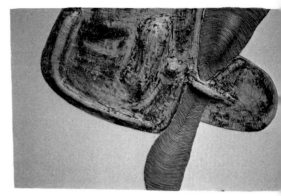

47. Untitled, 1965, gouache, ink, collage, 12¾ x 19½", Fourcade, Droll, Inc., New York.

48. Two Handled Orangekeyed Utensil, 1965, paint, papier-mâché, varnish on masonite, 16½ x 26⅜".

Two Handled Orangekeyed Utensil: Also a sexual image, closely related to Hesse's paintings and to the machine drawings. The gray shape which hangs from the top edge has both indentations and projections in its surface, and the orange cord-wrapped "handles" fit through a slot in the heavier form. This is generally a more ponderous piece than the others, lacking their humor.

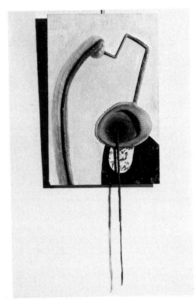

49. An Ear in a Pond, 1965, paint, cord, papier-mâché on masonite, 26⅜ x 17¾".

An Ear in A Pond: This too is a fundamentally two-dimensional concept, more of a "built-up painting" than the later ones, except for the fact that the pink "ear" form in the lower right is in quite high relief; from its center dangles a red double string wrapped for over half its length in another cord; beneath it is a painterly area which mortally confuses the rest of the relief. The colors here seem ill-conceived; an acid green and chartreuse outlines the background "machine shape"; the ground outside is a warm pinkish white, while inside it is a cool grayish tone, further undercutting the fact that the green lines are three-dimensional and tying them back to the surface. This piece is important primarily as a prototype for all the later sculptures from which cords and strings dangle the surface.

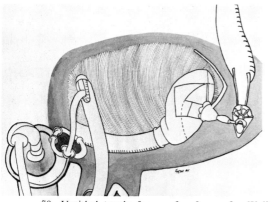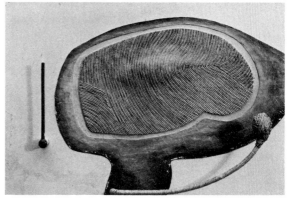

50. Untitled (study for or after Legs of a Walking Ball), 1965, inks and gouache, 11¾ x 16½",
Fourcade, Droll, Inc., New York.

51. Legs of a Walking Ball, 1965, paint, cord, papier-mâché, metal on masonite, 17¾ x 26⅜".

Legs of a Walking Ball: An image very close to several machine drawings; the three-dimensional possibilities are somewhat tentatively explored via the cord-wrapped orange central portion where the cords are used like lines, changing direction and contradicting the actual surface contour. For the first time, however, the surface is pierced (rather than merely built up) by two metal rods—a red one at the left which begins in a ball, and an orange cord-wrapped one at the right which is longer and ends in a wrapped oval. The larger form is once again firmly rooted to a two-dimensional backing through a "stem" which is cut off by the lower edge, and the fact that the right side of the oval is truncated by the right edge.

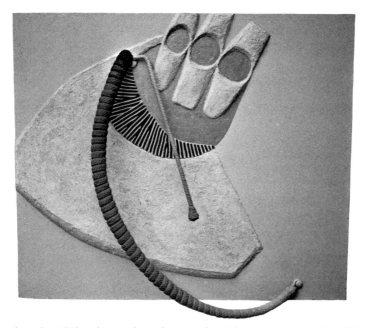

52. Oomamaboomba, 1965, paint, cord, cord-wrapped metal, plaster on masonite, 21¼ x 25⅝".

Oomamaboomba: The image is still contoured, painted and drawn, but it is boldly divorced from its robin's egg blue ground and successfully pulled out into real space by the cord and cloth-wrapped pink curve. There is a vaguely mask-like, primitive, or decorative African aspect to this piece which might have inspired the nonsense title. The chartreuse against tan and the black-and-white stripes, the whiplash of pink, provide more of an impression than a concrete associational image. The level of abstraction reached here is rather higher than the other pieces to date.

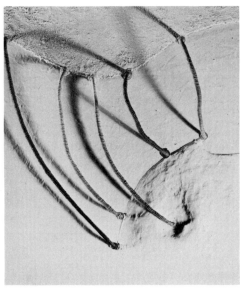

53. Tomorrow's Apples (5 in White), 1965, painted concretion, enamel, gouache, varnish, cord-wrapped wire, papier-mâché on masonite, 25⅝ x 21⅝".

Tomorrow's Apples (or *Five in White*): This is the first piece to be simplified to the point where the autonomous character of a relief is expressed. The curved white ground, being monochrome, intrudes less on the three-dimensional elements. It is also an integral part of the composition, as the five bent cord-wrapped rods (blue, pink, red, blue, yellow from left to right) begin and end at its contours, arching over the central flat-painted channel, with the exception of the third line which plunges into a circular dent in the pitted lower surface. The upper surface is a different texture—flatter and more grainy. The lines effectively spring off the surface, leaving behind shadows which appear to bend and shape its topography.

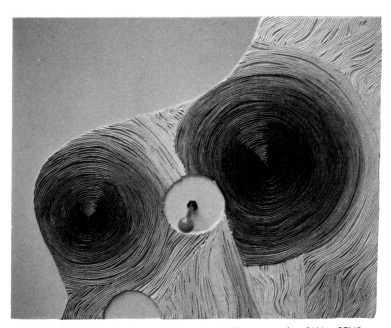

54. 2 in 1, 1965, cord, glue, paint, wooden ball on masonite, 21¼ x 27⅛".

2 in 1: Its painterliness marks this as another early piece. Here too there is a reluctance to separate the whole forms from the "painted" ground. The two cord-wrapped, dark-centered purple "breasts" connect easily with the cord-wrapped mottled white and lavender ground with its very beautiful linear convolutions, but there seems no reason for the shape underlying the cord; that is, for the flat pink background, which is forced forward by cutout areas in the relief (which also unsatisfyingly cut off the relief form) and the addition of a red ball which pops out of a hole between the two "breasts." There is something almost delightfully eccentric about this piece which is spoiled by a naive insistence on nonsculptural concerns.

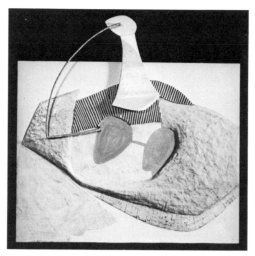

55. H + H, 1965, enamel, gouache, alcohol-varnish, ink on masonite, 21¼ x 27⅛".

H + H: Like *An Ear in a Pond,* it is rather confused, with a certain fussiness arising between the combination of two- and three-dimensional forms. The white phallic shape added to the top and tied by a metal rod to the two red breast (or brassiere) shapes it pierces, is the leftover piece of Doyle's sculpture mentioned above. There is a bird-like aspect to the white "head" and the pink "wing" at lower left, but the painted areas (ink, gouache, enamel, and varnish) seem flatly and unconnectedly imposed on the relief, and the only interesting formal aspect of the piece is the way the white projection clips the colored shapes against the white background. The title stands for "half and half," referring to a pipe tobacco used by Doyle, and the fact that his work is included in hers.

56. Cool Zone, 1965, aluminum and painted cloth-bound cord, 15 x 15", cord 45".

Cool Zone: The circular "peace symbol" is aluminum, all gray, though shiny on the pattern and dull on the ground; the fat double magenta cord hangs almost to the ground. This was the most fully sculptural piece executed in Germany, the only one freed from the rectangular ground, and as such it relates more directly to work made in New York the following year, especially the untitled hoop piece (fig. 69). Despite a certain obviousness, it is a simple idea clearly executed.

57. Pink, 1965, painted cord, papier-mâché, button on masonite, 21⅝ x 25⅝".

Pink: One of the most effective images Hesse made at this time and surely one of the ones she proudly called "weird." My associations are with insects, monsters, crustaceans. Except for the tiny pink spot (a real button) buried in the gray vertical, it is also Hesse's first monochrome sculpture. She seems to have begun to think of the figure as more completely separate from the ground at this time. The gray arc appears to peel away from its backing. The button might be seen as another point where the relief is "tacked" to the surface, as it is by the squirming white-to-gray tendrils which also seem to be struggling to escape from their surface.

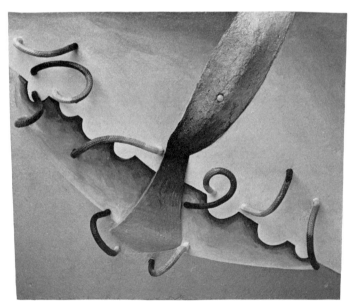

58. C-Clamp Blues, 1965, painted concretion, metal wire, bolt, painted plastic ball on masonite, 25⅝ x 21⅝".

C-Clamp Blues: Even given the fragile "crotch" image from which dangles a very light ball, and the tiny pink navel—a projected ball—above, it is perhaps unforgivable to see a play of words on the fact that Hesse suffered from severe cramps at this time, as well as on the old jazz classic— "The C-Jam Blues." Isolated from criticism, she was free to associate on all levels, yet of course *C-Clamp Blues* is also an accomplished abstraction and this is surely how she wanted it seen. The rough-textured surface is almost invisibly divided into three bands of color—a warm gold at the top, a paler yellow white, and a cooler gray at bottom. There is a hint of circular motion in the surface around the points from which the V-shaped wires emerge from the surface. The image is extremely simple, and extremely mysterious.

44

59. Up the Down Road, 1965, aluminum paint on styrofoam, cloth-bound cord on masonite, 27¼ x 21¼".

Up the Down Road: Here again conceptual clarity indicates the progress Hesse had made in these few months. By this time she knew just what to do with the relief form. The very rough grainy ground is aluminum paint on a kind of styrofoam, unmodulated except for what could be accidental furrows and pits here and there, although these are (conveniently and clearly, not accidentally) horizontal and vertical, a very subdued contrast to the vibrant and smooth purple plastic wire which scrawls rapidly across and above the surface like a single stroke of the pen, while simultaneously dividing the white area into two almost symmetrical interlocking shapes.

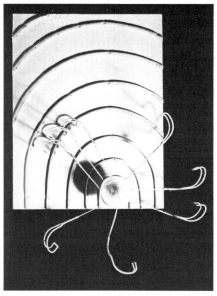

60. Eighter from Decatur, 1965, paint, cord, and metal on masonite, 27⅛ x 21¼".

Eighter from Decatur: A coolly logical white surface regularly divided by yellow embossed arcs is then mischievously undermined by eight silly double pink hooks on white stems emerging from a graded pink "breast form" (which harks directly back to *Ringaround Arosie*). One of these hooks hangs boldly but precariously to a yellow rib; the others fan out to the wall. The wit and gaiety of this piece separates it from all the other German reliefs. The title is slang for a throw of the dice, like snake eyes, boxcar, etc.

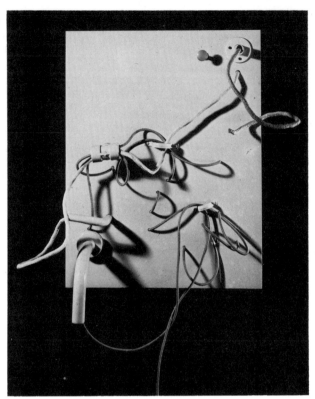

61. Top Spot, 1965, flexible metal cord, electrical cord, metal hardware, paint, plastic ball, porcelain socket on masonite, 27⅛ x 21¼".

Top Spot: Shows a similar exuberance and also indicates how free Hesse had become to invent, imagine, and laugh at her medium. A scribble of curly lines (narrow white tubing or coated wiring) playfully appears from and then disappears into the surface, to emerge again in another area. Entangled with them, but dominating them, is a fatter wrapped cord graded very light to dark blue. It travels through three "tunnels" (found metal hardware,) painted white like the ground) and ends in the center of a blue knob with a white center (like an eye) at the top right. At bottom left, the white wire travels the opposite direction, exiting from the background via a faucet-like pipe to hang all the way to the floor where it makes a loop on the ground.

In May, Hesse received the first public approbation of her new work from an informal show given by Herr Scheidt to present his artists' work to friends and the local art world. Hesse's reliefs and drawings were in an old greenhouse, hung free from the rafters, "like things growing. Really lovely" (Doyle). "Show went well," she noted. "I sold 2 Tom maybe also 2. I will also show August 6 in Graphics Room in Kunsthalle Düsseldorf." On May 19, she and Doyle went to Hameln, her mother's hometown; she saw the house she was born in and had lived in as a child; the present inhabitants would not let her inside. She met two of her mother's school friends and heard stories about the family—all dead. It was an upsetting trip. Then she got bronchitis, enjoyed visits from Ray and Mary Lou Donarski, Sylvia Stone, and Al Held. They all went to Bern for an exhibition of work by Duchamp, Malevich, Kandinsky, Doyle and, to her amusement, Albers. There she also met "the lady who in 1935 made the fur-lined teacup"; (Meret Oppenheim later sent her a collage). They also went to Held's show in Basel. Hesse loved Switzerland and they toyed with the idea of moving there.

In the meantime, she was working hard for the Düsseldorf show, "relaxing little . . . Have three more pieces to do . . . I fear the New York scene." July 3:

62. Hesse in her Kettwig studio, 1964–65.

"Worked like crazy"; July 31: "Have fourteen objects and fourteen terrific new drawings"; August 2–3: "Moved work to Düsseldorf and hung show"; August 4: "Worked like crazy and did five more groovy drawings"; August 6: "Our opening." And the diary entries virtually stop here, with no account of the opening or of her feelings about the show's reception. On August 10 they went to London, on the 16th to Dublin; she lists what she saw without comment.

The German period had provided a lonely but crucial apprenticeship. It was, in fact, fortunate that the seeds of Hesse's mature work emerged and could first be nurtured away from the New York scene, away from the pressure of an art world becoming increasingly incestuous and competitive, away from the advice and criticism of well-meaning friends, and away from the influence of new shows. The distance she had traveled between the first and last of the German reliefs was phenomenal, especially when one remembers that they were executed by a woman who had for several years been unable to work steadily, unable to clarify her ideas with any conviction. She returned to New York with her drive and ambition undiminished, with a body of respectable work behind her, a head full of new confidence and ideas, and an image of herself as a sculptor.

63. Hesse at the opening of her one-woman show, Düsseldorf, August 1965.

SEPTEMBER 1965–MAY 1970

They got back to New York in early September, and by September 30— ''Almost one [piece] complete in U.S.!'' This year was to be an immensely important one. Realizing that a change of scene was not going to help their failing marriage, renewing friendships as an artist in her own right, and finding that her friends were excited by and interested in the transparencies of her German pieces,[10] Hesse began to work in earnest. Even her first New York sculpture shows a marked difference from the German works, as though setting foot on Manhattan sidewalks had focused (if narrowed) her energies. To some extent her friendship with Sol LeWitt, his encouragement, and the example of his new Minimal work were important, but the sources of all her New York pieces are to be found in the German reliefs. They could have led in either of two directions: towards the funky fetishistic aspect or the monochrome structural aspect. It is a measure of Hesse's extremely personal approach that they never fit either category, though they were now subjected to a new rigor and directness, a new interest in ''simple'' and ''serial'' concepts.

64. Untitled, 1965, painted iron, wood, c. 10'6" high.

65. Long Life, 1965, papier-mâché, epoxy, cord and enamel over beach ball and hose, 20" diameter, hose 7'.

Untitled: A six foot pole rises from a rimless spoked wheel set a few inches from the ground and graded from a black base to a pale gray top. The weightlessness and exaggerated height provided by the pale-topped (i.e., disappearing) pole is compounded by the raised base. Unlike the German works, it is freestanding and monochromatic, but like them it is tightly bound with cord. The found machine-part image is transformed into a fetish with unexpected directness. Its exaggerated height anticipates the "Whitney icicle" piece of 1969 (fig. 197). Before she died Hesse had the spoke piece destroyed.

Long Life (November): Here Hesse compulsively wrapped cord around a large beach ball that sits impassively on the floor; a heavy cord-wrapped tube, or hose, protrudes from its top, lying for some length on the floor and then rising to the wall above, where it is "plugged in." The ball is black and the hose grades from black to dark to light gray, again becoming weightless as it rises and merges with a light-colored wall. The umbilical imagery also found in some of the German works is unescapable here in combination with the title, but the object itself is at once disturbingly detached and disturbingly physical, its matter-of-fact presence countered by its lugubrious content in a way that demonstrates Hesse's already intelligent control over reconciled opposites. This piece too was eventually destroyed.

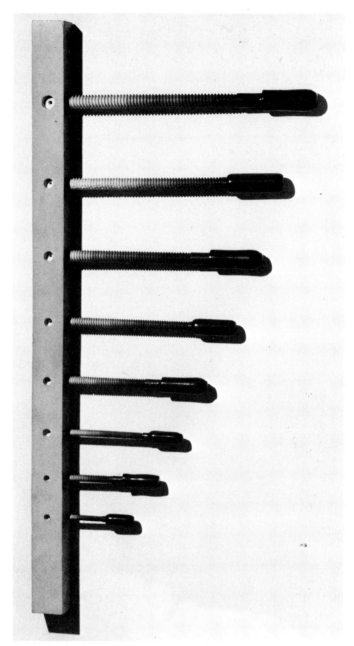

66. Untitled, 1965, acrylic on wood, 45 x 22 x 2½".

Untitled: Completed in October 1965, this was Hesse's last "colored" piece. She found the eight screw-threaded projections around the studio and made the rectangular bar from which they protrude. (Later she wanted to destroy this piece too because the "found" elements weren't uniform but, luckily, she did not.) The only material involved is wood, since the wrapped-cord effect is already simulated by the screw threads. The post is graded purple, light to dark, bottom to top, while the projections grade light to dark from the post out into space. As in all of these new works, the tonal gradations are used for sculptural rather than descriptive purposes. Where the spoke piece was made weightless by a light top, here the thick dark ends delimit the side boundaries and counterbalance the strong but paler (and thereby somewhat dematerialized) vertical from which they emerge. The phallic dowels and circular holes retain the sexual imagery of the reliefs, but what was previously a funky curved line has changed to linear austerity, straight and regular patterns. The holes and the capped protrusions are contrasted, but the latter's inherent aggressiveness is subtly tempered by hanging the piece sideways, so that the holes, rather than the rods, are frontally asserted. This is also the first piece in which Hesse so directly explored the rectangular-rounded contrast.

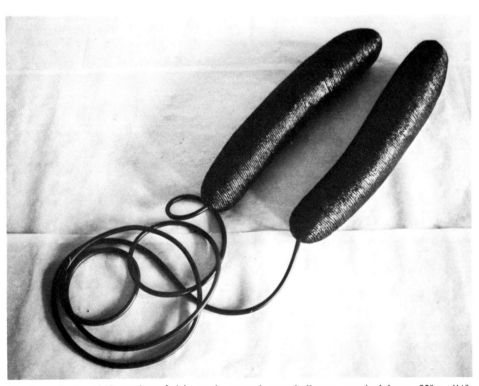

67. Ingeminate, 1965, papier-mâché, cord, enamel over balloons, surgical hose, 22″ x 4½″ diameter, hose 12′.

Ingeminate (November): Two sausage-like, enamel-sprayed, cord-wrapped black forms attached to each other by black rubber surgical hose. The humor of this piece is closely related to the German "machine" drawings, but in an extremely pared-down form, so that it is all the more unexpected. Whether the humor lies in the "funny" (visceral or sexual) shapes, or in the helpless entwinement, the shiny surfaces, the uselessness, the double image, depends on where the viewer's and the artist's imaginations meet. The title means "doubled, redoubled," or "to emphasize by repetitition," the first verbal indication of what was to become a major characteristic of Hesse's esthetic.

68. Several, 1965, acrylic, papier-mâché over rubber hose, 7' x 11" x 7".

Several (November): A reiteration of *Ingeminate*'s motif, more successful and less schematic than the previous New York pieces, as though Hesse's friends' favorable responses to the first works (which reflected, in turn, her own first responses to the Minimal tendency) had permitted her to move back, at least temporarily, to a more personal imagery, confident that she could handle "straighter" pieces as well. *Several* is seven gangling papier-mâché-over-rubber hose "sausages" of different lengths and curvatures. They are painted different gradations of shiny black and dark gray and are hung randomly from their strings on the wall like a bunch of chiles in a Mexican kitchen. There is an endearing lack of pretension to *Several,* though some of its curiosity results from its fairly large scale. The lackadaisical approach to a hanging position predates by two years the so-called "anti-form" movement, and the weight of the darker tones at the top of the forms stressed their "hangingness" from the strings which attach them to the wall.

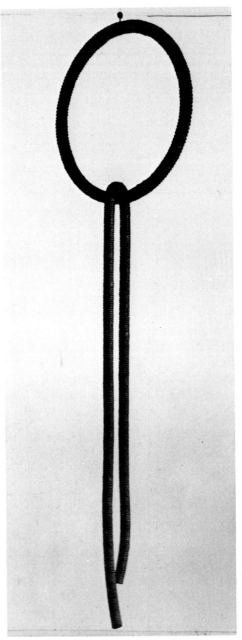

69. Untitled, 1965, enamel-painted cord over wood or metal and hose, Fourcade, Droll, Inc., New York.

Untitled (November): A large cord-wrapped black hoop hanging from the ceiling; looped over its lower edge is a limp, hose-like strand of the same thickness as the ring, one end hanging slightly lower than the other; both ends almost reach the floor and both are lighter than the black and dark gray middle section. The model for this piece could have been the German *Cool Zone* (fig. 56), in which an identical motif was presented in a more decorative manner; or, further back, several 1960–61 drawings, such as the one on the John Heller brochure (fig. 22). With that connection it can also been seen as a rather wistful stick figure, with a childishly drawn round head and limp, sheepish limbs. Moreover, it is a clear and formally exact sculpture, the proportions and the contrast of the two shapes providing a subtle psychological effect.

54

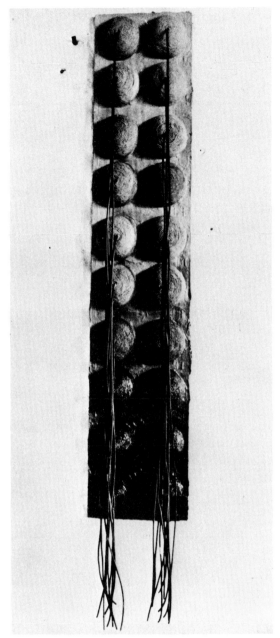

70. Ishtar, 1965, wood cord, paint, rubber, 36 x 7½ x 2½".

Ishtar (December): The first piece to incorporate a formal vocabulary which Hesse was to use consistently for the next two years—the repetitition of circular or hemispherical or "breast" forms from which strings, cords, or rubber lines emerge and hang down. It has obvious precedents in the German reliefs. I have never felt that the scale of *Ishtar* is quite right; there is a vague unease in its exaggerated and crowded verticality, which for my taste borders on the "fussy." However, its expert formal use of string line redeems it. The progressively accumulated weight and line toward the lower edge and the lighter (in tone and detail) top area are most effective. Its total length was perhaps necessary for the accumulative aspect to become apparent.

Hesse's diary of December 12, 1965, reads: "My yearly fall into the pit of darkness is upon me. . . and as I am working constantly with a great intensity it is mounting inside. The intensity with which I work is translated then into the gloom of despair. All my stakes are in my work. I have given up all else. . . . I do feel I am an artist—and one of the best. I do deeply . . . With my work I have one person here and one there, artists who know me and think I am good. Most others don't know me as an artist and give me no credit at all and I can't take this." Her marriage was by this time almost non-existent. Doyle was seeing Jane Miller, who was to become his third wife. Hesse was panic-stricken at the prospect of abandonment, and at the same time buoyed up to face it by her increased confidence in her work, a confidence still and always importantly rooted in the mutual respect of several close friends, LeWitt prime among them. She was also making new friends on her own. Through LeWitt she met Bob and Nancy Holt Smithson in January 1966 and Dan Graham (who ran the short-lived Daniels Gallery where LeWitt and Smithson had shown early in 1965). I began to take her seriously as an artist and a person then, sensing a transformation not only in the work, but seeing for the first time the tremendous reserves of strength which she herself continued to doubt. Hesse also knew Mel Bochner, Don and Julie Judd, Dan and Sonja Flavin, Robert Ryman, Bob and Sylvia Mangold, the Donarskis and Will Insley; she found an affinity between her work and that of Frank Lincoln Viner. She continued to see Al Held and Sylvia Stone, David Weinrib, Grace Wapner, Ethelyn Honig and, always, Rosie Goldman. Grace Wapner recalls that around this time Hesse found some object in the street—a broken pipe or something—which made an immense impression on her; she called it a "nothing" and said that what she wanted to make was "nothings" (or perhaps to raise "nothing"—herself?—to great heights). She was beginning to have a clearer picture of how to go about this. After dinner one night with Bill Giles and Lee Bontecou she wrote: "I am amazed at what that woman can do. Actually the work involved is what impressed me so. The artistic result I have seen and know. This was the unveiling to me of what can be done, what I must learn, what there is to do. The complexity of her structures, what is involved, absolutely floored me."[11]

Hang-Up (January 1966): In a 1970 interview Hesse called this "the most important early statement I made. It was the first time my idea of absurdity of extreme feeling came through. It was a huge piece, six feet by seven feet. The construction is really very naive. If I now were to make it, I'd construct it differently. It is a frame, ostensibly, and it sits on the wall with a very thin, strong, but easily bent rod that comes out of it. The frame is all cord and rope. It's all tied up like a hospital bandage—as if someone broke an arm. The whole thing is absolutely rigid, neat cord around the entire thing. . . . It is extreme and that is why I like it and don't like it. It's so absurd to have that long thin metal rod coming out of that structure. And it comes out a lot, about ten or eleven feet out, and what is it coming out of? It is coming out of this frame, something and yet nothing and—oh! more absurdity!—it's very, very finely done. The colors on the frame were carefully gradated from light to dark—the whole thing is ludicrous. It is the most ridiculous structure that I ever made and that is why it is really good. It has a kind of depth I don't always achieve and that is the kind of depth or soul or absurdity or life or meaning or feeling or intellect that I want to get." *Hang-Up* is the major early piece from any viewpoint, perhaps rivaled only by *Contingent* in Hesse's entire oeuvre. Based on a six-foot stretcher found in the studio, it can be seen as a comment both on her own past and on painting as a medium, its emptiness and its "dependence upon the support" (a critical cliché of the mid-1960's). Like the German reliefs, *Hang-Up* deals with a tension between two- and three-dimensional spaces; it is a pictureless picture from whose surface a drawn line escapes into real space. The use of a graded tone is very subtle as it plays in the double space the object occupies. The upper left corner of the frame is the lightest, the lower right the darkest, the other two corners medium gray. The bound wire follows a similar up-to-down gradation, but as it is drawn into space it becomes darker, and as it is drawn to the floor it is darker still, as though dragged down by its own weight. The title was suggested by a friend; the artist later wished she could change it to something less "cute."

71. Hang-Up, 1966, acrylic on cloth over wood and steel, 72 x 84 x 78″.

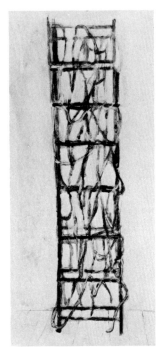 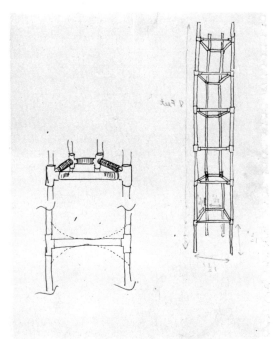 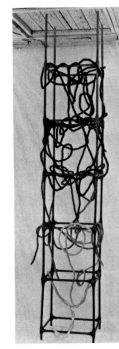

72. Untitled (after Laocoon), 1968, gouache, pencil, 22 x 15½", Fourcade, Droll, Inc., New York.

73. Study for Laocoon, 1966, pen and ink, pencil, 12 x 9", Fourcade, Droll, Inc., New York.

74. Laocoon, first version, March 1966, underneath second version.

Laocoon (March): (A second title appears below this one in Hesse's notebook—"Structured Snakes," later mercifully replaced.) Ray Donarski helped her build the plastic pipe armature which in her small studio reached from floor to ceiling. Hesse worked on this, her first major freestanding sculpture, for a long time, and discussed it with all of her friends. I remember having strong reservations about the first version. There were then fewer coils, and no matter how they were arranged they looked forcedly composed. The "irrational" element was not powerful enough to conquer or balance the rational structure, and something was wrong with the proportions—the thinnesses and thicknesses. The very soft, cloth-wrapped wires were each graded similarly from heavy black at bottom to nearly white at top, but not at quite the same rate, so there was an optical mixture, while the structure was graded in the opposite direction. Soon afterwards, Hesse remade the whole piece, wrapping the structure as well as the wires in cloth. The pipes had previously been covered with papier-mâché and "made fat" only at the joints. Now the whole piece was colored light gray without gradation. The addition of many more "snakes," chaotically looped and tangled around the now heavier structure, pulled the piece together. The obvious contrast of thin shiny pipes against fuzzy ropes was eliminated and the piece became more solid, more sculptural, more of a whole. Yet in the first version, there was an element of pathos, that *personnage* aspect of a spindly creature helpless in a tangle of things it could neither control nor understand, and this was lost when the piece became "better sculpture."

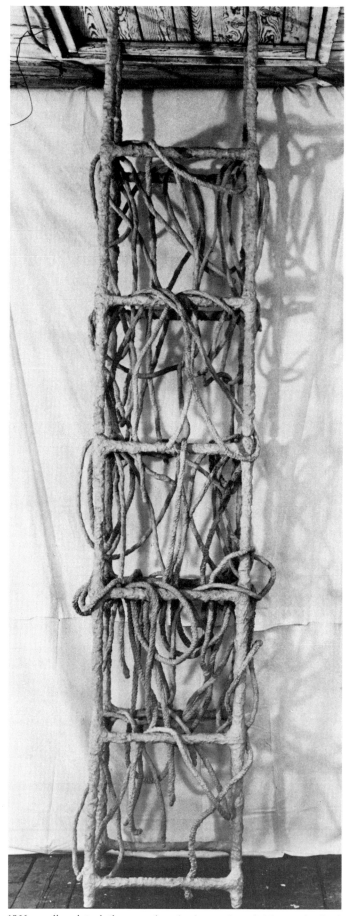

75. Laocoon, 1966, acrylic paint, cloth-covered cord, wire, papier-mâché over plastic plumbers' pipe, 10′ x 24 x 24″.

76. Total Zero, 1966, rubber, plastic, epoxy,
acrylic, polyurethane, papier-mâché over
inner tube, metal, 2′ 3″ x 2′ 3″ x 3′.

77. Untitled, 1966, three net bags with
painted papier-mâché, weights,
42½ x 11½ x 6″.
78. Vertiginous Detour, 1966, enamel,
rope, net, plaster, 23″, ball 40″
circumference.

Total Zero (February): An inner tube was made lopsided (a bulge on the right) by the addition of papier-mâché, bound and covered in paper, and then painted the glossy black Hesse favored at the time. From the upper part of its bulbous side emerges an abruptly tapered rod, twisted to form a loop in the middle and extending a couple of feet out—an absurd squiggle with a kinesthetic effect; its black-to-pale gray might be read as air escaping from the tire and disappearing into thin air. It was suspended by a narrow chain from the ceiling, against a wall, so that sculpturally it was closer to the German reliefs than any other works of this time. Perhaps an attempt to repeat *Hang-Up*'s success in wall and real space, it lacked the former's impact. I recall Hesse's friends being less enthused by *Total Zero*. Even the title referred to someone she didn't like, and the whole piece had bad associations of a difficult personal time for her; she eventually disliked and destroyed it.

Untitled (Not Yet),[12] *Vertiginous Detour,* and *Untitled* (March): The drawing in Hesse's original list does not quite resemble the finished piece called or not called *Not Yet,* since the nine black fishnet bags filled with, but not full of clear soft plastic around weights, appear to be hung within a frame or on a rectangular panel, whereas the finished piece hangs in a tear-shaped group against the wall. None of these three bag pieces is a major work, though Hesse was fond of *Vertiginous Detour,* a large net hung from the ceiling free of the walls and containing a shiny black papier-mâché ball from which emerge hard shiny strings of different lengths; these tentacles poke through and extend below their net container, and raise associations (octopus, hairy head, hairy testicle) which, for better or worse, bring it to life with a touch of absurdity not found in the other two bag pieces. *Untitled* has three black fishnets with an irregular lump of shiny black painted papier-mâché in the bottom of each; one lump is almost a ball; the other two are more irregular, rather rock-shaped. The idea of a light linear net holding such heavy looking objects was a good one, but not thoroughly worked out. In 1966, however, Hesse seems to have intended to follow through on these pieces. A note reads: "Not yet possibilities inside, more mysterious, epoxy a surface, try paper wrapping from Sol (tried something—so far too like Christo)."

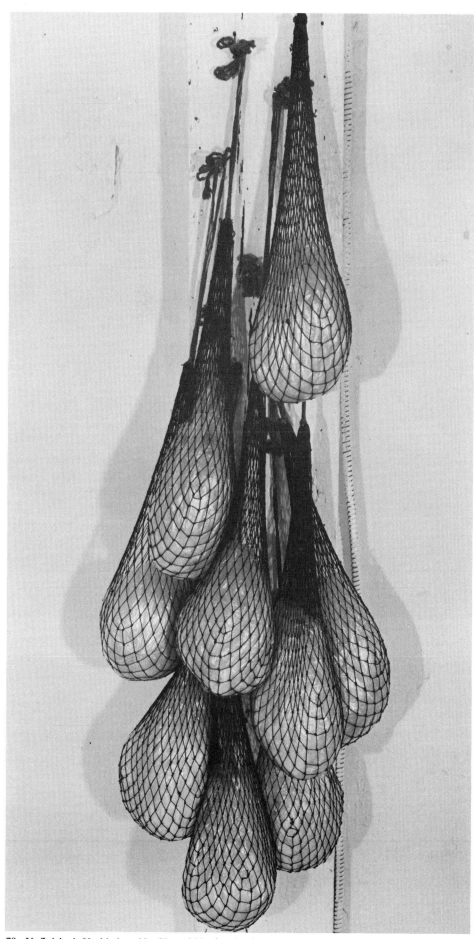

79. Unfinished, Untitled, or Not Yet, 1966, nine dyed net bags with weights and clear polyethylene, 72 x 24 x 14″.

Ennead: Often misdated 1965, though probably executed after March 1966[13] since it does not appear on her chronological work list which ended at this point, *Ennead* concretizes a concept mentioned earlier in Hesse's notebooks: "rope irregular (like snake hung) while working on Laocoon hang from ceiling to floor ad infinitum; cord room—like new piece going and coming every which way." It is a vertical plaque with a grid of tiny raised hemispheres from the centers of which strings emerge, straight at first, then tangled down towards the floor, where they are hooked up across a corner onto a single nail on a perpendicular wall. "It started out perfectly symmetrical at the top and everything was perfectly planned. The strings were gradated in color as well as the board from which they came. Yet it ended up in a jungle of strings. . . . The strings are very soft. I dyed them. Even though they were in perfect order, even though I wove the strings equally in the back, they were so soft they went different ways. The further it went toward the ground, the more chaotic it got; the further you got from the structure, the more it varied. I've always opposed content to form or just form to form. There is always divergency. . . . It could be *arranged* to be perfect." The title, which means "a group or set of nine" implies that order; once the piece was complete, however, she realized its implications. A note from May: "cords everywhere. Will do one that does not come from a form—that is endless, totally encroaching and irrational with its own rationale even if it looks chaotic." These notes describe *Right After* (1969) (fig. 208) and Hesse's last rope piece (1970) (fig. 218); *Ennead*'s plaque itself, like *Ishtar,* can be seen as a prototype for the circle drawings.

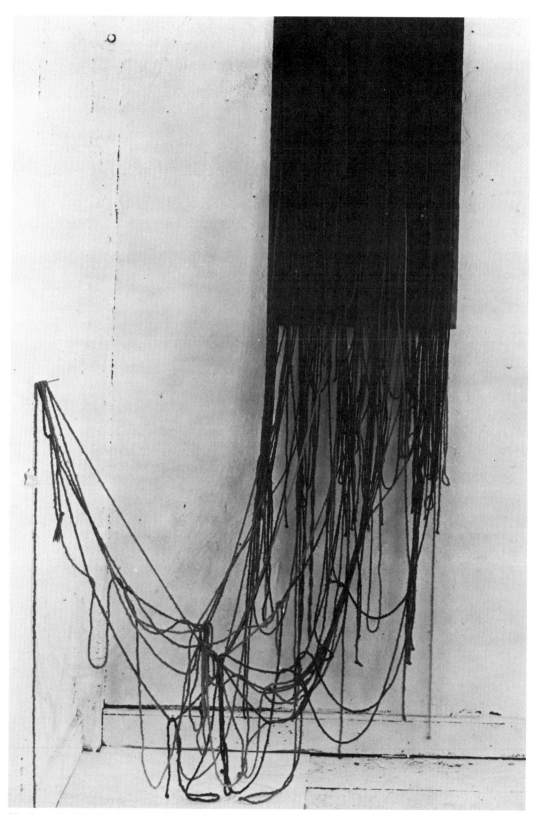

80. Ennead, 1966, dyed string and painted papier-mâché, 36 x 22 x 1½″.

81. Compart, 1966, acrylic paint, cord over papier-mâché and masonite, 48 x 9 x 12″.
82. Untitled, 1966, acrylic paint, cord and papier-mâché over masonite, 33 x 10–12 x ½–2¼″.

83. Untitled, 1966, acrylic paint, cord over papier-mâché on masonite, 9 x 9 x 2".
84. Untitled, 1966, acrylic paint, cord over papier-mâché on wood, 7½ x 7½ x 4".

In the spring of 1966, Hesse was making small rectangular reliefs enclosing circles in various ways. While the color was not graded, the reliefs, utilizing the wound cord technique of *Ringaround Arosie* (fig. 46), frequently appeared in multipartite series which produced a similar effect, with formal permutations taking the place of tonal ones. *Compart,* a black, four-part piece (fig. 81) involves a serial progression in size (9 x 9"; 10 x 10"; 11 x 11"; 12 x 12"), in the amount of space between the plywood panels (1", 2", 3"), and in the manner in which the three circles are divided onto four panels. A smaller peice, light gray, including two circles cut at different places (fig. 82), is also hung with a larger interval between the second two than the first two panels; the center of the second circle seems to completely disappear into space. While there is a clear connection to the work of LeWitt or Judd, these reliefs bear Hesse's own obsessive stamp. Two other small single gray reliefs (figs. 83, 84) almost identical, hold a single "breast" shape in much higher relief; these were originally planned as three increasingly large panels, each with a full circle, and were still in progress in January 1967.

It was also around this time that Hesse began to search for more esoteric titles, inspired by the recent purchase of a large thesaurus. A poetic list of possible titles ("marking time, nice question, liar's dice, make sense, last not least, fairly fast, 3 of a kind, pride's profile") was never used, and was replaced by more "intellectual" words like those drawn from the thesaurus category "circular motion," referring to the forms she was using and also, perhaps, to my choice of the word "eccentric" for the forthcoming exhibition she would be in: "circumnavigation/circumflexion/circuit/evolution/circumscribe/circuitous, devious/*rotation*, gyration, convolution/vortex, maelstrom, vertigiousness, vertigo/rotate, box the compass, gyrate/unfoldment, evolution, inversion/circle—cordon, cincture, cestus, baldric/(complex circularity) convolution, involution, undulation, sinuosity/coil—labyrinth/wind, twine, twirl, entwine, undulate/meander, indent, contort/involved—labyrinthine/in and out/eccentric." Above "Several" in her notebook, she wrote "abundant"; "Intertwined Vortex" and "Metronomic Regularity/Met-ro-no-mic irregularity" appear inside the cover. Another list includes some titles she did use: "Vertiginous Detour/box the compass/baldric/labyrinth/Ennead/Several/ingeminate/biaxial/diatic dyadic/dithyletic/bigeminate/ingemination-repetition/ennead—a group or set of nine."

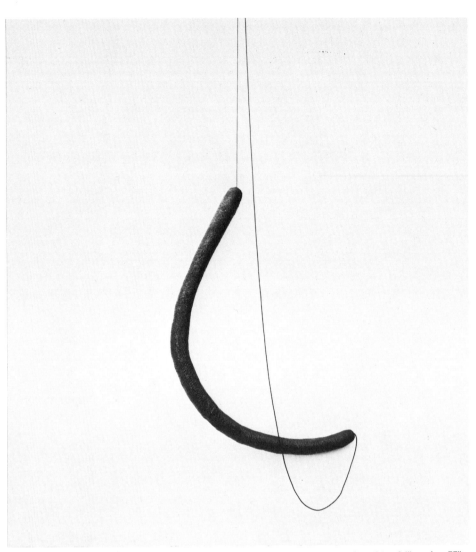

85. Untitled, 1966, enamel paint, cord, over papier-mâché and balloon, string, 31 x 26″, string 77″.

At the same time, Hesse's use of materials was slowly becoming more sophisticated. She had begun by using homemade papier-mâché—newspapers and paste; a friend then brought her some of the kind sold in stores—bits of paper in a plastic bag—and she mixed that with wood chips and epoxy, at one time applying the concoction over egg boxes. A series of five interesting but minor hanging pieces from early 1966, with a dominant "sausage," "boomerang," "gourd" or "strangulated penis" shape, were made from papier-mâché over balloons (figs. 85–87). When one friend saw these, her reaction was "slight horror. I was really shocked at their strong sexuality." Robert Ryman traded a painting for an "unwrapped" or unfinished boomerang which was still a white papier-mâché shell. He liked it better than some of the finished pieces: "It was all there; she didn't really have to put string around it; it was just what it was; she liked it that way too but wouldn't sign it or consider it complete." Another of these pieces (fig. 86), a more gradual curve, was deliberately broken at the end so that its tip hangs from the cord that the whole is wrapped in.

Among the "possibilities" Hesse listed that spring were "Large balloon papier-mâché off of wall; chain—another smaller attached and on floor" (perhaps another attempt at *Long Life*); "Stove pipe . . . relief pieces. Like Vietnam board collage[14]

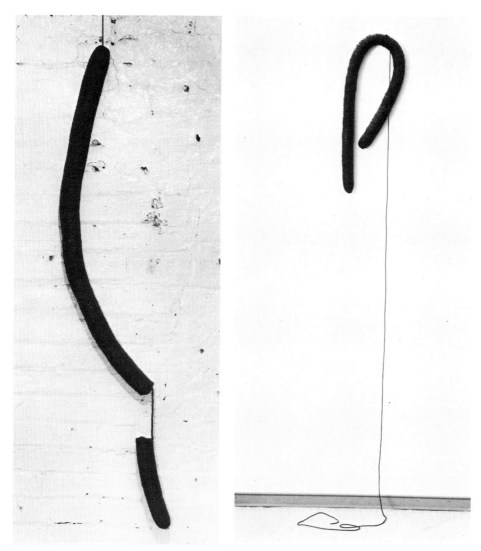

86. Untitled, 1966, enamel paint, cord, over papier-mâché and balloon, 46½ x 11½ x 2½".
87. Untitled, 1966, enamel paint, cord, over papier-mâché and balloon, 9¾ x 2 x 98¼".

and glue with wood chip. (Can even attach papier-mâché balloons onto board and incorporate.)'' She got Ryman to show her how to frame her drawings cheaply with glass and tape, and gradually, through friends, she acquired sculptural training and a knowledge of carpentry and materials with which, as a married woman, she had been unfamiliar. Around this time she visited Marisol's studio and here, as at Bontecou's (and Sylvia Stone's) she found a female model for this kind of work; she wrote in her diary: "Marisol does all her work herself. She will try anything. Experiment with any media, incorporating all things. What she does tho is leave too much on the surface. Design, decoration. Mystery is lost. . . . It sits, can expect it and there it is, a ring or necklace, a shoe, a glass or mirror. When her pieces hide something from the viewer we look at it differently.''

In the middle of that winter Hesse's marriage ended; Doyle moved across the street to his studio, which was difficult for her. She was teaching art to psychiatric patients and Ethelyn Honig was sharing her studio. For a while the artist and writer Ann Wilson, also ending a marriage, shared her living quarters, and Hesse saw a good deal of her circle, which included critic Gene Swenson,[15] artists Michael Todd, Paul Thek, and Joe Raffaele, writers Fred Tuten and Simona Marini. In contrast to LeWitt, Bochner, *et al.*, these friends encouraged the ''fetishistic'' aspects of her work. Paul Thek compared it to Lucas Samaras', which pleased her.

88. 1965–66 sculpture photographed in Hesse's Bowery studio.

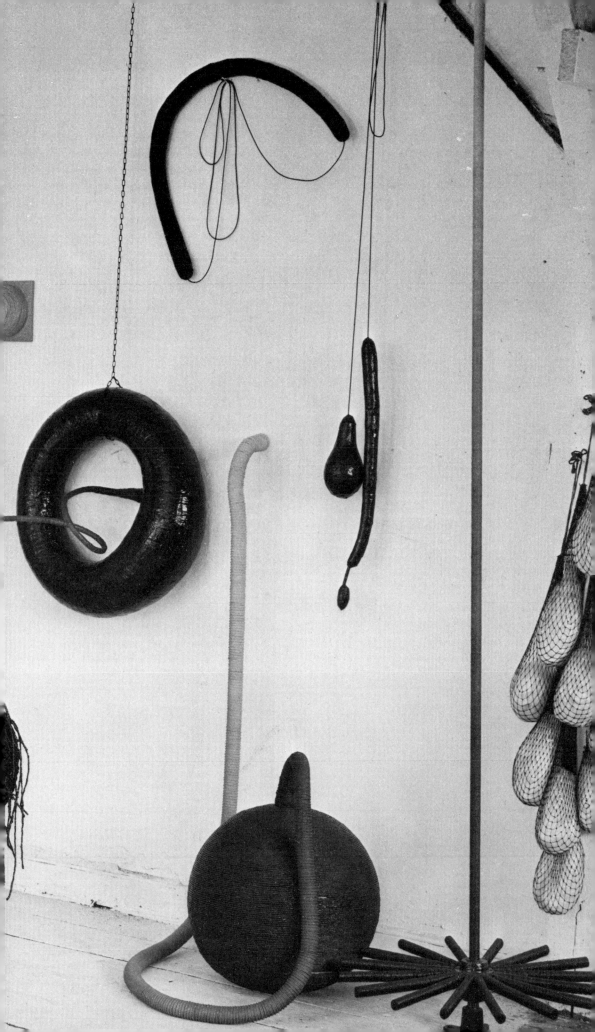

At this point two opportunities to show the new work presented themselves. During that winter I had been struck by the manner in which Hesse and Frank Lincoln Viner were working both within and outside of the current geometric tendencies, and I began looking for other artists confronting that dialectic. Donald Droll of the Fischbach Gallery offered me their new space on 57th Street for the opening show in September 1966, and I dreamed up the unfortunate title "Eccentric Abstraction." The spring before it took place, both Hesse and Viner were asked to be in another small group show at the Graham Gallery, organized by Joan Washburn. Still more unfortunately titled "Abstract Inflationism and Stuffed Expressionism," it also included Jean Linder, Philip Orenstein and Marc Morrell. Hesse showed *Hang-Up, Long Life,* and *Ishtar.* The show's flippant title influenced the way the work was seen: Robert Pincus-Witten described *Long Life* as a "slapstick ball and chain which might easily pass for an anarchist bomb designed by a color-blind obsessive-compulsive" (*Artforum,* May 1966), while John Gruen saw *Hang-Up* as a "stylistically uncertain wall-hanging" (*New York,* March 13, 1966). It was, however, a lively show, and Hesse's work was well received among artists.

She was, in fact, acquiring a growing underground reputation. "It's wild," she wrote, "I have many critics writers believing in me before I have really shown —Lucy [Lippard], Mel [Bochner], Gene [Swenson], [Robert] Smithson, all want to write about it—wild. Mel says he has heard much talk about my work." In 1966 dealers Klaus Kertess and Dick Bellamy came to her studio, and someone told her that the collector Robert Scull had cited her when asked "what's new and good on the scene," though he never bought anything. Her confidence was also boosted by the fact that she disliked Doyle's show in June at the Dwan Gallery, though she was acutely jealous of his place in that gallery which also handled LeWitt, as of that spring, and took on Robert Smithson in September. ("My whole world is in Dwan," she wrote at that time. "She [Virginia Dwan] does not accept me as an artist.") Hesse also felt that even her best male friends did not take her seriously when other men were around, and her contradictory feelings about where she stood are reflected in two diary entries. The first described an evening at the sculptor Ruth Vollmer's with Brian O'Doherty, Barbara Novak, Will Insley, Bob Smithson, Nancy Holt Smithson, and Mel Bochner. "Smithson and Mel described and highly praised my work. Necessary because 1) I am relatively unknown 2) am woman. Am sure that exists for all, however. I must drop that thought as totally meaningless." The second entry repeats a chorus she often used to fortify herself: "I am excited. Going away [to visit friends in Easthampton] . . . work, organizing . . . My work is good, I am pretty, I am liked, I am respected."

Hesse's "main summer piece" was *Metronomic Irregularity* for the "Eccentric Abstraction" show. At first she had wanted to show *Laocoon,* but in June, after seeing the space, she noted "lousy ceiling . . . my big piece Laocoon will not be right with all the gadgetry above." The necessity to make a new large piece produced a mingled fear and excitement, as indicated by such diary entries as: "Lucy wants me to do a big piece for show. It scares me to have it put that way. A finality also like an examination"; "Lucy—as earlier thought a space filled, my environment, ambiance, space. Anything I want to"; and later, "Anxiety increasing about the show. My work broken on way or there." She was thinking in terms of structures "seen three different ways" and existing simultaneously on "ceiling, side wall, floor." She wanted to work with cord or wire—"cord hung loosely, tightly, connecting, disconnect vertiginous regularity"—which then turned inside out to become *Metronomic Irregularity,* or the antithesis of *Ennead.* In August she ordered the cloth-covered wire and made several drawings and a model; the piece itself would have to be constructed in the gallery.

70

89. Untitled, 1966, gouache, 12 x 9″, Fourcade, Droll, Inc., New York.

The same month, in a needed respite from anxiety, Hesse went to visit the Honigs on the shore at Loveladies, New Jersey. One day she did sand castings on the beach with Ethelyn Honig and her daughter Deirdre: "Eva made triangular shapes, and with her fingers made long holes which, when reversed, became protuberances, slightly obscene, on a flat surface. There were about four of them. Unfortunately they were of plaster of Paris and were destroyed because of their fragility." It was also on this visit that she began to make the profoundly beautiful wash and ink circle drawings which continued through 1968. They provided another outlet for her energies, less frustrating than the sculpture, and important since drawing had always been crucial to her. There are indications that during the winter of 1965–66 she was searching for a drawing style that would parallel and give birth to new work the way the German "machine" drawings had produced the first reliefs. She had continued to make variations on these into mid-1966 (fig. 89), but their relationship to the new sculpture was too distant. When she arrived at the circles, a motif already present in the three-dimensional work, she may have missed the freedom of the more automatic imagery she had always used, but this could not have lasted long, since she extracted from this very simple formula—primarily rows of circles with or without centers—an endless internal vitality that made each one different (figs. 90–100).

90. Untitled, 1966, gouache, 9 x 11¾″, Fourcade, Droll, Inc., New York.

The drawings can be divided into two predominant types: the first consisting of rows of usually concentric circles contained in a visible or invisible grid; the second, larger or "target" circles, one or few to the page, also contained in rectangular compartments. There also are the mavericks—those in which all the grids are not filled by circles, or the circles cover four of the grid squares, or pale diagonal lines cross the grid; some are almost (but never quite) mechanical in execution; some are centered by pin pricks, presumably to add threads or strings later, and so on. They exclude no shade of feeling and formal diversity. Some are open, light-filled fields of little dark-or-light centered circles. Some are dark, ominous, almost invisible, the precise delineation of the circles absorbed into the cloud of wash until the drawing is carefully perused. These come into focus almost like Ad Reinhardt paintings—a possible influence, since the "black monk" was a friend of Ruth Vollmer's and much admired by LeWitt, Smithson, myself, and by Joseph Kosuth, also a friend of Hesse's at that time; Reinhardt's retrospective, for which I wrote the catalogue, was at the Jewish Museum in the winter of 1966–1967. I remember talking to Hesse about him, but of course she too was already at home in those shadowed areas.

Touch, both in sculpture and drawing, was so important to Hesse that it pervaded everything she did, even the simplest of ideographs. Impressed as she was with the deadpan "working drawings" of friends like LeWitt or Bochner, even in her graph paper series (also begun in 1966) where the tiny squares are simply filled with single circles or x's in pen and ink (figs. 101–105), the effect is not one of detachment. A rectangle of graph paper filled with hundreds of minute circles produced not a mechanical but a highly *textured* surface. The process, the activity itself, always emphasized her obsessiveness. (She claimed she could never make a "representational drawing," although in Maine the next summer she did studies of unshelled clams which are unique in her oeuvre–fig. 105.)

During the summer of 1966, things seemed to be progressing in favor of a new and balanced life, focused entirely on her work. (She took my son Ethan for a walk and enjoyed it, saying, already in the past tense, "it would have been nice to have a little boy.") Although some of her work was falling apart ("two pieces; two other pieces discolored from the varnish") she remarked "so what. They are not wasted. I went further in the work that followed. I take more care technically, I plan and figure out more wisely." She also saw a great deal of a small group who met several times a week—the Smithsons, Dan Graham, LeWitt, and Bochner in particular. They too felt that this was a "crucial time," a "fertile period," and came together out of common need as well as common interest. LeWitt was the oldest and to some extent the center of the group, "interested in other people's ideas, open to discussion," Bochner recalls. LeWitt's encouragement was invaluable to Hesse, although their relationship was not always a simple one.

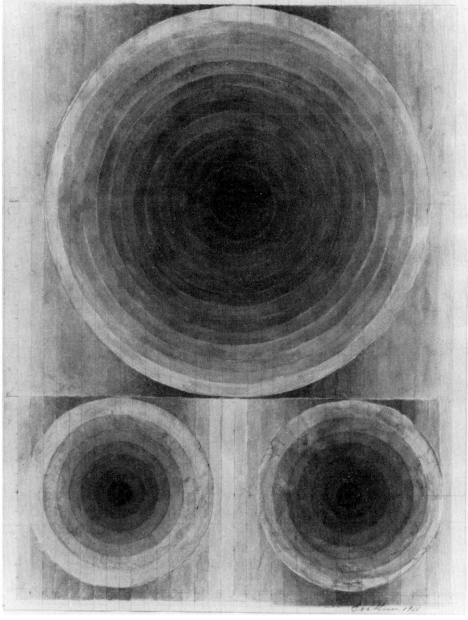

91. Untitled, 1966, ink wash and pencil, 12 x 9½", Xavier Fourcade, New York.

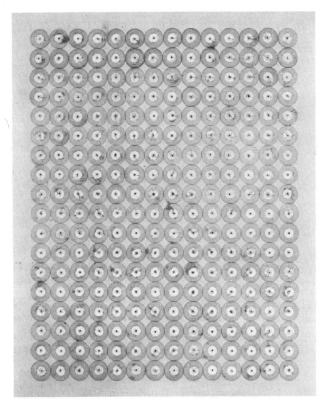

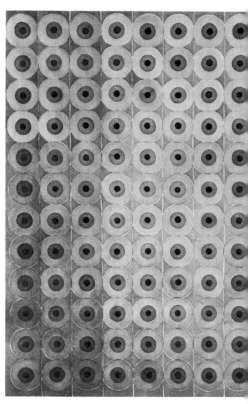

92. Untitled, 1966, ink wash on cardboard, 9½ x 7¾", Steingrim Laursen, Copenhagen.
93. Untitled, c. 1966, ink wash, 12 x 8½", Steingrim Laursen, Copenhagen.

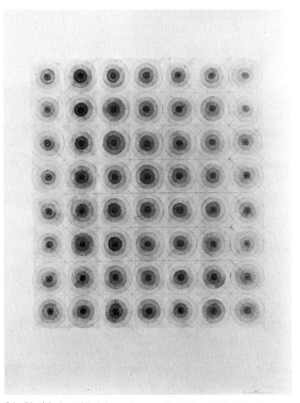

94. Untitled, 1966, ink wash, pencil, 11⅞ x 9½", The Museum of Modern Art, New York, Gift of Mr. and Mrs. Fischbach.
95. Untitled, c. 1966, ink wash, 10¾ x 13½", Paul F. Walter, New York.

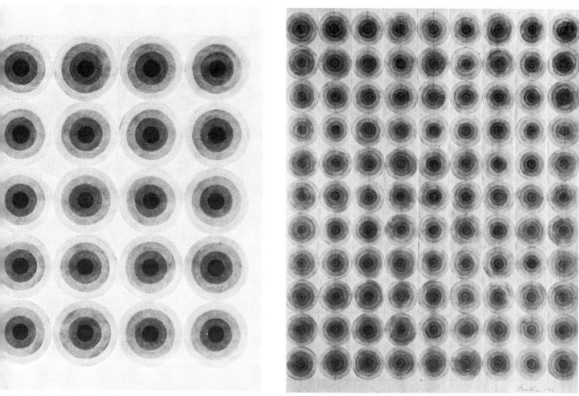

Untitled, 1966, ink wash, 12 x 9", Mr. and Mrs. Murray Charash.
Untitled, 1966, ink wash and pencil, 12 x 9", John J. Reiss, Milwaukee.

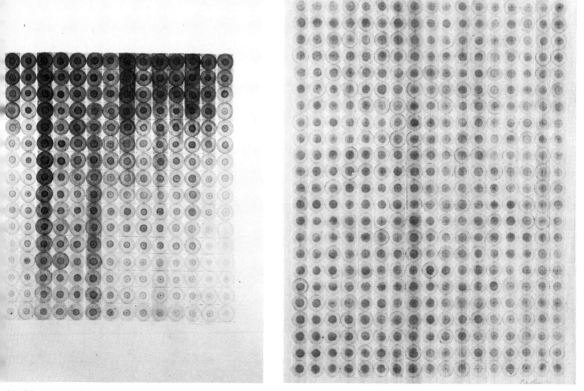

Untitled, 1966, ink wash and pencil, 8¾ x 7½", private collection, New York.
Untitled, 1966, ink wash, 12 x 9", Racelle Strick, New York.

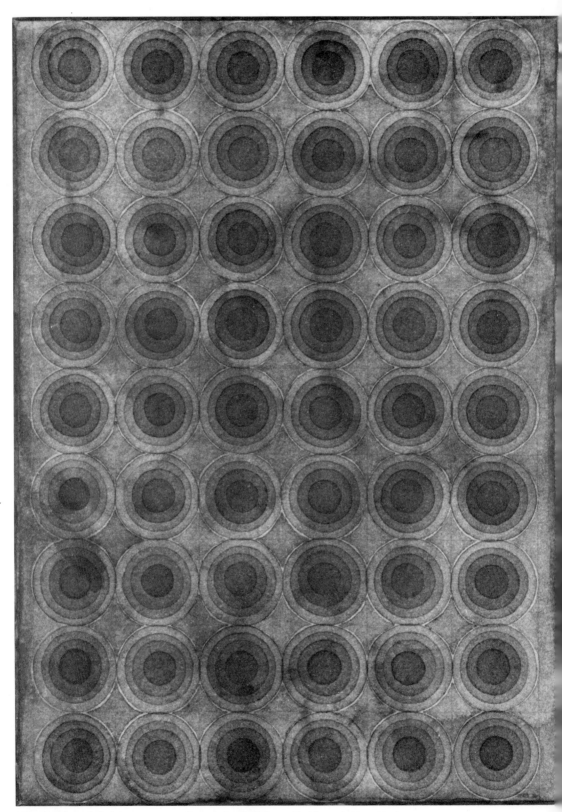

100. Untitled, 1967, ink wash on cardboard, 9 x 6½″, Lucy R. Lippard, New York.

101. Untitled, 1967, ink on blue graph paper, 11 x 8½″, Dorothy and Herbert Vogel, New York.
102. Untitled, 1967, ink on blue graph paper, 11 x 8½″, private collection, New York.

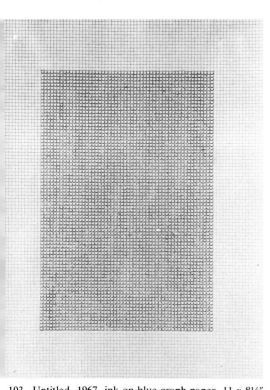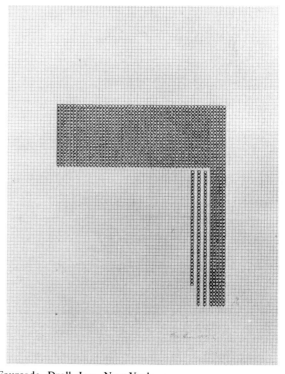

103. Untitled, 1967, ink on blue graph paper, 11 x 8½″, Fourcade, Droll, Inc., New York.
104. Untitled, 1967, ink on blue graph paper, 12 x 9½″, Fourcade, Droll, Inc., New York.

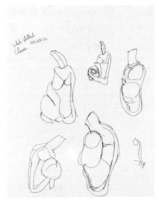

105. Whole Shelled Clams, Atlantic, 1967, pen and ink, 10 x 8″, Lucy R. Lippard, New York.

On August 16, she received a terrible blow, one which only the prospect of the important show coming up could begin to assuage. Her father died in Switzerland, and all the terrors of her first parental abandonment surfaced again. With admirable strength Hesse could, even in the lowest depths of despair, relieve some of the pressure by intelligent, if agonizing, verbalization of her predicament, and then return to her studio and transform all those feelings, doubts, and burdens into fine abstract sculpture. The fall of 1966 she was very tense, a combination of her anxieties about the show, her father's death, her usually suppressed envy of her rapidly succeeding male friends, her personal longing for a satisfying relationship with a man, and her lingering emotions for and anger at Doyle. The "Eccentric Abstraction" show opened September 20 and her fears turned out to be well-founded when the piece was installed. Hesse placed each tiny wire in its hole on one plaque and then attached it to a hole on the next. As this process continued, the stress on the panels increased, and after two days, when she was placing the last wires in this tedious process, the piece burst off the wall. Hesse was hysterical. Donald Droll, with whom she had been "rather shy," came to the rescue, took her out for a drink, calmed her down, and became from then on a close and supportive friend. LeWitt and Bochner, who had hung the panels for her, blamed themselves for not realizing the tension; they then bolted the piece to the wall and Hesse repeated the construction process. The damage was negligible but the experience was traumatic.

106. Eva Hesse with her father, Wilhelm Hesse, at the opening of "Abstract Inflationism and Stuffed Expressionism" at the Graham Gallery, New York, March 1966.

Metronomic Irregularity I, II, III: The "model" differs from its finished version not only in that there are two panels instead of three, but in that its orientation is vertical rather than horizontal. The two gray plaques are drawn into a grid with a hole at every intersection; from each of these holes on one plaque, to another hole on the second, runs a white cotton-covered wire. In the model, some of the holes are skipped, and the wires over the empty space (the distance a little narrower than the size of a third plaque) are quite tangled, as though a random system had been used. In *Metronomic Irregularity II,* the major version, the three panels are square and the two spaces between are the same size as the panels. The wires run much more regularly, presumably from a hole on one panel to its counterpart, or opposite, on the next one, and so forth. The central panel does not seem to have twice as many wires, but sends or receives some from one side, some from the other, with some overlapping. The wires here are not tangled, but form graceful irregular waves, difficult to follow to and from their sources. *Metronomic Irregularity III* was made after Hesse had traded the first version to Robert Smithson. (She was sorry not to have kept it for herself.) In this third version, the replacement of the empty spaces with two more panels, set back from the original three, detracts from the airiness of the wires, which are dark this time, and makes the whole piece too static and solid for its small scale. *Metronomic Irregularity* could be called one of Hesse's last "paintings." Having used line with this much freedom, but still against a planar surface, she was later able to follow the implications into real space with *Right After* (fig. 208).

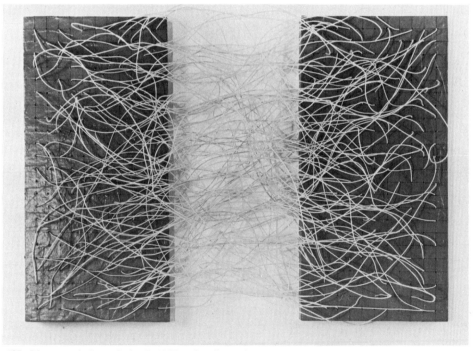

107. Metronomic Irregularity I, 1966, painted wood, sculpmetal, cotton-covered wire, 12 x 18 x 1".

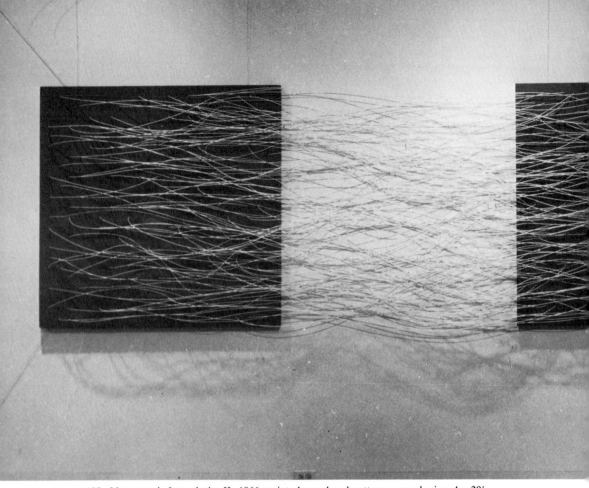

108. Metronomic Irregularity II, 1966, painted wood and cotton-covered wire, 4 x 20'.

In 1968, Hesse seems to have returned to the possibilities suggested by *Metronomic Irregularity*. A note suggests "cast 4 x 4 x 4 ecc. abst. with hose in each hole. hose ⅛ clear hose." Drawings from around summer 1968 show three other variations, all with the wires, straight lines this time, running from wall to floor, in two cases from one square panel to another (figs. 110, 111), and in the third from four flat bars on the wall to four on the floor, each containing five holes, the lines moving directly from one to another (fig. 112). Among other things, Hesse was playing with the variations in where the lines from the top could connect at the bottom, how far they could extend onto the floor, how dense these lines could be. Still another and much freer version (an undated sketch, but probably later in 1968) suggested a series of horizontal lines strung across each other from wall to wall or across a corner and hung from them, square "patches" with very long strings hanging to the floor. This was to be 35' long and the wall to wall lines were "one long wire" (fig. 113).

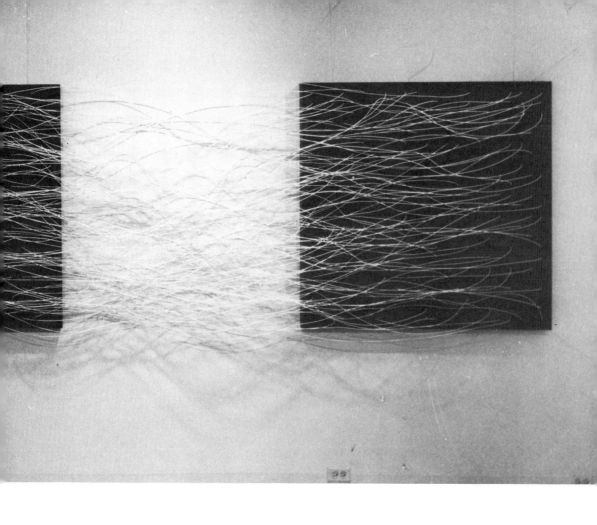

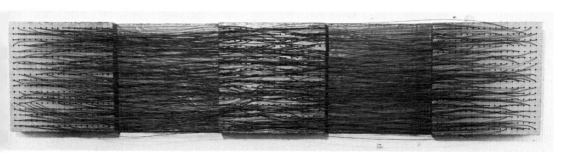

9. Metronomic Irregularity III, 1966, painted wood, sculpmetal and cotton-covered wire, 10 x 50 x 2¼".

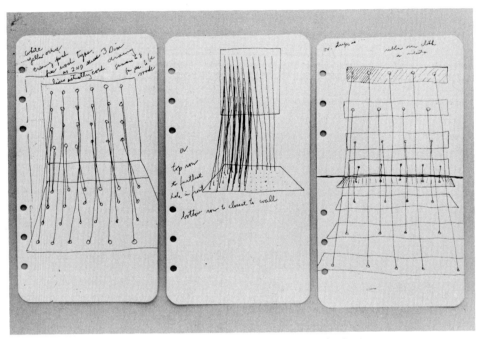

110–112. Notebook pages, 1967–68, pen and ink, 6¾ x 3¾″, Fourcade, Droll, Inc., New York.

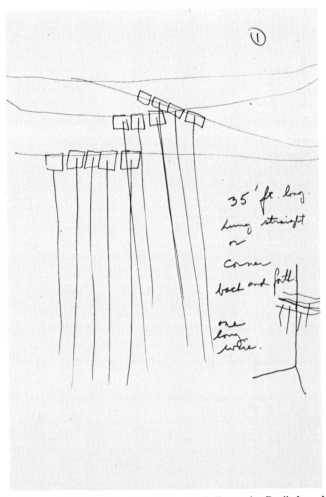

113. Notebook page, 1967–68, pen and ink, 8⅞ x 5⅞″, Fourcade, Droll, Inc., New York.

At the time, I was somewhat surprised at the precision of *Metronomic Irregularity II*, although that same precision amounted in fact to the maze-like obsessiveness (image merged with process) I found one of the most attractive aspects of Hesse's work. I was even a little disappointed, selfishly, not because the piece wasn't beautiful, but because I had conceived this exhibition in terms of the more organic character of Hesse's work, paralleled one way or another by Viner's floppy pop-colored envelopes, Louise Bourgeois' overtly sexual latex membranes, Alice Adams' giant chain link womb form, Bruce Nauman's exhausted rubber streamers, Don Potts' undulating wood and leather sculptures, Gary Kuehn's frozen-to-melted conjunctions and Keith Sonnier's vinyl-versus-wooden enclosures, one of which "breathed." *Metronomic Irregularity* wholly overshadowed *Several* (fig. 68), which was a radical piece in its own right, and *Ingeminate* (fig. 67), which were also shown. I was not trying to "create a movement," but rather to indicate that there were emotive or "eccentric" or erotic alternatives to a solemn and deadset Minimalism which still retained the clarity of that notion. I had traveled on both coasts looking at work, with Hesse's image at the back of my mind. *Hang-up*, with its awkward shift from the geometric, would have been just fine; *Metronomic Irregulurity*'s delicacy and assurance, its understatement and focus on structure, put me in the frustrating position of a critic whose generalizations have been proved untenable. I have since come to prefer that position to anything else, but in 1966 I had been writing only a year and this was the first exhibition I had organized.[16] In the text accompanying the soft vinyl announcement of the show, I expounded what I had had in mind (and what the artists had subtly denied by their work): "These artists are eccentric because they refuse to forego imagination and the expansion of sensuous experience while they also refuse to sacrifice the solid formal basis demanded of the best in current non-objective art. . . . Eccentric abstraction thrives on contrast, but contrást handled uniquely, so that opposites become complementary instead of contradictory. . . . In eccentric abstraction, evocative qualities or specific organic associations are kept at a subliminal level, without the benefit of Freudian clergy. . . . Ideally a bag remains a bag and does not become a uterus, a tube is a tube and not a phallic symbol. Too much free association on the viewer's part is combatted by formal understatement, which stresses a non-verbal response and often heightens sensuous reactions by crystallizing them. . . . Eva Hesse's intricately controlled labyrinth and tight-bound, paradoxically bulbous forms do not move, but their effect is also [like Sonnier's] both fixed and potentially changeable. The finality of their black to gray gradations is countered by an unexpectedly unfixed space and their mood is both strong and vulnerable, tentative and expansive." Mel Bochner's review in *Arts Magazine* (November 1966) was, in its Smithsonian tone, perhaps more appropriate to the work shown: "Eva Hesse's work was the best in the exhibition. It has become more involuted since her last showing and like all good work is not eccentric at all or any other epithet. . . . The result [of *Metronomic Irregularity*] is not chaos but a structure ordered in itself yet unavailable to comprehension. The totality is mind-boggling. It is a fabrication of entanglement, a logical fiction. Regular, remote, and lifeless. Her other pieces, atrophied organs and private parts, encased in string and painted black are not garish or horrifying. The lacerated shiny surfaces have a detached presence which is real. Hesse's work has an awkwardness similar to that of reality which is equally empty of inherent meaning or simplistic contrasts." David Antin, reviewing the show in *Artforum* (November 1966), liked *Metronomic Irregularity* less than the other two pieces and was not enthused about either, while Hilton Kramer in the *New York Times* (September 25, 1966), later an admirer of Hesse's, saw its imagery as "second-hand . . . [it] simply adapts the imagery of Jackson Pollock's drip painting to a three-dimensional medium." Several years later, the "Eccentric Abstraction'' show was touted as the source of ''anti-form,'' a pontification deriving strictly from hindsight. But these artists did lay the groundwork, and while most of us were unaware of it at the time, Flanagan, Dibbets, Long, and Beuys were making similar combinations in Europe.

Waiting for Gretchen Lambert to come and photograph her work around the end of 1966, Hesse wrote in her diary: "Almost one year's work. There is lots. It is good! Very Good. A most strange year. Lonely, strange—But a lot of growth and inward search." On Christmas Eve she inscribed a new hardbound notebook: "It is a fitting ending for another strange, bewildering, sad and yet strangely productive year. A final abandonment. And Daddy's death. And now on to work, and other changes, changes for another start." Her friends urged her to leave her loft, which dragged so much of her past into her present. She was often alone in the building; two sculptors across the street masturbated at their window, and someone was shooting at her back windows with a BB gun. She was frightened and unhappy there, but also psychologically rooted to the spot. It was still her home when she died.

Professionally, however, things were going well. Donald Droll had bought *Several* out of the ''Eccentric Abstraction'' show, and *Ishtar* was sold to Florette Lynn. A Texas collector was supposed to buy *Metronomic Irregularity II*, but this fell through. There was interest in her work from Robert Doty of the Whitney Museum and from the Larry Aldrich Museum. She continued to gain the respect of her peers. (''Nancy [Holt] told me during beer party at Yale [after a December 14 symposium by Smithson, Judd, Morris, and LeWitt at which Hesse took copious notes] that Don Judd very much liked my work. Still so important to me. Took immediate effect.'') And she was soon to be represented by Fischbach, which during these years also showed Mangold, Ryman, Smith, and Bladen. Her notebooks were full of drawings for new pieces, many never executed, though similar ones were. In December, Mel Bochner's innovative ''Working Drawing'' show at the School of Visual Arts provoked ''a lot more drawings, measurements, etc.,'' though Hesse was never at ease with mechanical or scale drawing.[17] She was working on pieces combining simple progressions and hanging or looped rubber lines, and on smaller reliefs with magnets, washers, sculpmetal, and woodshavings. Some of the pieces sketched but never executed had a faintly mechanical flavor, as though some part of her wanted to go back to a more ''eccentric'' image, but the work of 1967, taken as a whole, is the most geometric, serial, and Minimal of her career. It was, in fact, Minimalism's triumphant year, a period of great excitement and discussion of the ''issues,'' and a certain success for LeWitt, Smithson, Ryman, and Mangold. In November 1967, Hesse was in the opening show of the storefront Museum of Normal Art, one of the multiple birthplaces of so-called ''conceptual art,'' a term coined (in that context) by LeWitt, and applied to the work of Graham, Kosuth, and Bochner, among others.

While Hesse was very much in the midst of all this, she was at the same time professionally somewhat apart. One aspect of her work these artists liked so much was that it was so different from their own, although Smithson felt particularly close to Hesse in 1966–67, when he himself was going through a ''crisis of abstraction . . . I couldn't accept the Reinhardtian dogmas; it was a turbulence that she comprehended.'' He felt his sculpture *Alogon* dealt with a ''surd state'' also present in her work, ''where things don't quite hold up in terms of a given abstraction. We would talk about contrasts, things playing off each other, while she was making *Laocoon*. Her work had a strong impact on me. I was counter to the prevailing minimal situation myself and she had some of that in her work, but it derived from a biological organism, a kind of mummification.'' He reproduced the first version of *Laocoon* and its Hellenistic ''source'' in ''Quasi-Infinities and the Waning of

Space'' (*Arts*, November 1966), where he said about it: ''. . . we discover an absence of 'pathos' and a deliberate avoidance of the anthropomorphic. Instead one is aware only of the vestigital [sic] and devitalized 'snakes' looping through a lattice with cloth bound joints. Everything 'classical' and 'romantic' is mitigated and underminded [sic]. The baroque esthetic of the original Laokoon [sic] with its flowing lines—soft and fluid—is transformed into a dry, skeletal tower that goes nowhere.'' While this text may say more about Smithson's esthetic at the time than Hesse's, it demonstrates the resolutely nonassociative approach shared by these artists—whether or not they considered themselves Minimalists. It is no surprise that in this company Hesse suppressed much of her emotive inclination, and it is fortunate that this suppression seems to have been just the right prescription. When she later moved back in a more expressionist direction, she was able to take or leave what she had learned of rigorous structuring during 1967.

All the work from this year is gray and/or black, predominantly a middle-range gray. The forms are usually very simple and very clear and the obsessive and modeled or detailed use of materials sustained her need for a more personal contact. However, in the course of the year Hesse was also persuaded by her friends to take a step which was basically foreign to her, but had become de rigueur for the Minimalists—that of outside or factory fabrication. Though her natural surfaces made industrial construction contradictory, it would enable her to work faster and more professionally (the latter particularly appealed to her); everybody else did it and she could work closely with the fabricators and control her own surfaces. She had many doubts (so did I) but fortunately, considering her future sickness, unsuspected at the time, she had the courage to try it. The decision, made then voluntarily rather than later involuntarily, probably guaranteed her completing several more works in her short lifetime than she would have otherwise.

At this point Hesse's dependence upon her notebooks drastically decreased. The entries became sparse and sketchy and after early 1967, very little of importance to her work can be gleaned from them, aside from drawings, and copious notes on materials, chemicals, and fabrication techniques. She continued to use her diaries as exercise books for her analyst, but that function too is more fragmented. This may have been due to increased communication with other artists and increased involvement in her work, or to her growing conviction that she would be famous. As early as summer 1966 she began to describe a disturbing weekend with two friends and stopped, noting that if people were eventually to read the notebooks, she did not want to be cruel or invade the privacy of others.

In any case, for the first part of 1967 the only entries worth mentioning are the following: ''January 7: I am working relatively well. The eagerness and enthusiasm is at its highest point. I have many small new pieces. I am awaiting the two large boards I ordered 3 weeks ago.'' (One of these probably became *Constant*.) ''File—how to keep one. Ask Mel.'' ''Painting can be extended to Ryman, Tuttle. If Art seemingly had rules they're all temporary and there to be broken.'' (A wise precaution against the then prevailing dogmatism.) ''My work surprised Lou S. It does that to everyone.'' And about the opening of the Whitney Annual: ''Crowded. Pieces themselves without people hardly had the room they needed. It was depressing, people knowing nothing, just there as a place to go, or the right thing to have seen. . . . I wanted to get away.''

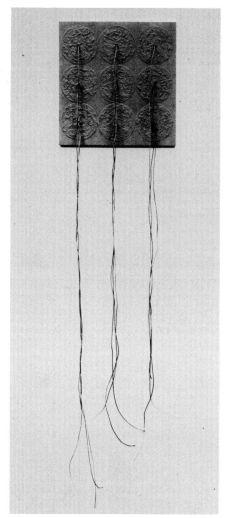

114. Ditto, 1967, sculpmetal on plexiglass,
wire cord, 15 x 14½", 70" with cords.

Ditto; Untitled; and *One More Than One: Ditto* is a nine circle grid of flattish sculpmetal
textures on smooth ground, closely related both to the circle drawings and to *Ishtar* (fig. 70);
from the circles' centers drop lanky rubber cords of varying lengths which fall in three
irregular triple lines, curling at the ends, longer at the left than the right. This hanging cord,
one of Hesse's favorite sculptural elements from the beginning, was used particularly often
in 1967, perhaps because it provided a foolproof way (along with the impasto surface) to add
an imperfect element to her symmetrical schemes. The lines in *Ditto* considerably aggran-
dize the scale of this small relief by incorporating into it all the wall space between plaque and
floor. They serve a similar function in two even smaller reliefs, variations on the same idea.
Untitled has a single dome of texture which fills all but the corners of its square plaque, is
hung quite high, and is extended by a single rubber line to the floor, where it curls once. Its
simplicity and its sadness are both inescapable. *One More Than One* has a crudely lunar
texture on a light gray horizontal box, hollowed out into two concave circles, in an "eye-
like" inversion of the "breast" theme, from the centers of which come two thick rubber
tubes or "tears" (actually a single line run through both holes) that reach the floor and can
hang straight or coil around each other. Compared to the preceding piece, this one is almost
baroque, more sensuous than austere, and its rubber cords have a weight and elegance that is
far more effective than the scrawny strings of *Ditto*. On a formal level these pieces represent
a simple solution to the problems Hesse was setting for herself about sculptures that included
several surfaces (two walls, wall-floor, wall-ceiling). They also evoke that unconsciously
wistful quality which is so much a part of her work, the fleeting impression of a small creature
with a long tail, a poignant image similar to that of the "lost balloon" in her 1961 painting (fig.
19). Nevertheless, these circles were always caught within the abstract rectangle and firmly
attached thereby to the wall; the evocative domes were low-lying and unassertive. The
content is always escapable, but also within reach.

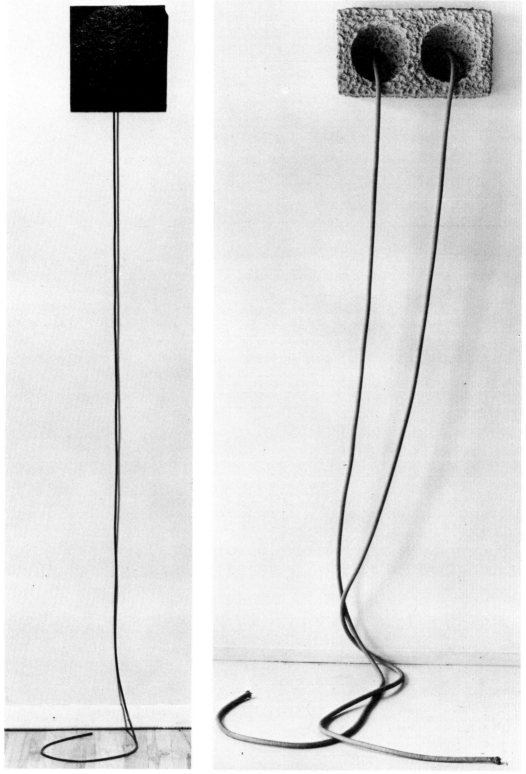

115. Untitled, 1966, woodshavings, glue, rubber tubing, 9 x 9″.

116. One More Than One, 1967, acrylic, papier-mâché, plastic cord, wood, 15½ x 8½ x 5½″.

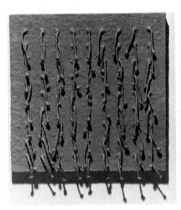

117. Untitled (Composition for Sylvia?), 1967, woodshavings, glue, acrylic paint, rubber tubing, wood, 12 x 10″.

118. Iterate, 1966, woodshavings, glue, string, acrylic paint, board, 20 x 20″.

119. Study for Sculpture, 1967, sculpmetal, cord, Elmer's Glue, Liquitex paint, varnish on masonite, 10 x 10 x 1″.

Constant; Untitled (or *Composition for Sylvia?*);[18] *Iterate;* and *Study for Sculpture: Untitled* and *Iterate* are probably both studies for *Constant,* one of Hesse's strongest pieces from this time. *Untitled,* because the scale relationship of its knotted tendrils and softly crusty plaque is so different, lacks the finished work's power, but has a peculiar humor and feisty presence of its own. A simple 4 x 4 grid protrudes into space and confuses itself as the rubber cords meet each other, finally almost obscuring the grid. *Iterate* has a finer surface and neater, less independent lines (string rather than rubber tubing) and its 9 x 9 grid does not activate the surface so much as divide it into parallel vertical sections.

Constant ("quantity that does not vary; number expressing a relation that remains the same for same substance in same conditions") is a typical product of obsessive activity (pulling the many cords through the surface and knotting them at the end) equalled by an obsessive surface, with the result that the piece is almost oppressive. Here the grid is 19 x 19 and the heavily rounded edges of the box-like relief, as well as the curly rubber lines, forces them out toward the viewer. The effect is one of vast space and the rubbery black shines ominously. Where in *Untitled* the rubber extrusions are clearly separate from their ground, in *Constant* the surface rills seem to extend naturally into the stubby extensions. *Study for Sculpture* is more subdued; its surface is just lightly modeled and a matte gray almost neutralizes the 9 x 9 grid of surgical cord extrusions, which, as in *Iterate,* hang straighter and have less life of their own despite the fact that each has two knots, one at the surface and one at the end. The masonite board was painted over in Elmer's glue, liquitex paint, and varnish; the resulting continuous surface is effectively muted.

Constant, 1967, woodshavings, glue, acrylic paint, rubber tubing, on board, 60 x 60 x 5¾″.

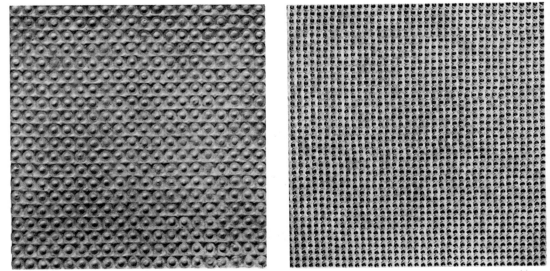

121. Compass, 1967, sculpmetal over steel washers and wood, 10 x 10 x 1¼".

122. Range, 1967, sculpmetal over metal grommets on wood, 12 x 12 x ¼".

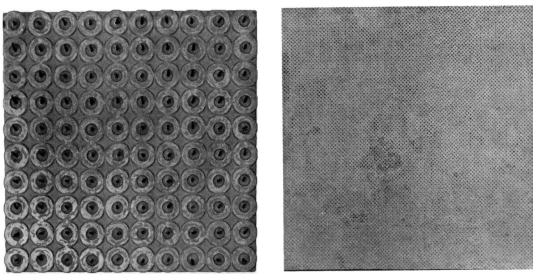

123. Cincture, 1967, sculpmetal over steel washers on wood, plastic tubing, 10 x 10 x 2".

124. Untitled, 1967, sculpmetal over steel washers on wood, 36 x 36 x 1".

Cincture; Range; Compass; Untitled; Untitled; Washer Table: All of the "washer pieces" resemble each other, although some are actually made of grommets rather than steel or rubber washers; these were laid in tight rows to cover completely a wood surface and then the whole was covered with sculpmetal. They recall the black circle drawings and the graph-paper drawings in both image and obsessiveness. They are almost drawings, or paintings, themselves, having little sculptural identity; even the boards are very thin, as though to further de-emphasize their volume. Some, however, subtly vary this theme. *Cincture* has a plastic extrusion coming from the center of each steel washer, and *Range,* being made of grommets, has a surface that glistens where the sculpmetal did not adhere to the raised rims. The washer table came about when LeWitt made Hesse a large square table painted white with a gray grid and told her "now you owe me a table." He provided the surface and she made the piece on it with black rubber washers.

125. Box with washers, grommets, etc., from Hesse's studio.

126. Washer Table, 1967, rubber washers on wood, 49½ x 49½ x 8½".

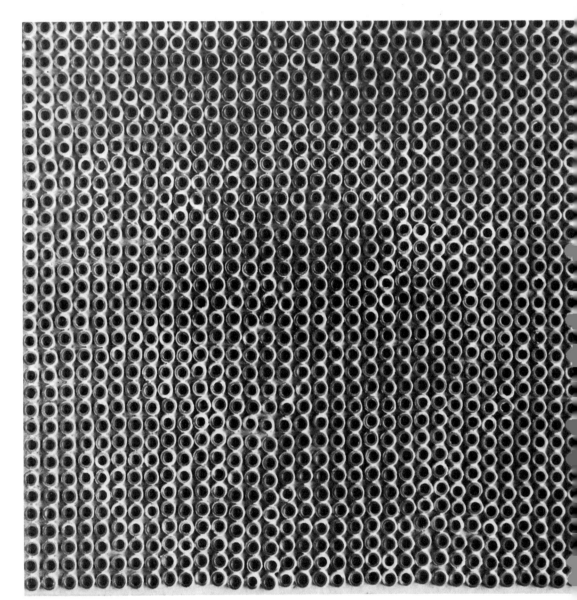

127. Untitled, 1967, sculpmetal over steel washers on wood, 8 x 8″.

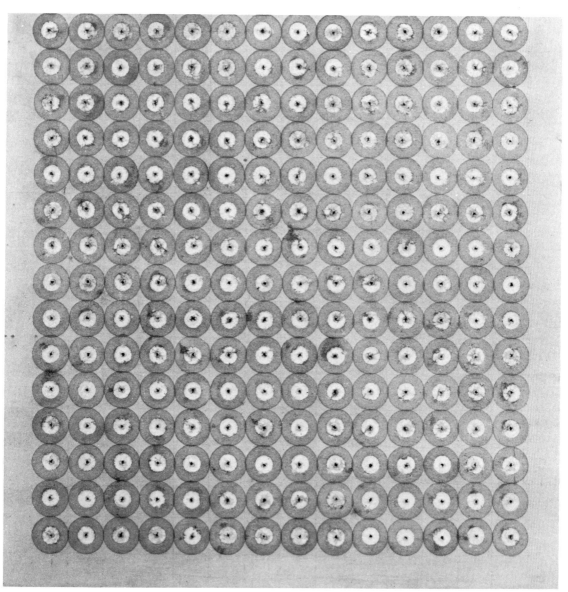

128. Untitled, 1967, ink wash on cardboard, 9½ x 7¾", Steingrim Laursen, Copenhagen.

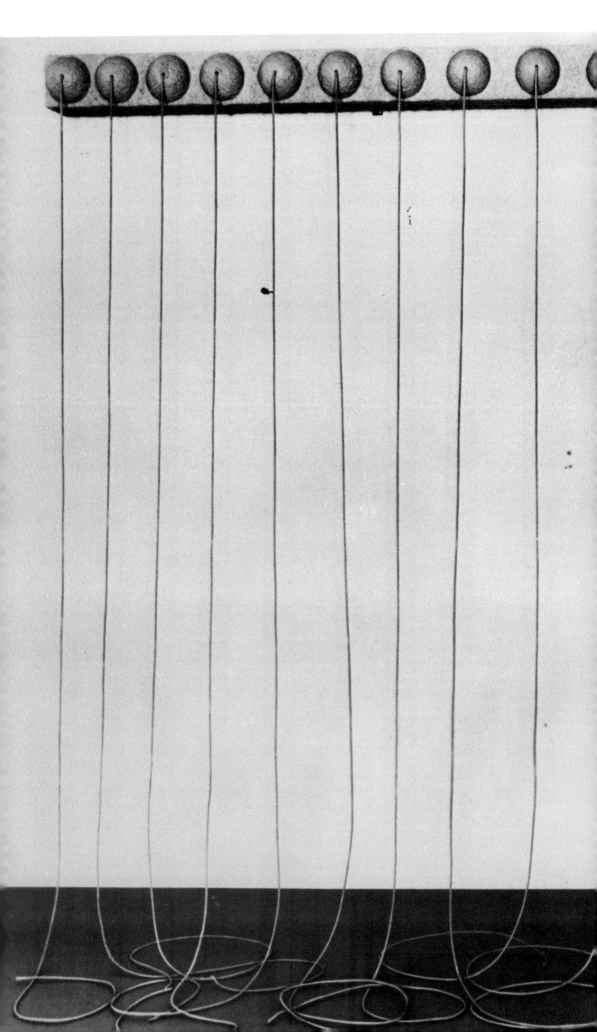

129. Addendum, 1967, painted papier-mâché, wood, rubber tubing, 5 x 119 x 6″, cords 84½″.

Addendum: By far the major piece of this year, it was shown in November 1967, in Finch College's "Serial Art" show. A prime mixture of so-called "logical" arrangement and random results, with a sensuous middle ground provided by the low domes, the texture, and the elegantly drooping cords, it went right to the heart of what "serial art" was about—*addition,* or addition to the point of absurdity. John Perreault wrote in the *Village Voice* (December 14, 1967) that only Hesse "sees, questions, and in a way relishes the absurd implications of this new cliché": and Charlotte Willard in the *New York Post* (December 9, 1967) quoted Ferenczi; "Pure intelligence is, in principle, madness." Hesse's own description of the piece, in the best detached and Minimal tone, was read by the artist onto an acoustiguide tape:

"The title of this work is Addendum; a thing added or to be added. A title is after the fact. It is titled only because that is preferred to untitled. Explanations are also after the fact. The work exists only for itself. The work must then contain its own import.
The structure is five inches high, nine feet eleven inches long, and six inches deep. A series of seventeen, five inch diameter semi-spheres are placed at increased intervals. The interval progression is as follows: ⅛, ⅜, ⅝, ⅞, 1⅛, 1⅜, 1⅝, 1⅞, etc. The semi-spheres are attached to the structure. They become unified with the structure by means of the repetition of form, and progressive sequence of placement. Equally unifying factors are the surface texture and the rope pulled through the center of each form. The three separate units are then made into one. The monochrome color is a light neutral gray. The chosen nine foot eleven inch structure, the five inch diameter semi-spheres and the long thin rope are as different in shape as possible. The choice of extremely different forms must reconcile themselves. To further jolt the equilibrium the top of the piece is hung seven feet high.
"The cord is flexible. It is ten feet long, hanging loosely but in parallel lines. The cord opposes the regularity. When it reaches the floor it curls and sits irregularly. The juxtaposition and actual connecting cord realizes the contradiction of the rational series of semispheres and irrational flow of lines on the floor. Series, serial, serial art, is another way of repeating absurdity." Originally, Hesse had planned the last line as her entire statement; it was to be repeated "three or more times."

Magnet Boards: It consists of four one-foot square shallow boxes, or trays, laid horizontally. Each bottom surface is divided into a grid with holes at each intersection; the grid units differ in each section, one is 11 x 14, another 11 x 15 and two are 10 x 13. One box holds twelve of the rough little gray painted magnets, each with a round hole in the center, but no lined grid or holes show under the uncovered part; one box holds 108 of these magnets, the third holds a "full set" of 143 magnets, and one is empty. Thus the piece is much more complicated and irregular than is immediately evident. In fact, until I wrote this, I had never questioned its symmetry, which I now find exists only as an impression. This would be so even if the ambiguous placement were changed. Levels of "imperfection" are more obviously carried through in the brushy surface of the sculpmetal grounds, the irregular lines, the lopsided magnets and the potential variability. All of these factors are skillfully controlled and used, perhaps, to point up once again the absurdity of things adding up, and not adding up. A notebook drawing indicates that the original idea may have been to hang the boxes on the wall as a relief and connect them by wires in a manner resembling *Metronomic Irregularity*.

et Boards, 1967, sculpmetal on wood and magnets, 24 x 24 x 2″ (four units, each 12 x 12 x 2″).

131. Untitled, 1968, test pieces in mixed media in glass and metal case, 14⅝ x 10¼ x 10¼".

Three Untitled Glass Cases: The idea of putting her small and test pieces into a glass pastry case came from LeWitt, who had found one in a store on the Bowery and put Hesse's small gifts to him in it. She liked the way it looked, and made the second one herself, as a "piece," and later a third one. A note from August 1967 reads: "Three levels—small pieces related by context by box which encloses them; otherwise independent. 1. rubber sheets. 2. sculpmetal. a) all rubber b) rubber, filler and sand c) rubber with filler and black and white powdered pigments." These are Hesse's most Surrealist works, due partly to the box format and partly to the juxtaposition of unlike or unrelated forms which produce, in turn, a "new reality." A natural outgrowth of early concern with collage, they are also very "precious objects," possible in this "play" context. The first case seems rather clinical because the floors are plain glass and there are two objects on each level, like removed organs lined up neatly for inspection—tubes sewed onto fiberglass cloth, a miniature umbilical bucket, a shiny visceral form emerging from a cut skin-like sleeve, a shallow rubber tray filled with bland plaster, another larger and empty lopsided rubber tray, a shriveled latex fish-like shape cast around a popped balloon. The second case has something of the same aspect except for the middle layer, which is like a landscape of rubber "grass" inhabited by a slumped rubber disc; the layer below is patterned with washers under the glass. The materials range from clay to rubber to plaster to fiberglass to screen to string to clear plastic tubes. The third includes a similar grouping, with three overlapping, almost flat objects on the top shelf, three still quite flat pieces on the second, four slightly higher-profiled pieces on the third, and, on the bottom, a gray-green latex scalloped screen curving up like waves and lying on a large gray plaster placque with numbers in it.

132. Untitled, 1967, latex test pieces in glass and metal case, 14⅝ x 10¼ x 10¼".

133. Untitled, 1968, test pieces in mixed media on latex and washers in glass and metal case, 14⅝ x 10¼ x 10¼".

134. Inside I, 1967, painted papier-mâché over wood and twine, 12 x 12 x 12″; Inside II, 1967, painted papier-mâché over wood and weights, 5 x 7 x 7″.

Inside I; Inside II; For Joseph: These pieces were made in the spring and summer of 1967. *Inside I* is one foot square and deep, with a regular but lumpy papier-mâché texture which thickens the walls of the box until it becomes a dominant sculptural presence. Deep inside is a tangle of stiff gray painted strings of different thicknesses which anticipate Hesse's late rubber string piece (fig. 218). The tangle of ''line'' is small in relation to its heavy, almost fortified container, which is deep enough so one has to look way *in* to see the chaos it conceals in its depths. *Inside II,* much smaller, not as deep, is similarly built, and the walls are spikier and even thicker than those of *Inside I.* They frame two heavy ''weights'' (perhaps rocks) wrapped in papier-mâché and bound into two rather messy, wholly mysterious and irregular egg-shaped packages of slightly different grays, which rest impenetrably, almost filling the floor of the box. *For Joseph,* a present made for the birthday of Rosie and Norman Goldman's son, is also inclined toward the organic; it is small, gray, with a rough surface (plaster over a cardboard box) and contains a lock of Joseph's hair, an overtly personal content making the gift the equivalent of the old-fashioned locket or brooch.

135. For Joseph, 1967, painted plaster over cardboard, hair in plastic, 3½ x 2½ x 4″.

136. Untitled, 1968–69, latex on wire mesh, staples, wire, rubber bands, 6⅞ x 3½″.

137–140. Assorted small and test pieces, 1967–69.

The second formal theme that runs through this year is that of the box, used not as a miniature stage as are the boxes of Joseph Cornell, but as a container, keeping, however, the air of mystery inherent in the box form. Hesse had gotten a large supply of magnets through Dan Graham, and used them in a piece which can be seen as a transition between the relief and the box form.

Other small pieces and test pieces dating from this period until the end of Hesse's life include two rubber boxes with oval plaster inserts, coiled springs rising from the centers, two tiny gray boxes (sardine cans) with intestinal tangles overflowing them, and one with a heavily textured surface which opens to display a strange lump (fig. 141), flat, ragged-edged resin "pancakes" lying in an overlapping row; two sets of double black rubber donuts on slanted grounds (and their wax prototypes), a twisted or chewed-looking shape like a volcanically melted bottle, wax trays, other discs and "chips," double clay tablets, bits and pieces of screening and latex overlaid or combined, a flat piece of fiberglass sprouting clear vinyl tentacles, soft boxes lapsing into non-rectangular forms, rubberized ropes and tendrils and mats and strips and sleeves and trays of various sizes and eccentric shapes, mysterious lumps and packets which might some day have found their way into larger scale or fuller expression had there been more time (figs. 137–40).

Aside from the washers, the only "found" object Hesse used after 1965 was a bumper for the bow of a boat—a canvas object like a stuffed starfish—which she must have figured was so unfamiliar that its "found" quality would not detract (fig. 137). In 1968, Ruth Vollmer took her to a marine supply store and she bought three of them there, one of which she gave to Vollmer. She added the strings to all three but epoxied only Vollmer's, so it is white and hard while the other two are natural beige (fig. 140).

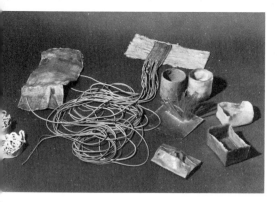

139.

140. Untitled, 1968, epoxied string and stuffed canvas 11 x 13 x 6″.

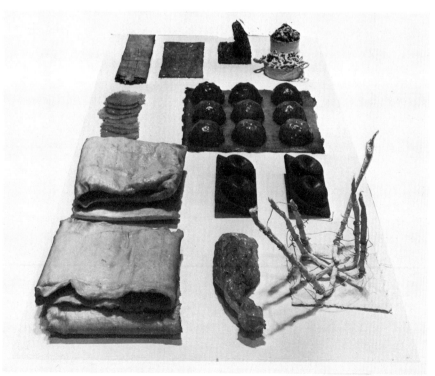

141.

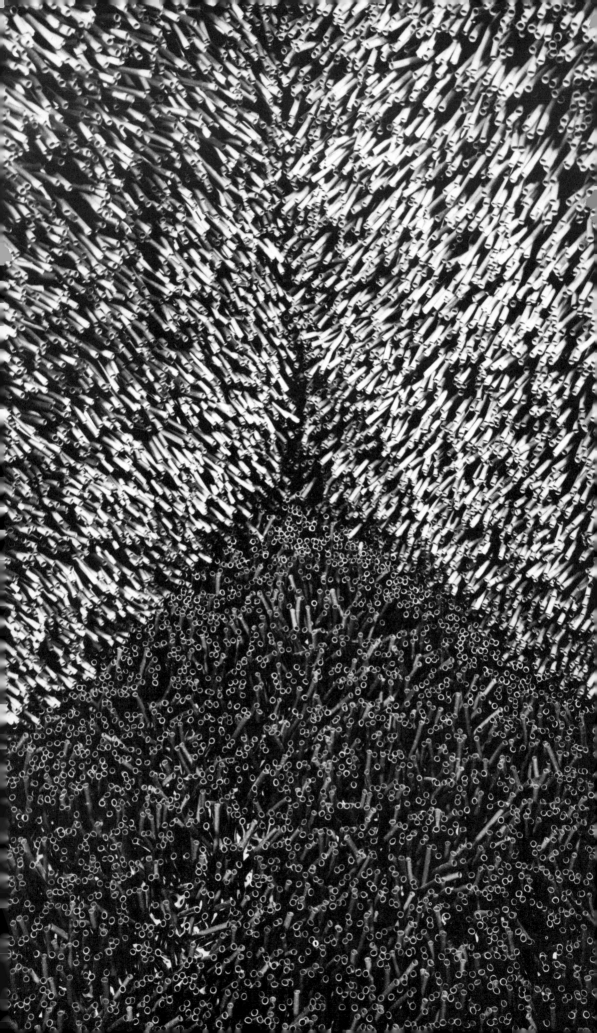

143. Accession II, 1967, galvanized steel, plastic tubing, 30¾ x 30¾ x 30¾″. (See fig. 177 for fiberglass version.)

◄ 142. Accession II, 1967, detail of interior corner.

Accession I, II, III, IV: This is not only the major box piece, but the first work fabricated. The small version, completed in June 1967, is a square (but shallow) box of grid-perforated aluminum through the round holes of which Hesse poked short lines of rubber hose; every hole was filled, and "all hose goes inward, inside box; outside box looks woven," she wrote to Rosie (fig. 145). Hesse was pleased with this image of a softly bristling interior hidden by a "woven" or relatively peaceful exterior. She made drawings of it and of a corner of its interior (fig. 144), and eventually there were four versions of this piece. The box frame of the large version (fig. 143) was fabricated in fall 1967 at Arco Metals in downtown Manhattan, where Smithson had been working. The gallery had provided money for materials, and it was made of galvanized steel (stainless being prohibitively expensive), with plastic extrusions. It was not a difficult piece to make, and Hesse got along well with the workers there. When the box was completed, she settled down to the task of threading the vinyl extrusions through the 30,670 holes, and on January 26, 1968 could write "box finished!" It was shown at the Milwaukee Art Center and the Chicago Museum of Contemporary Art in an exhibition called "Options," where people got inside the box and wrecked it. It had to be refabricated, and rethreaded, this time with the help of an assistant, and Hesse had just finished it the day she first collapsed. The third version (also large) was fabricated at Aegis in the summer of 1968 of a very thick milky fiberglass with air-drilled holes and clear plastic extrusions (fig. 177); the fourth and fifth are also small ones and were made in 1968. (The bristly sample Doug Johns gave her appears in fig. 138.)

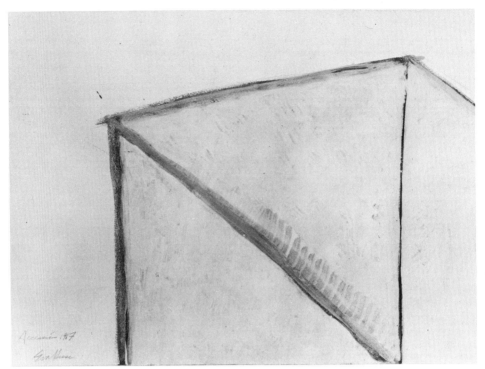

144. Accession, 1967, gouache and pencil, 11½ x 15⅜, Fourcade, Droll, Inc., New York. (See fig. 177 for related drawings).

Accession means "increased by something added," and indeed describes a box. All the versions are extremely palpable and tangible; the large ones are, in addition, secretive. Only when one leans over and looks inside (they stand 30¾″ high) is one subjected to the "feeling" more openly accessible in the rest of Hesse's work. It is the most impersonal of her sculptures. Where the smaller shallower version is more welcoming, and because of its scale even vulnerable, the large one is ominously absorptive. The bristles are soft, but the associations are thorny, and with its hard exterior, there is an unavoidably defensive quality. I have always been put off by the outside of the piece, although Sol LeWitt points out that its contrasts offer "the best of both possible worlds." Hesse herself eventually became less fond of *Accession:* "It becomes a little too precious, at least from where I stand now," she said in 1970. "Too right and too beautiful. . . . I'd like to do a little more wrong at this point."

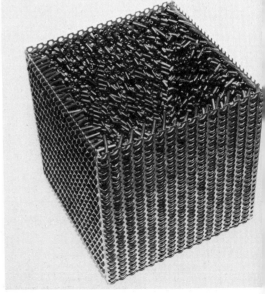

145. Accession I, 1967, aluminum, rubber tubing, 14¼ x 14¼ x 9⅛″.
146. Accession V, 1968, galvanized steel, rubber tubing, 10 x 10 x 10″.

147. Eva Hesse, winter 1967–68.

The summer of 1967 Hesse visited Ruth Vollmer in Southhold, Long Island and came to Georgetown, Maine to visit me, Donald Droll, and Roy Leaf. She spent most of the summer, however, in New York, working in the two small rooms which comprised the living quarters of her two-story loft. She preferred this to the upstairs studio. ("I work only downstairs. In my corner. It is really crowded with work and tools and all sorts of paraphernalia. Feel less lost and lonely there that way. Upstairs is unknown unfamiliar to me.") Her friend Dorothy James, who then lived in the studio below, remembers that "Summer '67 seemed to be a crucial time for her—attempted emancipation of thought from old and fairly recent 'scars'; the possibility of looking forward; assertion of herself as an individual artist." She had cut off her long and beautiful hair, which seemed symbolic of a "new image, fresh starts. There were several pieces in various states," James continues, "I think it was important then that the impetus and rhythm of working should be maintained, and to work on two or three, though without loss of intensity, seemed a safeguard against falling into emptiness and crises of purpose. *Accession*, the grid drawings, the sculpmetal piece and the first little showcase all had the advantage of being workable together in the room in which she then felt most secure and at ease . . . the point at which demands of scale and the vapours of resin forced her to leave this place of safety . . . would have been a landmark in Eva's mental landscape."

148. Interior of Hesse's Bowery loft, downstairs living and working quarters (from film by Dorothy Beskind).

149. Repetition Nineteen I, 1967, pencil on graph paper, 8½ x 10⅞″, Fourcade, Droll, Inc., New York.

Repetition Nineteen I, II, III: During the summer of 1967, Hesse wrote to Rosie Goldman that she was "working out an idea for a gas," illustrating it by little cylindrical "buckets" with hoses coming out of them. Not completed until a year later, *Repetition Nineteen* was to exist in three versions, though the one with hoses was never fully executed. (The bucket image itself appears in her notebooks as a doodle as early as 1956.) Several very complete drawings dated summer and fall 1967 show the squat bucket form with a false bottom, raised 3″ from the ground, from which emerged a long, rubber umbilical cord (figs. 149, 155). The shape was more cup than bucket, 8″ high and 8″ in diameter. One drawing calls for the material to be "sheet metal covered with sculpmetal"; there were to be "19 sections—to be placed at random (in a group) on the floor or (low level and not a particular base)." However, what was actually made that summer was a series of nineteen forms that were taller and thinner, lacked the cords, and were made of "aluminum wire, papier-mâché, Elmer's glue, polyester resin, Dutch Boy white diamond gloss paints." In September, Hesse wrote to Dorothy James in England, "Have painted all 19 two times since Wed. Even sanded some of the drips." Later in the month she sent her a Polaroid of this version, and it appeared on the color postcard which announced Hesse's first show the next year, labeled "first edition, 1967, each unit approximately 10 x 7" (fig. 152). In this letter, she wrote: "Last Friday 15 minutes before this place closed I bought liquid casting rubber and filler and separator. I experimented all weekend. It's a great media for me. . . . Today (I used it all up over weekend) I went to get a larger supply. Its possibilities are endless. I will cast my 19 pieces. Worked on little things during experimentation of different proportions of rubber to filler, thickness, etc. Can alter color also and translucency." At this point the metal and sculpmetal version was presumably junked, and the little latex buckets with cords, one of which ended up in one of the glass cases, appeared (fig. 150). Of the large ones (fig. 151), however, only four were made and they were sold separately. Originally they were a luscious cream color with a very long translucent cord from their depths. They are very soft, and fall all over themselves trying to stay upright, which makes them more openly humorous, more Oldenburgian in their slapstick positions, than the other versions.

So *Repetition II* was first going to be made in metal, then latex, and then was abandoned; Hesse resurrected it the following summer in fiberglass as her first piece at Aegis.[19] The fabricator remembers it as a "horrible failure"—a complete series of "*exactly* cylindrical fiberglass pots" with cords emerging from the false bottoms (each at a different height, so the

106

150. Untitled, 1967, test piece for Repetition Nineteen I, latex and rubber tubing, 3 x 3½ x 3½",
cord 40".

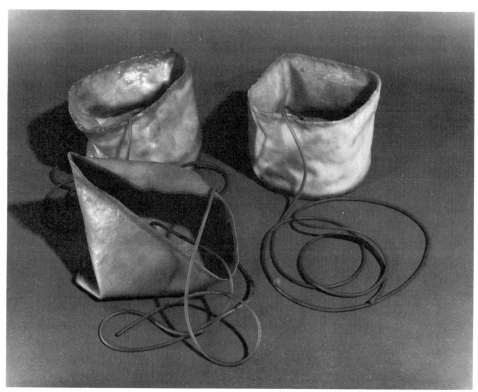

151. Untitled test pieces, 1967–68, latex and rubber tubing, each 5½ x 10¼–11", cords 18–26".

152. Repetition Nineteen I, 1967, aluminum screening, papier-mâché, Elmer's Glue, polyester resin,
Dutch Boy Diamond Gloss paint, 19 units, each c. 10″ x 8″ diameter.

cords appeared to be of different lengths). It did not follow one 1967 drawing in which the
"pots" themselves were different sizes. Hesse was appalled at its perfection, and the piece
was rejected. When they began again, the false bottoms and cords were omitted, and the
result was *Repetition III* (fig. 153)—the last and best-known version—completed in July
1968, a year after the first attempt; "work from which so much anxiety occurred is now being
constructively handled," reads her diary, and finally, "July 23 Finis large irregular version of
Repetition 19." This fiberglass version was shown in her first one-woman exhibition, and
The Museum of Modern Art acquired it a year later. The nineteen hollow cylindrical
elements, c. 12 x 20″, open at the top, sit on the floor in aimless but congenial disorder.
(The photograph reproduced here was Hesse's own placement.) Each unit is a different dis-
tortion of the regular shape they suggest when together. Each unit has been battered into a
different configuration. One is very nearly perfect, while another seems about to crumple.
Like schoolchildren in uniforms, or prisoners, or young trees in a nursery, they carry within

...etition Nineteen III, 1968, fiberglass, 19 units each 19–20¼″ x 11–12¾″ diameter.

them their exuberant individuality.

The character of each version of *Repetition Nineteen* is quite different, as size and the nature of materials changes its presence. The papier-mâché version is the most awkward and gawky, whereas when working with fiberglass, which is physically hard and ungiving, Hesse managed to retain the softness in both concept and color of the latex she had abandoned. The units are receptacles, and as such, they receive light and contain the shadows in their bases. Through a lucky fabrication accident, there were many little bubbles which gave them an inner glow. The light passes through the nubbly walls to alter shadows of its own. Hesse continued to try to find a use for the latex buckets. A notebook sketch shows them thrust out into space from a wall panel, the cords hanging; another suggests the possibility of setting them out at progressively longer distances from the panel, and an undated working drawing for this idea, without the buckets, seems to refer back to the purple wooden piece of 1965 (fig. 66).

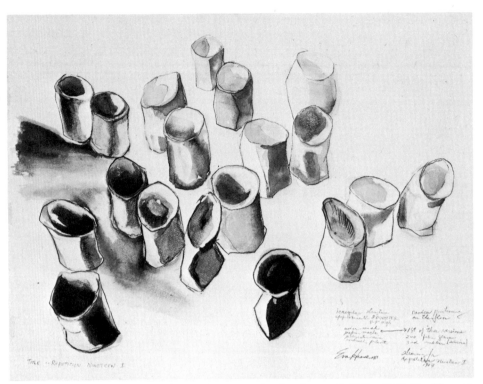

154. Repetition Nineteen I, 1967–68, gouache, watercolor, brush, pencil, 11¼ x 14⅞″, The Museum of Modern Art, New York, Gift of the Eva Hesse Estate.

The discovery in fall 1967 of latex rubber, even the Canal Street variety, was a breakthrough for Hesse. It enabled her to use a "sophisticated" material which was nevertheless tremendously sensitive to the touch. Dorothy James remembers having "the impression that work for Eva the summer of 1967 was a necessary rather than a pleasurable activity, and contrast this with the excitement she showed when first experimenting with liquid casting in rubber. . . . She had been conscious of her use of papier-mâché in *Repetition Nineteen* as 'kid's stuff,' in contrast to the use of 'real' materials which she admired in the work of others. Nevertheless she felt it dishonest to use materials in a way that hadn't been personally arrived at, usually through long and/or difficult processes. Before she found momentum and confidence in her own vision and methods, there seemed to be some conflict between the work she was then doing, and the idea of the work she should be doing to win the approval and admiration of a composite Judge/Parent/Fellow Artist figure." That autumn Donald Droll had told Hesse that if she was ready, Marilyn Fischbach would give her a full-scale show the next spring. Her reaction was: "Am scared. Am scared anyway so it makes little difference. . . . If I get going I mean really I might make it." (The show was eventually postponed until November 1968 because the new materials gave her so many ideas and led to so many technical complications.)

As soon as she had discovered liquid rubber, Hesse began a whole new body of work, fed by the material's possibilities. Latex is an immensely sensuous and flexible substance, and it incorporates (at least temporarily) lovely colors without getting into "color problems" in the Albers sense. Its hand-made surface allowed for those expressive vestiges shunned by Minimalism.

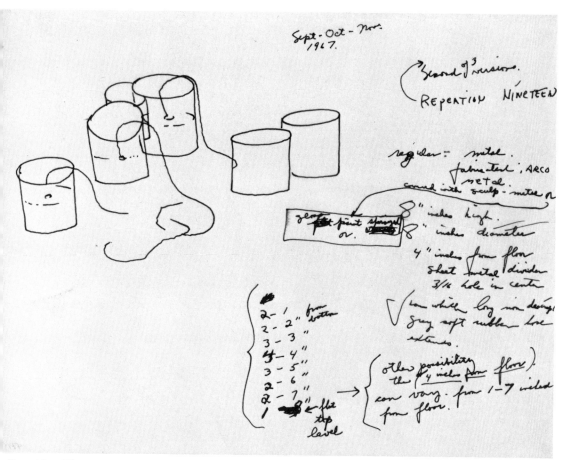

Repetition Nineteen (first of 3 versions), 1967, pen and ink on tracing paper, 8⅞ x 12″,
The Museum of Modern Art, New York, Gift of the Eva Hesse Estate.

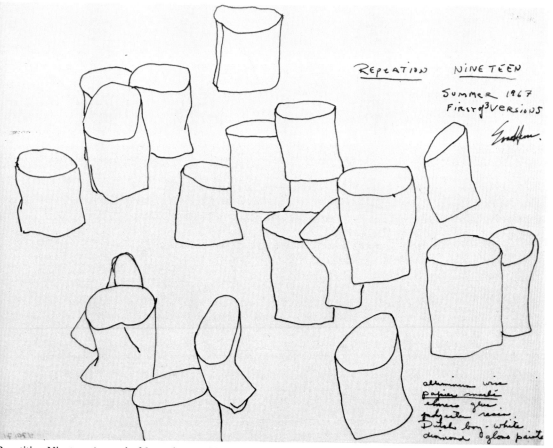

Repetition Nineteen (second of 3 versions), 1967, pen and ink on tracing paper, 8⅞ x 12″, The
Museum of Modern Art, New York, Gift of the Eva Hesse Estate.

157. Schema, 1967, latex, 42 x 42″, 144 units, each 2½″ diameter.

Schema: "Am in the process of casting a sheet of rubber (on Sol's table) 3′6″. On top of which sit semi-spheres 2 ⅛″ in diameter. It is all transparent to translucent, clear rubber. Looks like that vinyl type hose," Hesse wrote in September 1967. "It's a long process, painted on with brush and having to wait ½ hr. to one hr. between coats. Although this varies depending on size of what I cast, thickness etc. The sheet will need 10 coats." She learned the process herself in this first piece (which was preceded by two small versions, 9 ½″ square with nine hemispherical units), pouring and trying out the ratios of clear rubber and chemical thickener, drying the units on the radiator or in a muffin tin in the oven. It was completed in February 1968. One new factor, aside from softness, was the fact that the lumpy little hemispheres were not fixed on the mat, which endowed it with a certain sense of fragility and risk. Both this and its place flat on the floor may have been partially due to Hesse's friendship with and admiration for Carl Andre and his unfixed "rugs" of different metal plaques in a grid, but the idea itself is fundamentally a pictorial one, and another source is her own earlier work—the circle drawings, or reliefs like *Ditto*. While the two small "models" are perhaps more moving, *Schema* itself has an impressive scale and is more abstract; the hemispheres are multiplied on the larger mat to become elements of a pattern or field rather than independent presences.

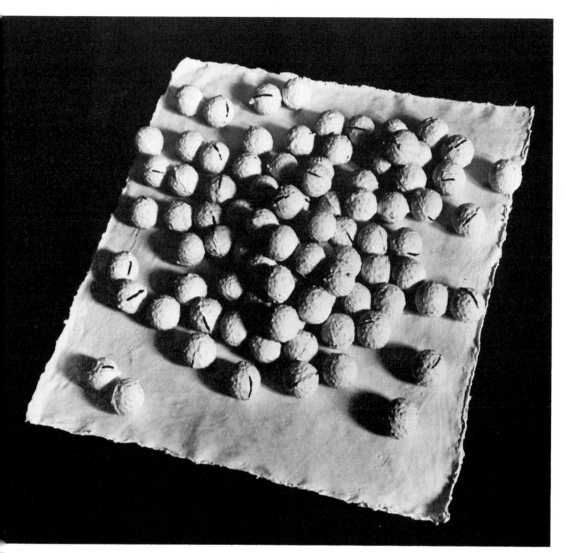

3. Sequel, 1967–68, 30 x 32", 92 units, each 2½" diameter.

Sequel: This followed *Schema* in the winter of 1967–68. (About the title she wrote "what follows after; continuation of a story or process or the like after a pause or provisional ending.") It was the first piece in which Hesse added powdered pigment to the latex. *Sequel* is similar to *Schema,* but the rubber is an opaque white, the moveable units are split spheres, made of *Schema*'s hemispheres (cast originally from a Spaulding rubber ball) put together so they didn't quite fit. The association with overripe golf balls is in a way unfortunate, but the nubbly surface was necessary to counter the matter-of-fact smoothness of the mat, with its tensely ruffled edges. The balls, vaguely centered, are tumbled onto it in a random pile—an assertively radical concept. As in *Schema,* the scale is modest, but just right, carrying a strong sense of body identification. A drawing dated September-October 1967 indicates that *Schema* and *Sequel* started as a single piece, colored like *Sequel,* arranged like *Schema,* and sat, not on the floor, but on a one foot high "table" exactly the same size as the mat. A slide taken by Dan Graham in 1967 of *Sequel* "in progress" shows that its balls were originally lined up in a grid like *Schema.* Hesse also did many experiments with larger rubberized hemispheres of different colors and sizes, some hard, some soft, which never culminated in a completed piece.

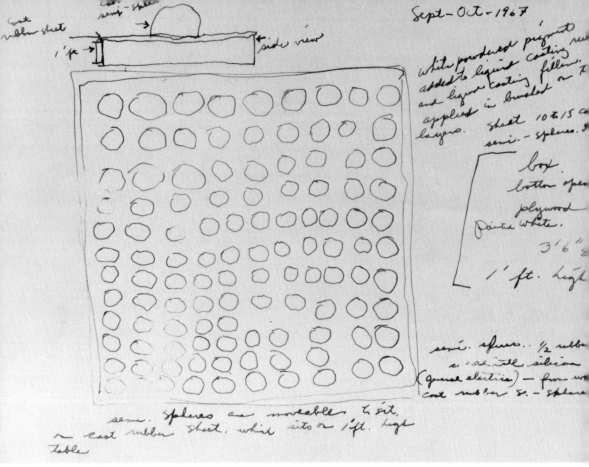

159. Study for Schema/Sequel, 1967, ink on tracing paper, 9 x 12″, Fourcade, Droll, Inc., New York.

While 1967 may have been Hesse's "serial" year, *Sequel* and a drawing with that date on it and another undated sketch indicate that her "anti-formal" tendencies were simply being held in abeyance. The first sketch (fig. 161) shows a sprawling snake-like form which was to be "plastic flat tubing positioned whichever way it may lie, filled with sand, sealed firmly at both extremes." The other (fig. 160) shows three versions of what appears to be the same material—coiled, and dropped, and drooping from wall to floor, reminiscent of Nauman's "Eccentric Abstraction" pieces as well as of Hesse's own *Several* (fig. 68).

January of every year was a terrible time for Hesse due to the anniversary of her mother's death. In 1968 Ruth Vollmer took her on a trip to Mexico City, where they saw Pre-Columbian art, climbed the pyramids, and visited markets and churches. Hesse, Vollmer remembers, was less interested in sightseeing than in absorbing the city's life. It has been suggested[20] that her last piece (fig. 221) was inspired by a group of Olmec sculptures seen at this time, but I doubt if this did any more than reinforce Hesse's predilection for the *personnage* image. At the end of the month, she went to Oberlin College "to give criticism," as she put it; she took Royce Dendler's class and spent time with the students. (She had applied for a teaching job at the School of Visual Arts by then; she was hired the following September.)

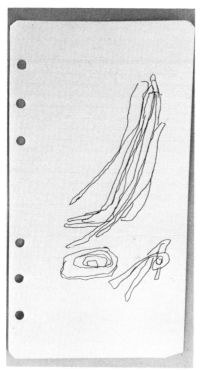

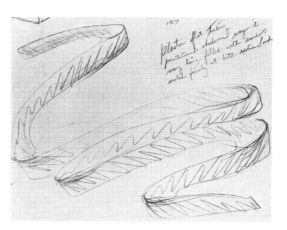

160. Untitled, c. 1967–68, pen and ink,
6¾ x 3¾″, Fourcade, Droll, Inc.,
New York.

161. Untitled, 1967, pencil on graph paper, 8½ x 10⅞″,
Fourcade, Droll, Inc., New York.
162. Model for Schema, 1967, latex, 9½ x 9½″, 9 units,
each 2½″ diameter.

During 1968 Hesse was increasingly in contact with other young artists whose
ideas were similar to her own. In March she exchanged studio visits with Keith
Sonnier, whom she had met through "Eccentric Abstraction." His wife, the artist
Jackie Winsor, was then also working in a direction that indicated concerns similar
to Hesse's, although their solutions were consistently dissimilar. Around the same
time she met Richard Serra, who had called her after seeing a photograph of
Hang-Up, which interested him. They also exchanged studio visits and he gave her
some advice about sources of materials and technical problems. The following
summer, when both were working at Aegis Reinforced Plastics on Staten Island,
they would go there on the ferry together and had long talks about art—technique
rather than theory.

For all of Hesse's determined testing and experimentation with materials, she
knew latex was not a permanent substance. *Sans I, Sans III,* and *Stratum* have, at
this writing less than seven years later, already disintegrated. Other latex pieces,
unless they have been kept away from light and heat, have lost the original syrupy
surface and color modulations and have darkened to a deep brown; eventually they
too will dry up, crack, and collapse into dust, unless some sort of fixative substance
is discovered quickly.

163. Sans I, 1967–68, latex, metal grommets, 6′ x 7″ x 1″.

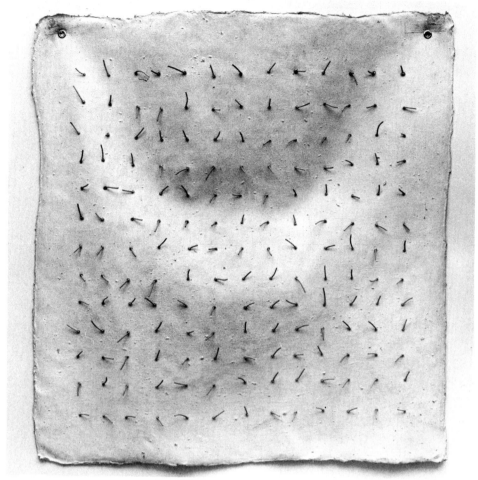

164. Stratum, 1967–68, latex, metal grommets, plastic tubing, 42 x 42″.

Sans I: A natural brown latex piece, originally quite translucent and shiny, it anticipates not only the huge fiberglass *Sans II,* which dominated her show, but the 1969 "window" drawings which drew, in turn, from much earlier drawings where irregular rectangles, repeated like panes, were a frequent motif. The beauty of *Sans I,* again that of a quirky personal vision, is that the double row of rectangles (or rather shallow trays of soft material, extending in a line of 24 over six feet) hangs tall and thin on the wall and then extends four of its units onto the floor. By this very simple method, what might have been a relatively ordinary Minimal or "serial" idea, takes on the wistful aspect of Hesse's other pieces, and works in two real spaces, i.e., out of the pictorial zone.

Stratum: This comes as close to a "painting" or a latex drawing, as anything Hesse did, and she chose the title because it meant "horizontal layer or section of material." In fact, there are two 1967 circle drawings which might be considered prototypes for it—wash grids, one with strings (fig. 165) and the second with plastic "tails" hanging from the center of each circle (fig. 166). (The first was bought in 1967 by the Weatherspoon Art Gallery in North Carolina, along with a Stella and a Gorky—a grouping which pleased her.) A third drawing, from 1968, simulates those strings in ink line (fig. 167). The circles are omitted in *Stratum;* an opaque beige latex square hangs on the wall by two grommets (buckling a bit at the top) and is patterned by an irregular 13 x 13 grid of short tails, knotted at the surface, which point every which way, intensifying the floppiness of the surface by having a further inquiring life of their own.

Latex is "painted" on in layers, lending itself to flat surfaces, and its use drew Hesse back toward painting, although she never for a moment considered oil on canvas again, wholeheartedly convinced as she was that "painting is dead." If one compares *Stratum* to *Constant* (fig. 120), for instance, the thin and flexible latex sheet to the heavy textured box, one sees how the sculptural aspect was mitigated in the former. Later that year fiberglass was to lead her once more into freestanding sculpture.

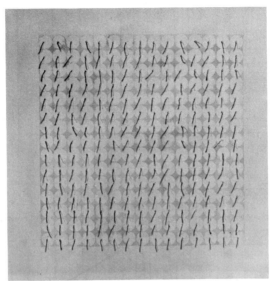

165. Untitled, 1967, ink wash and string, 15½ x 15½",
Dillard Collection, Weatherspoon Art Gallery,
University of North Carolina at Greensboro.

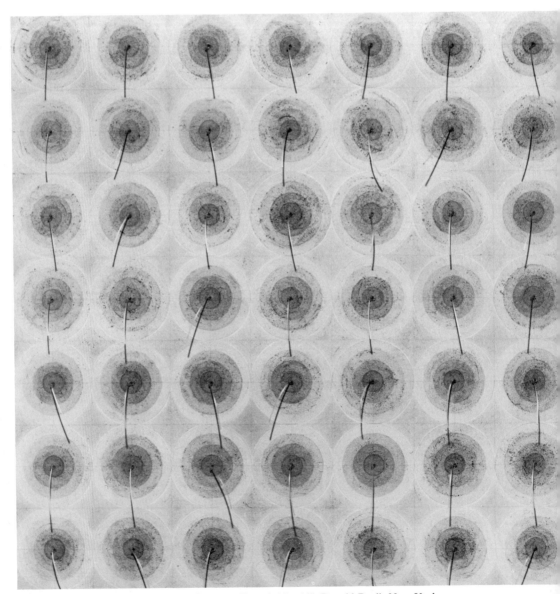

166. Untitled, 1967, ink wash and plastic on cardboard, 14 x 14", Donald Droll, New York.

118

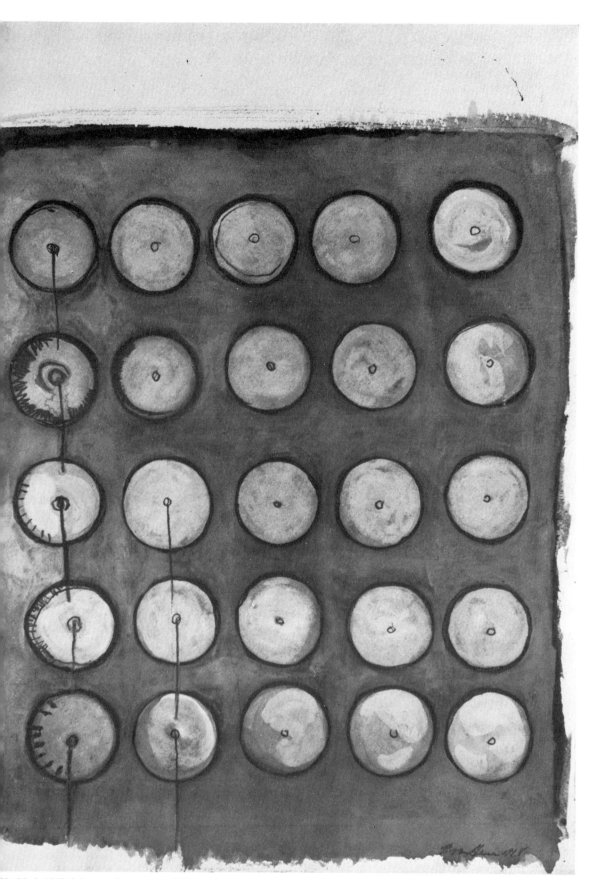

Untitled, 1968, ink, pencil, gouache, 15½ x 11″, Mr. and Mrs. Ernst Englander, New York.

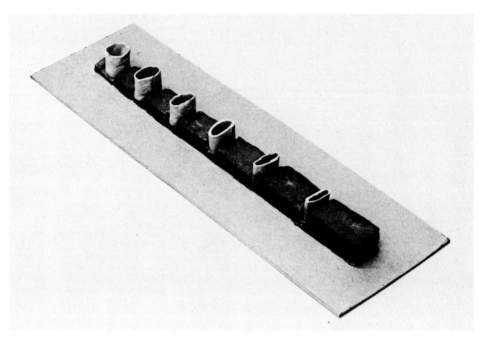

168. Untitled, 1968, unfired clay and painted cardboard, 13½ x 1¼ x ⅞".

Untitled: Sometime in the winter-spring of 1968, Ruth Vollmer gave Hesse some yellowish clay, from which she made one of her most beautiful pieces, although it was to be an anomaly in terms of her new work. It was the only time she worked in this medium, the flexibility, literal earthiness, and delicate colors of which might have greatly appealed to her had she further explored them. This piece takes to a particularly sensuous point the progression idea that had dominated her 1967 work. A long bar is broken into increasingly larger sections; an open cylindrical cardboard form inserted between the sections is squeezed to a flat sleeve as the distances grow and the interstices get smaller. It is a virtually kinetic use of materials. She planned a larger version which was never executed, probably because by the time it might have been constructed, she had abandoned such a strictly serial concept for a looser and more emotively manipulable form. Two working drawings exist in which it is designated for "clear or natural" fiberglass and polyester resin, to be 214" long, 6" high and 12" wide. In an inscription she referred to the cardboard units as "buckets," relating it to *Repetition Nineteen.*

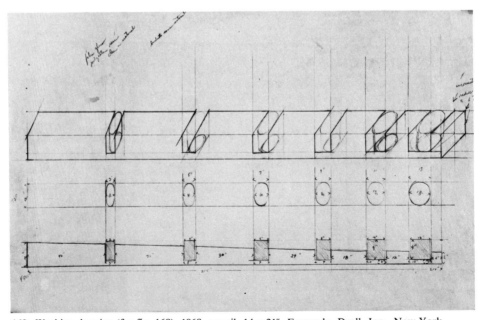

169. Working drawing (for fig. 168), 1968, pencil, 14 x 21", Fourcade, Droll, Inc., New York.

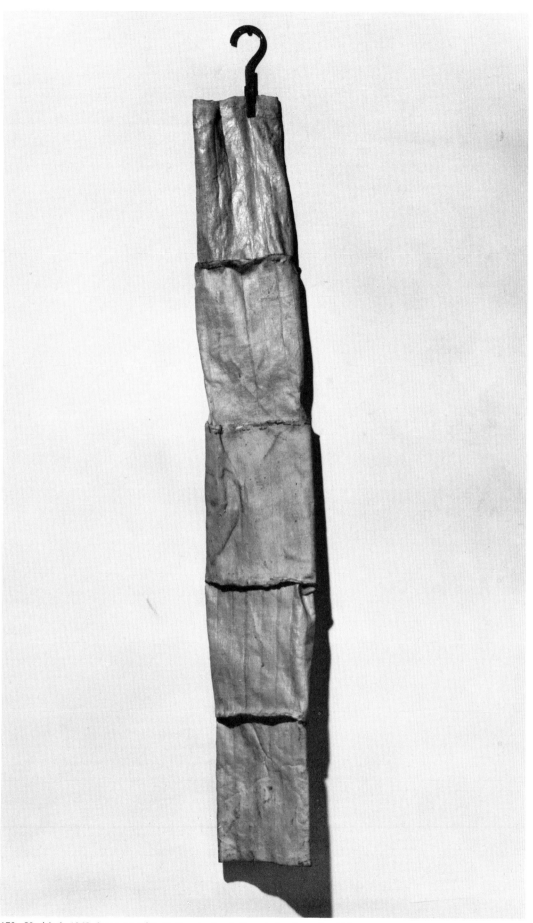

170. Untitled, 1968, latex on wire mesh, plastic clothespin hook, c. 9 x 30″.

171. Area, 1968, latex on wire mesh, metal wire, 20 x 3'.

Area was made rather hastily in the summer of 1968 for an American Federation of Arts circulating exhibition I had organized called "Soft and Apparently Soft Sculpture." It was constructed from the molds from which the large version of *Repetition Nineteen* was made—ten rectangles of wire mesh covered with rubber; there were supposed to be nineteen of them, "but it was a hot summer and I just couldn't get the 19 done. . . . I have a personal attachment when it comes from another piece," Hesse told Nemser. "I mean this was empty containers and you have that sexual . . ." The rectangles are roughly sewn together and the surface is "painterly," not only in the way the rubber is applied, but in the way it is dented and bent, as though it could take whatever life gave it, but would retain the marks. Like *Sans I, Area* "sits" against the wall, with seven units stretched out on the floor before it—an awkward but relaxed presence.

172. Seam, 1968, latex on wire mesh, metal wire, 9' x 4'.

Seam: Made around the same time as *Area,* it is hung the same way, but reverses the structural principle; two long rubberized pieces of mesh are sewn down the center. It was shown in the fall of 1968 at John Gibson's timely "Anti-form" show. Related to both *Seam* and *Area* are a series of "sleeves" which in turn relate to one of the last pieces—*Tori* (fig. 199); the sleeves were probably also derived indirectly from the sections of *Repetition Nineteen.* One piece, hung on the wall by a plastic clothespin, is a miniature *Area* of double thickness and five modules (fig. 170). These might be flattened versions of the rubberized but stiffer and smaller sleeves, or folded rectangles open at two ends, shown in a pile of four at Hesse's Fischbach show (Fig. 177). (They were to be sold in groups of four or five.) Many of these sleeves remain, but they exist as a piece only in the collection of Grace and Gerry Wapner; Hesse gave them a set of four that Christmas. She anticipated that the sleeves would collapse, as they have, but said it would be all right.

Accretion; Untitled: Accretion was the second piece completed at Aegis in summer 1968. The basic unit was a solid wooden tube; she made a small version of this in 1967–68 with the tubes painted a heavy gray. Six of them were strung through with very long lines of metallic gray plastic cord. There is a rare finished "representational" drawing of this sculpture which shows the poles balanced perpendicularly across a saw horse, cords just grazing the floor (fig. 174). Notes indicate that the poles were to be 41″ long, the saw horses would be translucent natural resin; the lines were also to be natural color. The saw horse didn't satisfy her, however, and she couldn't find anything that made sense to lay the poles on. (The box and parallel placement in the accompanying photograph were not her idea.) Two other, more casual drawings, both dated 1967, show this piece from different angles with an ambiguous base. Another shows the poles stacked up vertically in a tall thin box open at two ends, the cords trailing. Still another drawing, worked out in great detail, shows the fiberglass tubes coming up from the floor through what appears to be a topless and bottomless coffin-like box. Another written note, which may or may not relate to this piece, speaks of "fiberglass free forms over any materials—long irregular poles 2 kinds 1) with bottoms 2) long leaning without bottoms, taller than ones, strung together by rubberized rope."

Then Hesse decided against the cords because she had already used them so much. She finally decided the poles would just lean against the wall, a decision possibly influenced by John McCracken's leaning planks. The hollow clear (greenish in some lights) fiberglass poles, again molded on cardboard tubes, were enlarged to 58″ long and 2½″ diameter; fifty of them were leaned against a long wall in an irregularly spaced row. The units themselves have little individuality, unlike those in *Repetition Nineteen*. They are neither graceful nor stubby, solid nor fragile. The surface of each is slightly different from every other. It is their existence as a *crowd*, or repeated linear strokes in the space between wall and floor, that provides their impact. They transform a wall into a shimmering fence of light and subtle color, retaining their scale even when shown in a very high-ceilinged room, probably because their size is human, natural, predictable, and therefore harder to distort. The title, according to Hesse's notes, means "the growing of separate things into one."

173. Model for Accretion, 1967, 19 painted wooden tubes, each 20½ x 1″ diameter; 6 tubes with 128″ plastic cords.

174. Untitled (after Accretion model), 1968, ink wash, inscriptions, 11 x 15″, Mr. and Mrs. Adam Aronson, Saint Louis.

175. Accretion, 1968, fiberglass, 50 units, each 58 x 2½″ diameter.

From March through the fall of 1968, Hesse was preoccupied with planning and then, beginning in the summer, with executing her new fiberglass pieces for her first one-woman show, which was to be subtitled "chain polymers," an indication of her fascination with the mysteries of chemistry, materials, and advanced fabrication. In April 1968 she wrote, "If I can forever lose panic I know I am then capable of being great artist, great person. That terror stands so in my way. It is a haunting paralyzing experience, one of which I stand in dread of occurring, and when it happens it is even worse than what I anticipated." But around the same time she also wrote, "It is easy in my work now. I know the important things there, but in life, yet a way to go."

Hesse had first gone to Aegis on the recommendation of Robert Morris and Stylianos Gianakos early in 1968, accompanied by Ruth Vollmer. She discussed

possibilities with Doug Johns, the partner in charge of the art side of the business, and was given sample materials to study, but they could not start work until summer. Moving out of the studio this way was a major step for her, and she went to Aegis with some trepidation; this was a real factory, utterly male-oriented, and she expressed fear of "all those men with their great big sculptures." But it was necessary in terms of the professionalism she sought so determinedly and she hoped more professional craftsmanship would keep her pieces from disintegrating. Eventually she found it rewarding as well as frustrating to work with someone else. Doug Johns worked closely with her as a friend and as technical advisor on every piece from the summer of 1968 until her death. In the fall he left Aegis and devoted himself solely to Hesse's work, charging her a minimum fee and living in her studio early in 1969.

176. Sans II, 1968, fiberglass, 3'2" x 21'6" x 6⅛"; 5 units, each 38 x 86 x 6⅛" (see fig. 178 for detail).

Sans II: The third piece made at Aegis that summer was completed on October 27, 1968. "Fini! Turned out great!" Hesse noted. It was constructed from a gum rubber mold cast from her plaster model with a skirt of paper around it so the tops could be knocked off irregularly. Doug Johns remembers this was the first time he really understood what she was looking for. Spreading 430" across the wall, two rows of fiberglass units, each 38" and 6⅛" deep, *Sans II* is actually five separate reliefs hung together, the module the same shallow tray that appeared in latex in *Sans I.* But where the first version is a humble and flexible figure, *Sans II* is Hesse's largest and most detached piece. It is a triumph between the frontality of painting and the subtlety of surface possible only in three dimensions. The surface both refracts and absorbs light. It expands across a room in grand calm. A notebook page from 1968 says "Sans must have the materiality of fiberglass. edges. scale less tight, petty. vs. open and free. don't pressure self about this it will come when lifestyle opens up. It must it will one follows

128

through partially automatic.'' Above it she drew a triangle with its points labeled ''process,'' ''content,'' ''materiality.'' Elsewhere, she quoted something from a conversation with Carl Andre: ''real materials substance. materiality. anything worth doing is worth doing again and again.'' On Christmas Eve, 1968, she jotted down the idea of a single *Sans* ''tray''—''very large to lean against wall, off, not regular''; or of ten *Sans*-like trays hung vertically with no inside planes—''rubber skeletons.''

Unfortunately, due to its size and Hesse's relatively unknown status as an artist at the time, *Sans II* was considered impossible to sell as a whole and it was acquired by four different people. While the units are strong enough to stand alone or in pairs with ease, no one who has seen the original installation can feel that the effect of the parts is the same. As could be seen when three were shown at the Guggenheim exhibition, the work also suffers from being separated in that the fiberglass is discoloring at different rates under different conditions.

177. Front room, Hesse show at the Fischbach Gallery, November 1968. Foreground, Accession II; left, Accretion; right, Repetition Nineteen III.

Hesse's Fischbach show opened on November 16. In the front room were *Sans II*, *Accretion*, *Repetition Nineteen III*, and *Accession II*, all in clear fiberglass and a stunning combination in a large, light space (fig. 177); *Sans I*, *Schema*, *Sequel*, and *Stratum* were in the back room, with some drawings and a shelf holding one glass case, a latex "umbilical" bucket, four latex "sleeves" and the miniature model for *Augment* (fig. 180). I wrote the press release and a small statement by the artist dated June 1968 followed:

177a. Back room, left to right: Repetition nineteen test piece, "sleeves", Augment model, glass case (fig. 133).

130

"I would like the work to be non-work. This means that it would find its way beyond my preconceptions.

What I want of my art I can eventually find. The work must go beyond this.

It is my main concern to go beyond what I know and what I can know.

The formal principles are understandable and understood.

It is the unknown quantity from which and where I want to go.

As a thing, an object, it acceeds to its non-logical self.

It is something, it is nothing."[21]

The show looked beautiful and was a definite success. Hilton Kramer, having recovered from "Eccentric Abstraction," wrote in the *New York Times* (November 23, 1968) that it was a first show of "uncommon interest . . . a kind of demoralized geometry just barely rescued from complete dissolution by formal improvisations of an eccentric order." Emily Wasserman reviewed it at length in *Artforum* (January 1969) saying, among other things, that she had been aware only of Hesse's "trailing or wound twine pieces. . . . I found the sense of humor which informed most of these works a touch bizarre, though not at all anecdotal or coy. Their sensuousness was so restrained as to be almost shy. And yet . . . the formal intentions of the work were both assured and clearly felt." Although she did not have the automatic "anti-form" reaction one might have expected, she too saw form "demoralized," especially in *Repetition Nineteen:* "each dissolving away from that module, they defy and snicker at its obsessive rationality. . . . While the work does not at first impress or impose itself with an overbearing presence, I found that the after-impression was one of a subdued, though eye-catching vigor. Incorporating the conceptual with a wryly objective slant on that conceptualness in terms of her materials, and the processes she uses to shape them, Miss Hesse adds a new distinct accent to the current scene in sculpture." John Perreault in the *Village Voice* (November 28, 1968) called it "surreal serialism" or "anti-form." "The more you look at [these pieces] the uglier and more interesting they become. . . . One could call these new works Pathetic Objects . . . [they] are completely abstract and resist any kind of single-leveled interpretation or response. . . . Because of their harsh illegibility they provoke bizarre anthropomorphisms. The kind of queasy uneasiness they evoke makes one want to stroke them gently, to soothe and smooth them down and reassure them that they will not really disintegrate entirely. . . . Having one of these pieces would be like having a very, very neurotic pet, a threat to visitors, but completely dependent upon its owner's perceptual attentions to hold it together and keep it from slipping away into nothingness. Whether Miss Hesse intends it or not, her sculpture (or her anti-sculpture) causes very complicated emotions in the viewer. . . . Her works are questions rather than answers. They are bundles of eccentric contradictions, impossible to resolve on any merely intellectual level and therefore disturbing, tough and a meaningful assault upon our notions of both form and good taste. . . . Eva Hesse is an important new artist. . . . Her distinction is determined by how and why she lets her materials determine her forms." However, Lil Picard and Martin Last saw the work as "toys," and the latter, writing in *Art News* (November 1968) saw the fiberglass pieces as "wastebaskets," "ice-cube trays," and a "plastic iron maiden"; "There is a bland quiet pleasure to these loony pieces."

I have quoted the reviews at such length both to indicate how Hesse was seen "within the scene" and to show how clearly the real core of the work and of the artist usually communicated themselves. The only drawback was that people got so carried away with effect that they seemed disinclined to seriously analyze the formal intentions. Hesse's thoughts about repetition, about forms in isolation and similar forms repeated, fixed and unfixed, hard and soft, her variations on formal themes, her desire to make the sculptural elements absurd in themselves and in their multiplicity, were largely neglected for self-indulgent insights into the work's overall character.

Several pieces were sold. Hesse was invited to be in some important group shows here and abroad, prime among them Harald Szeemann's "When Attitudes Become Form" in Bern, Robert Morris' Castelli warehouse show, and Marcia Tucker's and Jim Monte's "process" show, as it was popularly known, at the Whitney. Hesse's involvement with materials and their attributes has been overemphasized because of her public association with other artists who were more dependent than she upon accidents of physical phenomena, and she worried that she was being imprisoned in a category which did not entirely suit her work. At the same time she enjoyed being in the company of artists whom she liked and admired, among them Serra, Sonnier, Andre, Smithson, and Ryman. "Everything is process and the making of my work is very interesting," she said later. "But I never thought of it as I was throwing, scraping, putting on the rubber. That was necessary to what I was going to get to." Her main interest in latex, fiberglass, and other flexible or translucent synthetics was their malleability, their near-ugly delicacy, and ambiguous textures. She told Cindy Nemser that she was not involved with "truth to materials . . . for instance I rubberized the cheesecloth in *Contingent* because the rubber needs more strength for permanency. To keep it very thin and airy I use a very very fine plastic, a very cheap plastic which is so thin, and clings together so when the rubber dries you have all this clingy linear kind of thing. If a material is liquid . . . I can control it but I don't really want to change it. I don't want to add color or make it thicker or thinner. . . . I don't want to keep any rules; I want to sometimes change the rules. But in that sense, process, the materials, become important and I do so little with them which is I guess the absurdity. Sometimes the materials look like they are so important to the process because I do so little else with the form. I keep it very simple."

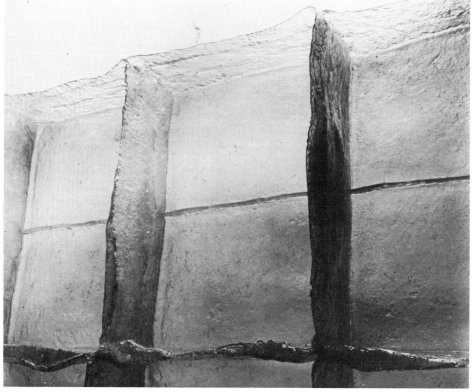

178. Sans II, detail.

179. Augment (on floor), 1968, latex on canvas, 19 units, each 78 x 40″; Aught (on wall), 1968, double sheets of latex stuffed with polyethylene, 4 units, each 78 x 40″.

180. Model for Augment, 1968, latex on cotton, 29 units, 8½ x 4½ x 2¾".

Augment; Aught: The modules for *Aught* and *Augment* are the same size, but made differently, the former being double rubber sheets stuffed with polyethelene drop sheets; the latter being rubberized canvas. The model (fig. 180) is latex on cotton, and there are 29 sheets in it as opposed to the 20 in *Augment.* (Hesse had wanted many more—"a thousand"—and her definition of the title was "Increase, make greater"; *Aught* meant "anything, whatever; any little part.") She worked on *Augment* for some time, vacillating about the amount of order or chaos to impose on the sheets. I remember one or more lying on the floor of her studio covered by a much thinner and paler layer of delicate, powdery, very soft and skinlike rubber (the powder was a preservative); the top layer was somewhat tumbled, and the image, though "strange," as she wanted it, too closely resembled an unmade bed, and was finally discarded in favor of laying the modules over each other so only the crinkled borders showed, and then turning back the last one to reveal that the surfaces were not, after all, like the visible borders, but smooth and slightly different in color. This solution contained a characteristic combination of order and surprise.

Similarly, *Aught,* which may have its source in *Stratum,* has a highly pictorial aspect and is hung on the wall like a painting, with a wrinkled border like a frame, though it perversely and unexpectedly bulges from the wall to maintain its sculptural identity as well. *Aught* as well as *Stratum* (fig. 164) and Robert Ryman's stretcherless paintings, have probably had an influence on the proliferation of unstretched and buckling canvases which appeared as an offshoot of the "anti-form" bandwagon. The pictorial/sculptural double role suggested in *Aught* was more subtly handled in 1969 by *Contingent* (fig. 209). The "dumbness" (a quality Hesse sought rigorously) of *Aught* contrasts with the elegance of *Augment,* and when they were shown together, as at the Castelli warehouse show in December 1968, they were often mistaken for a single piece.

135

The warehouse show, officially titled "9 at Leo Castelli," was held in the influential dealer's west side storage space, and became a midway landmark for something which had been titled by Robert Morris in the April 1968 *Artforum*, "anti-form" or "process."[22] It had been for several years one of those "ideas in the air" as yet not concretized. Artists working independently in their studios on both the east and west coasts, in Germany, Holland, England and Italy, were experimenting with the range of independence a material could be allowed when separated from permanent form. Flexible or scattered materials used not only to dilapidate but to disintegrate form were in wide use by 1968 when "anti-form" suddenly appeared as an idea whose time had come. It represented partly a reaction against Minimalism, replacing geometric rigidity with fluidity and indeterminacy, "new" and shiny materials with "old" or unprepossessing ones, an esthetic of order with one of apparent chaos,[23] although in fact, anti-form was not so much opposed to form as committed to introducing another area of non-formalist form to be dealt with, just as LeWitt and others had introduced a conceptual or gestalt content to oppose the anti-content "optical formalism" of the Green Mountain gang.[24] On a less interesting level it also represented a permutation of the 1960's "new materials" syndrome, which posited, at its most unspoken and superficial, the notion that if you couldn't find a style of your own, you could at least find a material.

In his *Artforum* article, Morris noted the "reasonableness of the well-built" and the tendency of modular art to "separate, more or less, from what is physical by making relationships themselves another order of facts." In opposition he offered "the process of 'making itself,' " which he himself had explored in a 1961 *Box with the Sound of Its Own Making*. "Of the Abstract Expressionists only Pollock was able to recover process and hold on to it as part of the end form of the work," he wrote. "[In the new work] sometimes a direct manipulation of a given material without the use of any tool is made. . . . The focus on matter and gravity as means result in forms which were not projected in advance. Considerations of ordering are necessarily casual and imprecise and unemphasized. Random piling, loose stacking, hanging, give passing form to the material. Chance is accepted and indeterminacy is implied since replacing will result in another configuration. Disengagement with preconceived enduring forms and orders for things is a positive assertion. It is part of the work's refusal to continue estheticizing form by dealing with it as a prescribed end."

181. Untitled multiple, 1968–69, latex over cloth
tape and balloon, 7 x 2½ x 2½".

It is indicative of the art world's evolutionary greed for the new that this very short article was so influential, and that certain questions, such as "what, if any, is the difference between a felt rectangle and a latex mat?" remained unasked. Critical response to the warehouse show demonstrated, in regard to Hesse, a classic situation in which exhibiting one's best recent work is not "politically" the wisest move. While Hesse's pieces looked beautiful in the vast, dim, concrete-floored space which dwarfed some of the larger works, their completion and assurance, seen among the most casual manifestations of "anti-form," made them look almost conservative. John Perreault called them "cruel and bland" (*Village Voice,* December 19, 1968). *Aught* and *Augment* followed fewer of the new "rules" than Hesse's *Sequel, Area,* or the two-year-old *Ennead* or three-year-old *Several.* But to those critics unfamiliar with the roots of this work, the supposedly "non-formal" pieces looked more radical because the relationship to Pollock, laid out by Morris in his article, was clearer. They concentrated on the supposed "absence of formal prejudice" and "indifference to style," and related the pictorial bias of much of the work to the "airiness and luminosity which has recently informed much current painting" (Max Kozloff, *Artforum,* February 1969) which I frankly doubt had anything to do with it. The impetus was far more toward a destruction or "dematerialization" of sculptural form, though those forms had originally been heavily influenced by abstract painting. In his last paragraph Kozloff found Hesse's and Bill Bollinger's pieces respectively, "slightly more picturesque versions of minimal sculpture" and "too emphatically purposeful to be placed within the overall sensibility," which should have been a compliment, but wasn't so intended. In fact, that same sensibility was shared by an early lead prop piece of Serra's which was by far the most traditionally sculptural (albeit one of the more effective) pieces in the show, as well as by Nauman's tape recording of a word series hidden in a steel beam, Kaltenbach's well-pressed felt form with a single crease, and so forth.

Hesse had "every right to believe she would be regarded as one of the major figures in that direction since she'd been working that way for so long" (LeWitt), but in fact she was not one of the first artists to be invited. Her work was clearly a precedent for just that "return to the emotive" and the flexible which made "anti-form" possible. Her "conservativeness" can be attributed to her independence and her advanced awareness of the *sculptural* possibilities of such materials and arrangements. Now that most of those piles look alike in retrospect, her position is more understandable. There is nothing brutal in Hesse's work, and her refusal to destroy form is consistent with the subtlety of her approach to materials. Also understandable is the omission of artists such as Smithson, Andre, Oppenheim, Viner, and Ryman, whose roles in this "trend" were never explored. Viner, with whom Hesse felt an affinity, was permanently omitted, probably because his ideas were too fantastic and his materials too garish, not chicly drab enough (the "natural look"); Ryman was soon enveloped by "anti-form" although his painting ideas had remained unchanged since the late 1950's, and until 1967 his work had been ignored because it was too old-fashioned and "expressionist." Smithson's, and later Oppenheim's, direct use of earth and other such materials, and Andre's "particle theory"[25] were used to advantage and so acknowledged by many of the above-mentioned artists. The relationship to Pollock was the same one Hilton Kramer had noticed two years before in regard to *Metronomic Irregularity.* The critical neglect of Hesse's achievements and refusal to take her as seriously as the other artists can probably be ascribed to the fact that as a woman, she couldn't *be* the "new Pollock." "She was very hurt by this first confrontation with art politics and anti-feminism, which was so obvious" (LeWitt).

Nevertheless, everything else was going so well for Hesse that friends had trouble understanding her increasing depression and exhaustion. It had begun in September. Since there seemed no psychological basis (and she did not, in any case, react with physical symptoms to psychological problems), we began to wonder if her tiredness, headaches, and vomiting were not caused by the fumes from the synthetics she was using. (Ironically, she had stopped Grace Wapner from using resins in 1962 because she was afraid they would all be poisoned.) She continued to work hard and to teach six hours a week at the School of Visual Arts, but later she remembered: "Xmas time 1968 I was so ill, Castelli warehouse exhibition, Bern Kunstalle, Whitney Museum, I was so ill. Had signs but would not recognize them. One can deny anything. Then it can dominate. Like you sleep lots, it progresses with time, you get headaches prior to which maybe five befall you a year . . . you throw up—first you ate something, then something is wrong, you didn't eat something. You don't throw up—till you throw up eating nothing. Keep going then to the collapse."

The collapse did not come until April. In the meantime, fabrication had allowed Hesse to accept assistance in her work and her bad health made that help mandatory. In the fall some of her School of Visual Arts students had helped her sand the fiberglass pieces before the show. Doug Johns worked with her in the studio, and from January 1969 she had a student assistant from the Great Lakes Colleges Association. Martha Schieve had seen *Sans II* in the Whitney Annual and although she was a painter, had chosen to work with Hesse because "it impressed me as the only thing that had any sort of human element in it. She was working with her hands." The first thing they worked on together, with Doug Johns, was "the icicles " as it was called while in progress.

Connection: Wire armatures were hung from the ceiling and fiberglass cloth wrapped around them in small hunks; Johns would mix a vat of polyethelene; it would heat up and be painted on very lightly with a brush. Hesse wanted them to "let it happen," the fiberglass to be left to the shape it was taking, and the element of chance to occur through the use of different people's touches. Johns' modules were always very tight, not accidental enough, while Schieve worked very loosely, "practically let it slide off the wire"; Hesse's modules were in between these extremes. She told them she was not after a decorative effect; when it was finished she was dissatisfied with the piece because it had come out "too beautiful," with too *much* variation. A little sketch, which has since disappeared, showed that the artist intended to keep all the modules hanging together, but two or three were shown for sale as "multiples" at the "Plastic Presence" exhibition at the Jewish Museum a year later. At Hesse's death the piece was still in a sort of limbo. Gioia Timpanelli recalls that Hesse considered the piece unfinished. "She wanted to do 'many, many, many, many more of them.' That's how she put it." Her executors, guided by her original intentions, have treated it as a single piece. Since it was completed before her first operation, the theory that it was executed partially as "a kind of physical exercise, squashing, or hand-over-hand manipulation . . . largely as the physical expression open to the artist at the time" is precluded.[26] Nevertheless, there is an extreme pathos to the twenty dangling units; they are attenuated remnants, skeletal in presence and implication, disturbing and even ugly, rather than "too beautiful." The title was a tentative one of her own. Linda Shearer has remarked in the Guggenheim catalogue how Hesse's anxieties about her "connections" to other people were formally articulated by "her relentless use of cords and elements which gropingly reach out to the viewer." Here the connections seem to have been cut, and the reaching organs wither on their wire stems in a manner related to the once organic barrenness of *Tori* (fig. 199), also begun in January 1969.

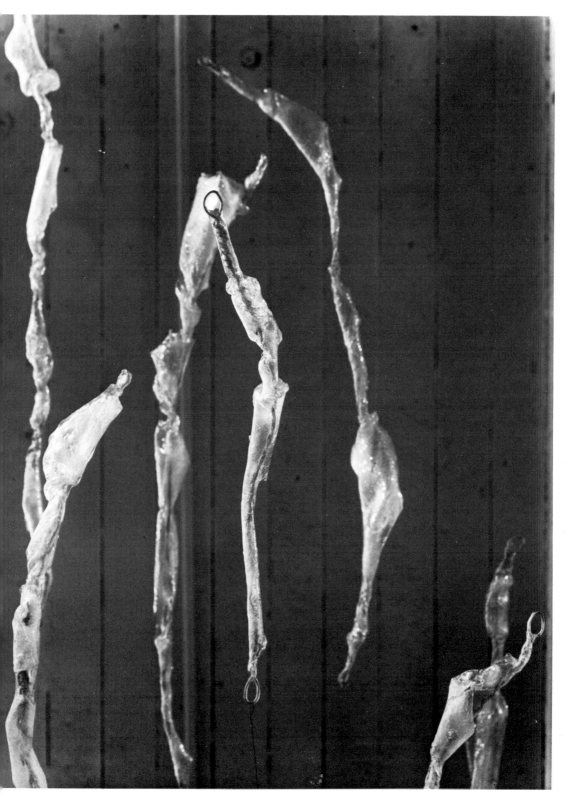

82. Connection (detail), 1969, fiberglass on wire, 9 of 20 units, each 16–65½″ x 3″.

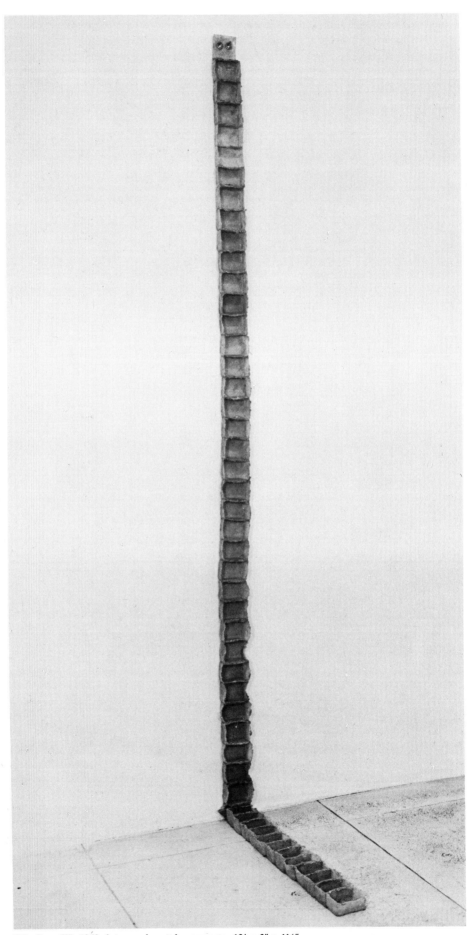

183. Sans III, 1969, latex and metal grommets, 13' x 3" x 1½".

184. Untitled, 1968, ink on stationery, 7¼ x 7¼", Fourcade, Droll, Inc., New York.

Sans III: Completed in January 1969 for "When Attitudes Become Form" at the Bern Kunsthalle, it is really a reprise of *Sans I* (fig. 163). The shallow latex boxes are smaller, the single rather than double line attenuates and exaggerates the original idea, but the proportions are pretty much the same. It was the last full-scale all latex piece and also the last that can be directly associated with Minimalism. Having pioneered alternatives to that tendency, Hesse allowed herself to move away from the compact wholism that had characterized the past two years of her work, and into a series of free-hanging, leaning, or lying pieces which were much more fragmented, dematerialized, and expressive. One of these, planned but not executed for a show I was doing in Seattle, related to *Sans III* in the way it came down the wall and bent onto the floor, but it was to be stringy, "all rubberized uneven (looks like foam deteriorated from Canal St. red pink orange kind that looked like Serra)."

Some of these reverted to ideas first established in older work. On November 14, 1968, two days before her show opened, Hesse had drawn a sketch on Fischbach stationery showing a bar-like panel on the wall from which swirled a mass of long thin gray rubber cords curling in a high tangle at the floor line (fig. 184). Another similar drawing showed the cords rolled up to the panel on the wall and then rolled down. These are based on an extant test piece in which a series of very long clear plastic tubings are sewn onto a cloth backing (fig. 138). While the drawing relates it to *Ennead* (fig. 80), the synthetic materials would have ruled out the chaos possible with plain string. A third version of this idea was begun early in 1969 when Hesse's assistant, Martha Schieve, helped to make a work in which a rubberized cheesecloth wall piece fed out a single row of nylon strings dipped in resin and hardened in an L shape where they met the floor, and, bent to its angle, extended across it. Some of these strings were longer, some shorter, but the basic position was that of *Sans I* and *Sans III*. Doug Johns remembers helping make two of these, one quite high off the ground, one lower: "She liked that it flowed down and hardened naturally, that it was straight and perfect but it had happened *naturally*." No one is known to have destroyed either one, and yet they no longer exist. Despite their fragility, Johns says they could not have fallen apart, but must have been destroyed accidentally, perhaps after Hesse's death.

141

Drawing had always been a means for Hesse to discover her deepest preoccupations, and there are drawings from 1968 which are not sketches for sculpture but relate to later work, predicting a looser direction as well as abandoning the circle in favor of lopsided boxes within boxes or lined up "window" forms. Having extensively explored the circle and graph paper, she seemed to be groping for a new focus and taking her sources from sculpture. Two transitional steps may have been the lovely warm brown and white "window" drawing with crooked rows of imperfect circles within the frame (fig. 187), and a gouache of wavering horizontal bars, a sort of sketchy Venetian blind with a few circles at the ends which make some of the flat bars into quasi-poles and define a vaguer center (fig. 188). Another (fig. 185) echoes the seamed surfaces of *Area,* consisting of rectangles of different sizes bound together into one long vertical, and another (fig. 189) harks back to the more detailed work of 1961 as well as anticipating the beginning of the Woodstock series in 1969. Yet another blurred pink and white drawing shows a trapezoid, or rectangular mat in perspective (fig. 186).

185. Untitled, 1968, ink and gouache, 16½ x 11", Fourcade, Droll, Inc., New York.

. Untitled, 1968, gouache, 11½ x 15¾″, Fourcade, Droll, Inc., New York.
. Untitled, 1968, gouache, 12 x 12″, Dr. and Mrs. Edward Okun, St. Louis.

Untitled, 1968, ink and gouache, 15 x 11½″, Fourcade, Droll, Inc., New York.
Untitled, 1968, gouache, pencil, silver ink, 22 x 15½″, Fourcade, Droll, Inc., New York.

190. Untitled, 1968, ink, gouache, 13 x 13″, Arthur Cohen, New York.

. Untitled, 1968, gouache, 11 x 15″, Roy R. Neuberger, New York.

192. Untitled, 1968, gouache, pencil, 14¾ x 11″, Dayton's Gallery 12, Minneapolis.

193. Untitled, 1968, gouache, pencil, 15½ x 11″, Fourcade, Droll, Inc., New York.

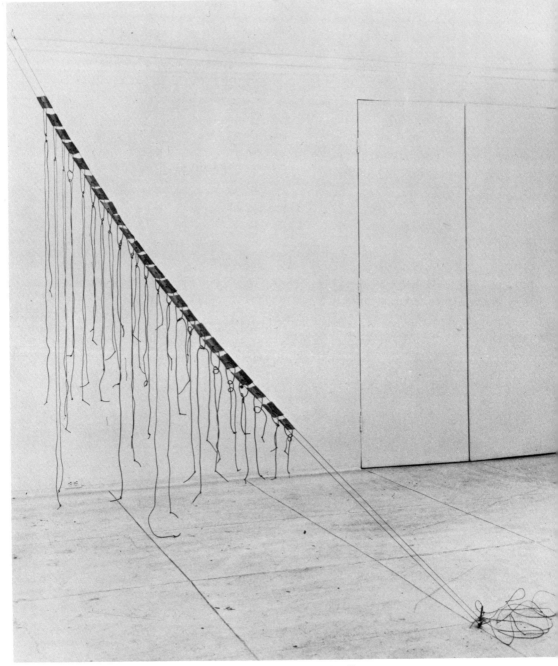

194. Vinculum II, 1969, latex on wire mesh, wire, staples, string, 16' x 3".

Vinculum II: Completed in January 1969 for the Bern show (which opened in March), it is a delicate ladder suspended in space by thin diagonal rubber lines from the meeting point of wall and ceiling to the floor, where it is attached in a tangle of string. (A sketch suggests that there was a choice between hanging it against the wall—"attached as several"—or "strung out," as is the finished version.) The square "rungs," miniaturizations of the screened ladder sections in *Vinculum I* (fig. 195) are rubberized wire mesh. Hanging from each one is a loop with long trailing irregular ends, some of which touch the floor; the longer lines are more or less at the top and the shorter at the bottom, so a rough triangle is formed. The image of precariousness, or physical decrepitude, is stressed by these dangling, broken ends —possibilities cut off, or pessimistic comments on the success of the climb. "It is very taut," Hesse said of it. "It is attached from the two angles so there is a lot of tension, and yet the whole thing is flexible and moves." Her title notes are "link, that which binds; bond, tie, connecting medium." The tenuousness of that connection is reflected in the fragility of the piece. It is, perhaps, about risk, or about weakness, physical and temporal.

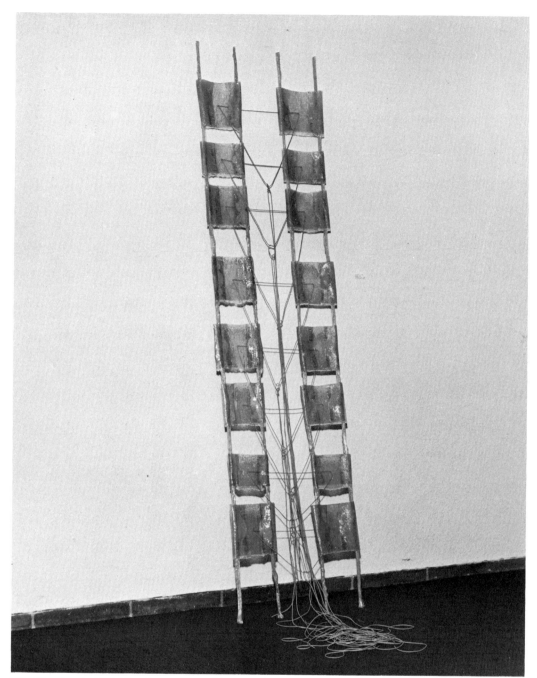

195. Vinculum I, 1969, fiberglass, rubber tubing, metal screen, 8' x 8" x 2'.

Vinculum I: Finished in February or March, though according to the title it was begun before *Vinculum II*. It too has "connection" as content, although there is a sketch of it without the laced rubber lines that form the connecting inverted triangles and end in an untidy pile on the floor—an excessive detail which might better have been omitted. Schieve, Johns, and Hesse all worked on this piece from the beginning and Hesse was pleased with the way group interaction and elements of chance affected it. When she first had the idea, she asked Johns to make her a fiberglass pole, and he made her "a perfect pole," which she kept around the studio because it amused her so. What she wanted, of course, was an "imperfect pole"; in the final version the four tapering lines are more like saplings, or spindly legs at the bottom, horns at the top. Here the ladder reference is more obvious than in *Vinculum II*, though the irregularly spaced fiberglass and mesh "rungs" are translucent and fragile in their awkward way too. There is perhaps a reference back to *Laocoon* (fig. 75) in the grid-versus-loose-soft-line theme. Hesse was particularly fond of this piece, and saw it as "solid and staid and inflexible except for the hose, where *Vinculum II* is similar but totally flexible."

It was this period at the end of 1968 and beginning of 1969 to which Hesse was referring when she told Cindy Nemser: "I used to plan a lot and do everything myself. Then I started to take the chance—no, I needed the help. It was a little difficult at first. I worked with two people [Schieve and Johns], but we got to know each other well enough, and I got confident enough, and just prior to when I was sick I would not state the problem or plan the day. I would let more happen and let myself be used in a freer way and they also—their participation was more their own, more flexible. I wanted to see within a day's work or within three days' work what we would do together with a general focus but not anything specified. I really would like, when I start working again, to go further into the whole process. It doesn't mean total chance, but more freedom and openness." Schieve helped repair *Accession* and make the latex multiples (fig. 181): these Hesse described in a note dated November 2, 1968, as: "a gauze-like tape dipped in liquid rubber wrapped around a blown balloon. As a coat dries a second and third is applied. At some point during drying stage, balloon is burst; and another application of rubber is applied. At some point process is completed. Then powdered." The result was a group of strange shriveled "sleeves" the insides of which took on the color of the balloon, the outsides a fleshy color and ribbed pattern.

150

196. Expanded Expansion, 1969, fiberglass and latex on cheesecloth, 3 units of 3, 5, and 7 poles each, 120 x 180–240″ per unit·

Expanded Expansion: Completed February 28, 1969, it was made by laying cheesecloth on plastic, mixing the rubber, spreading it by brush one layer thick on the cloth, drying it, and peeling it off the plastic so chance determined the irregular edges. When the ten-foot fiberglass poles were made, they were laid down on the cheesecloth, fiberglass was laid over each pole, overlapping the rubber, and the resin spread on both sides. Martha Schieve recalls Hesse's "real honest use of chance. She didn't manipulate it, didn't try to keep the irregularities in the actual texture and at the same time didn't try *not* to have them happen." *Expanded Expansion* is as absurdly redundant as its title, and was intended to be even more so. "I thought I would make more of it but sickness prevented that. They could actually be extended to a length where one would really feel they were environmental. . . . It is flexible so you could push it very narrow or you could push it wide apart." It leans against the wall (as do her other pole pieces—*Vinculum I* and *Accretion*), but she also noted that it looked beautiful on the floor. The idea is a modular or Minimal one, but the piece itself, with its contrast of stiff poles and soft, tactile hangings, its potentially accordian-like movement, is not impassive, but hovers on the brink of function and association. It is a curtain and thereby hides something. "It has sort of like legs on it," she observed. "Maybe that is not so good. Possibly it potentially has quite a few associations and yet it's not anything. So maybe that increases its silliness . . . . It contradicts its ridiculous quality because it has a definite concern about its presentation. It can't just be a whim, you know. It's too considered."

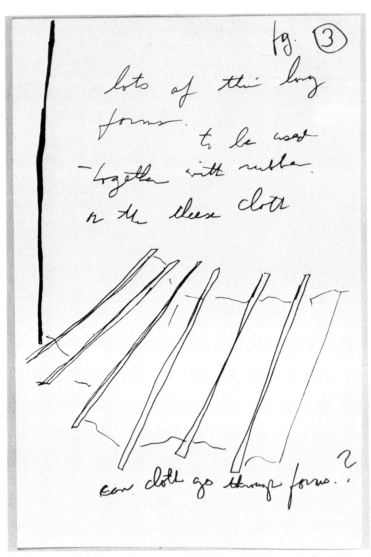

196 a. Study for Expanded Expansion, pen and ink, 9 x 6″, Fourcade, Droll, Inc., New York.

Untitled: This piece emerged from Hesse's dissatisfaction with *Connection* (fig. 182); she wanted to try some other ideas. It was still unfinished when she collapsed and Martha Schieve, who had helped make it, completed the last bit for the Whitney show. It is the least assuming piece Hesse ever made, to the point where in a huge and crowded museum room it almost isn't there at all. A twisted tentacle of colorless fiberglass hanging from the ceiling, it hits the floor with several feet to go (even with the highest ceiling) and coils there stiffly. She thought of this piece too in terms of unlimited expansion, as is indicated by a text found in her papers which appears to be about this and *Expanded Expansion:* "Intentionally two pieces of great contrast in form but similar in their thought and extreme position. Both are endless. If ceiling were higher or space on floor larger it could as well be continued and exaggerate its position more. The rubberized cheesecloth also could continue. Both take a stand on absurdity. Both by means of form as well. One is endless and yet a thin longish substance that is linked together and one feels the infinity to which it could extend. The other is opposite in form, large looming, powerful yet precarious. Its positioning as a unit or sectional units could take many stands. The flexible and also inflexible quality is there and in contrast."

The fact that this piece, and three out of the last six that Hesse made, were untitled is indicative of her failing stamina. "Wherever things are to be identified I do title them," she told Nemser, "and I give it a lot of thought most of the time because I don't like things being called untitled; that's a sign of uninterest, and I am interested. I try to title them so it has a meaning for me in terms of what I think of the piece and yet it's just like another noun. I use the dictionary and thesaurus. I use a word for its sound but they don't· have a specific meaning in terms of content."

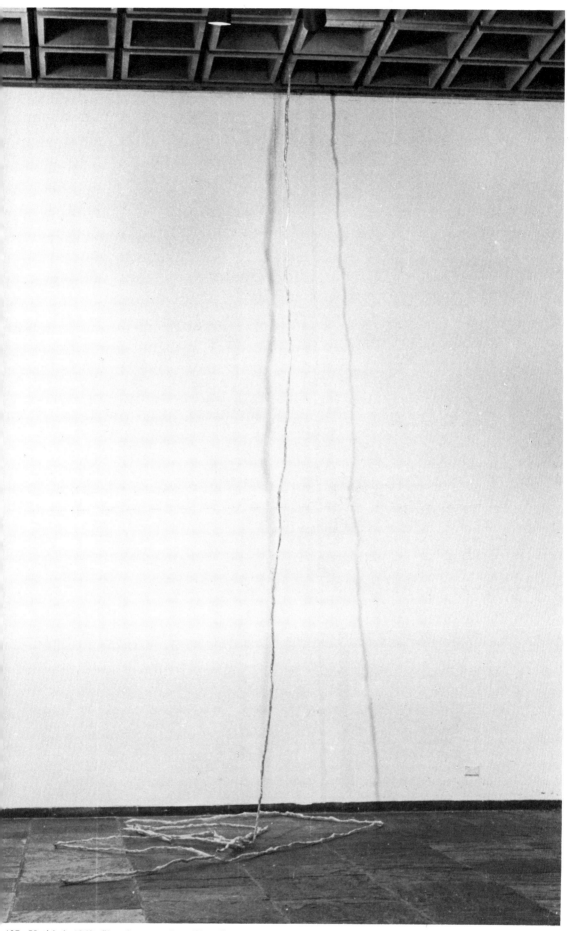

197. Untitled, 1969, fiberglass on wire, 62′ x 1″.

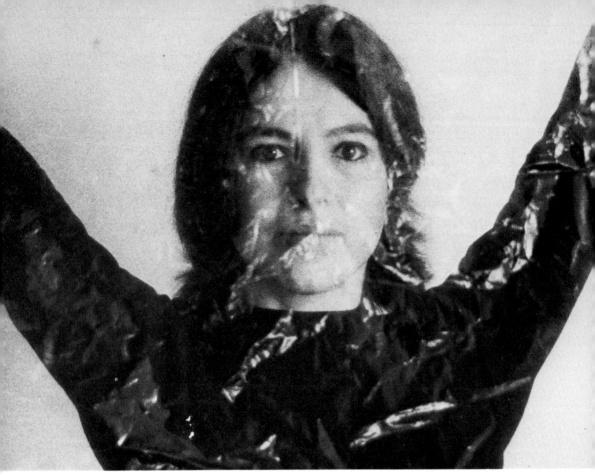

198. Eva Hesse, 1969.

In March Hesse wrote "Sick" in large letters across her diary. But the pressure of shows she wanted so badly to be in kept her going until April 6, when she collapsed at Donald Droll's loft, where she was just finishing the repairs on *Accession*. It was immediately obvious that afternoon that she was seriously, physically ill, though convincing her various doctors that this was not a depression was not an easy task. She went to Ruth Vollmer's home and was not admitted to New York Hospital until April 10, when what seemed like an endless round of testing began. When they finally discovered the brain tumor, they operated immediately. It was now April 18; in another day or so she would have been dead. Fortunately she remembered nothing but a few vague impressions from that time. When she awoke she recalled only "change of head gear, bandage, wrappings, care, very tender care, time—vague, and very real things. Space orientation all off —totally inaccurate and unaware, dislocated. Never afraid. Someone always there, never aloneness. . . . No one knew what condition I'd be in after the operation. There were so many possibilities. Also in terms of my personality—and my psyche. To myself I seem pretty much the same (not depressed or anxious). I look at the past 3½ years with a kind of amazement. All that has come to pass. My changes. Inside and outside. I can be proud. Am I? And certainly I can live alone and be within myself."

One of her first thoughts was that she didn't *have* to be an artist to justify her existence. "I could live without it. And then one of my second or third thoughts was film. . . . I had just seen *Weekend* and I wasn't that moved. But I saw it a second time and I was as moved as I could be by anything. . . . I had never tried to make a film. I don't know what made me think that was physically easier. . . . I have so little content in my work in terms of reality. For me it is very much that but it is not visible. It is abstractly that way, and in film, although my film would be very abstract, there is some closer connection. I mean you have to use some kind of imagery to do it through connectiveness of people or whatever I would choose. And it would give me another vehicle, a vehicle of content. Chances are it would be sparse, but I am sure in the first one I would use people. . . . I have some kind of personal avoidance of using a camera because in my family there was a lot of photography being done. . . . It is sort of in vogue now. Everybody is doing it. Sometime I would like to try it.''

Nevertheless, Hesse's art was the most important thing she had, and after the operation, however little she admitted it to herself, she knew that if she was going to realize her capacity for making great art, she had to do it right *now*. She completed six more major pieces and many drawings before she died, overcoming obstacles that would have demolished most people. In a curious way, Hesse gained strength from her predicament. The possibility of death had broken down certain barriers life had always imposed on her. Gioia Timpanelli, who had met her only in late 1968, could barely believe Hesse's accounts of her own weakness, anxiety, and dependence in the past. She found her immensely strong and clearheaded, as though "this was the first time she was *really* living on all levels." Along with Droll, Vollmer, David Magasis and Naomi Spector, she was one of Hesse's greatest supports that last year. It was also at this time that Eva and her sister "found one another again''; while convalescing, she stayed with Helen, her husband Murray Charash, and their children, Ruth and Marc, at their home in New Jersey, and became "so much a part of all our lives."

A month after the operation Hesse attended the opening of the Whitney show in a wheelchair from the hospital. Finally titled "Anti-Illusion: Procedures/Materials" rather than "process," due to the artists' complaints about being yet again categorized, the emphasis of the exhibition and catalogue was still decidedly on process. Marcia Tucker wrote that Hesse "has found that because she is concerned with creating personal forms, she must use only materials that she can make herself. The plastic, fiberglass, rubberized cheesecloth and gauze from which her pieces are modelled are neither cast nor moulded. They are made by putting the raw material on the floor and shaping it, adding layers until the proper substance is attained." *Vinculum I, Expanded Expansion,* and the untitled fiberglass "icicle" were installed near Ryman's huge brushy cardboard painting, and few, if any, of the reviewers who noted the "gestural aspects" of the show as a whole were aware that these were two of the major sources of such new freedom.[27]

The summer of 1969 Hesse's studio was too hot and she didn't want to be alone. Yet she felt good; she had come close to death but had escaped with the removal of what she thought was a benign tumor. Now she was going to relax, allow herself a leisurely convalescence and time to get back into sculpture, have a vacation. She went to visit Grace and Gerry Wapner in Woodstock. After returning to the city she and Gioia Timpanelli decided to spend the rest of the summer at Gioia's cabin in Woodstock, with occasional trips back to New York. This period was planned by both friends as "a whole regimen around work." It rained every day for weeks, and they took tables out on the screened porch because it was too dark in the cabin. Hesse had her drawing tool box with her—filled with little bottles of ink, stubs of pencil, wax, colored pencils, brushes, all of which "she practically knew by name. I liked seeing her with her objects," says Timpanelli, "because she had a serious relationship with them—childlike, intuitive. And she was very serious about good enough materials. The paper had to be good; even though she couldn't spend money, she would treat herself to that because it was serious. We worked hard and we laughed a lot. We really *lived* every single day. As the summer went on, she was concerned about all the shows coming up."

It must have been around this time or soon afterwards that Hesse wrote: "The lack of energy I have is contrasted by a psychic energy of rebirth. A will to start to live again, work again, be seen, love. I fight sleep to respond to this real excitement that is frustrated because there is so little I can do. I'm told and know I must let all those who have asked to help me do so now. It's another new thing to learn. I have held general help at abeyance too many people and how and what to say or do. There are about 8 people who have done so much for me. Really I have an incredible group of close friends and friends. For this long since April 6 I have never been alone months I have lived with friends. I have tremendous new feelings although there is confusion they are strong black, white, none gray."

199. Tori, 1969, fiberglass on wire mesh, 9 units, each 30–47 x 12½–17 x 10¼–15".

Tori: Begun in January 1969, two of its units were complete by February and six were completed in March. Since the remaining three were finished in August, this was probably the piece to which Hesse returned when she could briefly work on sculpture again. It was made of chicken wire, pulled over and pinned at the ends, bent subtly by touch—Hesse's own, although Johns and Schieve helped to cover them with fiberglass and resin. Johns recalls "it was one of the toughest to make; the stuff kept sliding off the screens, or its weight would crush the screens." The nine empty receptacles, their surfaces scarred, frozen at the moment of splitting open, lie as though discarded on the ground, tossed carelessly against each other in a defeated version of *Repetition Nineteen* (fig. 153). Formally they also refer back to the rubberized sleeves (fig.177a) and *Area* (fig. 171) of 1968, but here the image is a painful one. Hesse chose the geometrical definition of the word, which she heard from Robert Morris: "a surface or solid generated by the revolution of a circle or other conic about any axis." But there are two other definitions of "torus"—the botanical: "the swollen summit of the flower-stalk, which supports the floral organs"; and the anatomical: "a smooth rounded ridge or elongated protuberance, as of a muscle; *spec.* the *tuber cinerum* of the brain." It is impossible not to read into these broken and barren forms—like seed-pods past their prime—the downward plunge of Hesse's life at this time.

156

In Woodstock, Hesse began a series of drawings which began on half sheets and then went into full (14 ⅞ x 22 ") sheets, some of which were completed back in her studio. The first one she made was *For Gioia* (fig. 200), which closely resembles work from 1961 with its compartmentation, pattern, delicate, subdued color and washed and scumbled surface. The small drawing she gave to David (Dudy) Magasis, shows how most of them started—full of color and self-indulgent expressionist brushwork which was then worked over until she achieved the rigor she wanted (fig. 201). This one she considered "too easy, too pretty, too much of the past," and it was only for love of a good friend who really liked it that she decided not to destroy it.

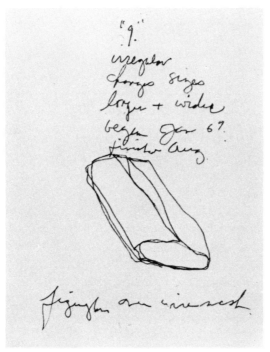

199a. Study for Tori, pen and ink, 6¾ x 3¾", Fourcade, Droll, Inc., New York.

"The Woodstock drawings are absolutely the kitchen sink," Gioia Timpanelli recalls. "They had in them everything in the cabin. When she'd begin, she'd move freely. There were times when she'd work on more than one at a time. Sometimes there were six or eight of them on the floor. They were hung on the walls, they had to get harder and harder. Their beginnings were incredible—highly colored, complex, intricate. They started in a very familiar place but she knew they were going somewhere else. She crayoned on them, used colored pencils for incisions, scratches. She used some of the liquitex and caseins I was using. Some of them had a real paint quality and that bothered her. She'd *break* that surface with pencil lines. . . . As far as she was concerned, painting was dead. I don't think she'd ever have gone back to painting, unless she could paint in a brand new different way. If she hadn't been out of her studio she probably would have been making models instead of drawing that summer, although she never contemplated abandoning drawing. In October, we went to Andrews Nelson Whitehead and bought a *huge* quantity of good paper and then we bought *lots* of quart bottles of ink."

Many of these 1969 drawings (figs. 202–207) resemble "windows"; prototypes from 1968 (figs. 190–193) bring out the image still more clearly. In the Woodstock series, the centers are more often open, or "blank." However, it is the touch, the working of the surface, the pale but intense color, the *density* of the finished drawing that dominates the compartmented or "paned" and bordered structures. When they were shown at Fischbach in March 1970, as Hesse's second one-woman show, Hilton Kramer stressed their romanticism and said they were "at once fragile and yet very firmly conceived," (*New York Times,* April 18, 1970) which could be taken as a metaphor for the way the artist was living her life at the time they were made. Some of the "windows" are dark, opaque, offering little respite from the surface, the present, reality. Others are delicate and light-filled, with pastel colors, grayed but not muddied, floating the rectangular structure into another, fantasy, space, while the scratched and nervous borders insist on this, the "realer," space. The layering of the fragile washes (some including gold and silver inks) parallels the layering of latex or fiberglass which produced works like *Contingent* (fig. 209) which was completed after or simultaneously with this series and shares its preoccupation with light. While the sculptures change and the drawings are relatively static, the execution in some of them is so precise that the light seems actually to flicker over the passive, painted surface. When she used a grid in the "window" series, it too quivered with life, each square different from the next, or lopsidedly divided into inequal scale. Sometimes bands of rectangles separate smaller rectangles or divide the page in half; sometimes the borders themselves seem like angular halos of light; sometimes the heavy, rhythmic scratching at the surface betrays the tension and inevitable content behind the image.

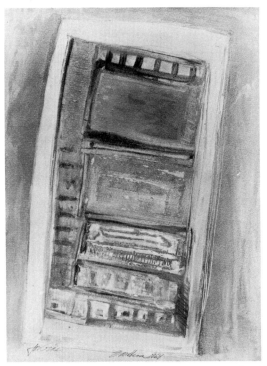

200. For Gioia, 1969, pencil, wash and mixed media, 14⅞ x 11″, Gioia Timpanelli, New York.
201. Untitled, 1969, gouache, pencil, 22 x 14¾″, David Magasis, New York.

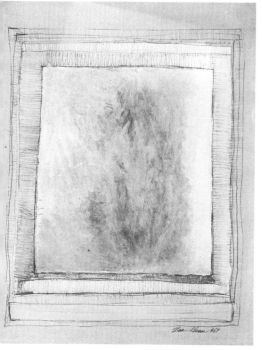

02. Untitled, 1969, gouache, pencil, 23 x 17½", Fourcade, Droll, Inc., New York.

03. Untitled, 1969, gouache, pencil, 21⅞ x 17¼", Paul F. Walter, New York.

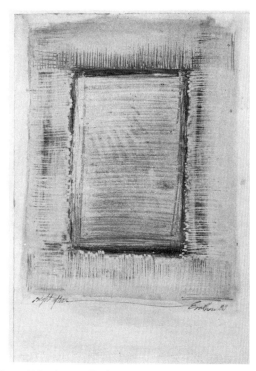

04. Untitled, 1969, gouache, pencil, 22 x 17", Mr. and Mrs. Henry Feiwel, New York.

05. Right After, 1969, gouache, pencil, 22 x 14⅞", Constance C. Wittkoff, St. Louis.

206. Untitled, 1969, gouache, pencil, 22⅛ x 15¾″, Mr. and Mrs. Ronald B. Lynn and family, Teaneck, N.J.

By August, Hesse was having headaches again. She was tired and slept in the afternoons, "slept as though she weren't going to wake." However, she went back into the city, not because she was sick, but because she wanted to get to work. But within a few days, the symptoms recurred so violently that she went right back into the hospital. Her second operation was on August 18th. When she came out, she had radiation treatments for about two weeks, and later, chemotherapy with Dr. William Schapiro.[28] She was still optimistic, and as soon as she could, she began to work again on the airy web of fiberglass skeins that had hung in her studio since the previous winter, when Schieve remembers that she was already concerned that the piece was "too pretty." She called it (and a drawing unrelated to it—fig. 205), *Right After*.

207. Untitled, 1969, gouache, 23 x 17½", Galerie Ricke, Cologne.

Right After: "The idea totalled before I was sick. The piece was strung in my studio for a whole year. So I wasn't in connectiveness with it when I went back to it, but I visually remembered it. I remembered what I wanted to do with the piece and at that point I should have left it, because it was really daring. It was very, very simple and very extreme because it looked like a really big nothing which was one of the things that I so much wanted to be able to achieve. But coming back to it after a summer of not having seen it, I felt it needed more work, more completion and that was my mistake. It left the ugly zone and went to the beauty zone. I didn't mean it to do that. . . . My original statement was so simple and there wasn't that much there, just irregular wires and very little material. It was really absurd and totally strange and I lost it. So now I'm attempting to do it in another material, in rope, and I think I'll get much better results with this one." Doug Johns recalls it being done in three pieces, three sessions. He would saturate in resin the 100–200′ long fiber, some 20′ at a time, then hand it up to Hesse, who would festoon it from the hooks and nails spotted all over the ceiling: "Once it was up, that was it. It was very spontaneous and we had a great time."

One of the problems with *Right After* is the beauty of the material, relaxed loops of fairy tale gossamer thread. But in Hesse's dark, shabby, low-ceilinged studio, Gioia Timpanelli recalls, "it was magic, a fantastic absurdity." When it was shown in a black room at the "Plastic Presence" exhibition in the Jewish Museum, it became much too jewel-like, to Hesse's distress, although she liked the fact that near it was her friend Tom Clancy's work, which she saw as "heavy and masculine" as opposed to her "delicate feminine" piece (Bill Barrette). It was, however, well-received. Robert Pincus-Witten wrote in *Artforum* (January 1970) that it "carried the exhibition for me," that Hesse had made a "central contribution" to new American sculpture, and that her "forms are strong, suggestive, intellectually focused; [it] surpasses any piece in the show."

208. Right After, 1969, fiberglass over string, 6½ x 10 x 16′.

Contingent: Begun in November 1968 with the help of Schieve and Johns, *Contingent* was not completed until a year later. In the fall of 1969, although Hesse no longer could teach at the School of Visual Arts, a group of students came down for what was to be a one-day stint of assistance, as she wanted to show the piece in an exhibition at Finch College. Two of the girls sewed pieces of cheesecloth together, because they were too narrow, and the boys rubberized. When it became clear that more help was needed, Bill Barrette and Jonathan Singer volunteered; they became her regular assistants, with Barrette continuing to be a kind of technical custodian and to install most of the shows after her death. He remembers that when they arrived, a couple of sections had been made, one of which was a single prototype with small fiberglass ends which had been made through the trap door in the ceiling and was too long to hang in the studio. This was made in 1968, and exists now as a separate "piece"; Hesse also gave a long sheet of rubberized cheesecloth to Naomi Spector, a friend who worked at Fischbach; it was to be hung perpendicular to the wall.

They made five or six sections, with Johns advising them on the right amount of ultra violet inhibitor (so the latex would deteriorate as slowly as possible), on how to bond the resin, and generally overseeing the process. Altogether, many test pieces, with different kinds of cheesecloth and rubber, were made. Schieve remembers the technique resembling that of *Expanded Expansion:* "the pieces on top came last, they weren't there at first." Hesse told them ways of cutting off the fiberglass so it was "irregular but not forced, so it would look 'dumb.' She was pretty up at that point," Barrette recalls. "It was only with the other pieces that she began to relinquish control. At first she was very reluctant to let anyone work on it. Sol [LeWitt] talked her into it, said there was a long historical precedent. Finally she got over feeling queasy about having people help her on other than the mechanical things."

A drawing dated January 15, 1969 (fig. 212) represents one of the first ideas for *Contingent,* although the test modules were already under way. "That was much thinner" she told Nemser, "and it had either end wire mesh underneath the fiberglass and it was going to be on hardware that turns. And there were going to be many in a row. . . . I did a whole group [of sketches] in one time. . . . I always did drawings but they were always separate from the sculpture or the paintings. . . . They were related because they were mine but they weren't related in one completing the other. And these weren't either. They were just sketches like I tried something else and it worked. . . . It was also not wanting to have such a definite plan. . . . It is just a quickie to develop it in the process rather than working out a whole model in small and following it—that doesn't interest me." Four quite finished drawings and annotated working sketches on yellow lined paper were among Hesse's papers. They clearly relate in proportion and material to the finished piece, although the drawing style—very loose and modeled—makes the components appear much rounder, even phallic, and anthropomorphic (fig. 213). Notes and another drawing indicate that she may once have thought of it as a single piece hung against the wall: "stand up on lower section holes to attach to wall not necessarily straight can lean forward." The middle section was to be "rubber clutched together with rubber wires or cord or staples mixed. nothing form however it falls naturally"; and "top held up or fallen over either way." Related to this idea is also a drawing for a large vertical rectangular piece which would be "narrow very long overlap as gets on the floor," hung from "middle ceiling to floor then to wall."

Contingent finally consisted of eight glowing composites of rubberized cheesecloth and fiberglass run through various proportional and textural changes, the light catching each translucent sheet a different way, producing different colors. One piece is much longer than the others; "I could have cut it off but I said no—so it will stand different." It hangs from hooks in the ceiling. ("They were the hooks that we used while we were making it . . . they weren't there as decoration and I don't believe in changing them to get nicer hardware.") *Contingent* is different in every space it hangs in, but holds its own even badly hung and lit in a Guggenheim Museum bay. Hesse originally did not want an even number of units, but Johns told her it was too late to add to it; a different batch of rubber would change it too much.

Contingent is at once more detached and less associatable than most of Hesse's work, transcending the whimsical to make a statement that is grand simply in its existence, and, at the same time, is as profoundly personal or intimate as a work of art can be. It incorporates the qualities and textures of the new and the old, of the battered and the beautiful. With the opaque weight concentrated in the middle of the piece, it seems from some angles to hover in mid air, or to disintegrate at both ends.

The piece (and not a "mockup" or "prototype"[29]) was shown at Finch College's "Art in Process IV" in fall 1969, and it dominated the show. Hesse's catalogue statement read:

Hanging.
Rubberized, loose, open cloth.
Fiberglass—reinforced plastic.

Began somewhere in November–December, 1968.
Worked.
Collapsed April 6, 1969. I have been very ill.
Statement.
Resuming work on piece,
have one complete from back then.
Statement, October 15, 1969, out of hospital,
short stay this time,
third time.
Same day, students and Douglas Johns began work.
MORATORIUM DAY
Piece is in many parts.
Each in itself is a complete statement,
together am not certain how it will be.
A fact. I cannot be certain yet.
Can be from illness, can be from honesty.
irregular, edges, six to seven feet long.
textures coarse, rough, changing.
see through, non see through, consistent, inconsistent.
enclosed tightly by glass like encasement just hanging there.
then more, others. will they hang there in the same way?
try a continuous flowing one.
try some random closely spaced.
try some distant far spaced.
they are tight and formal but very ethereal. sensitive. fragile.
see through mostly.
not painting, not sculpture. it's there though.
I remember I wanted to get to non art, non connotive,
non anthropomorphic, non geometric, non, nothing,
everything, but of another kind, vision, sort.
from a total other reference point. is it possible?
I have learned anything is possible. I know that.
that vision or concept will come through total risk,
freedom, discipline.
I will do it.

today, another step. on two sheets we put on the glass.
did the two differently.
one was cast—poured over hard, irregular, thick plastic;
one with screening, crumpled. they will all be different.
both the rubber sheets and the fiberglass.
lengths and widths.
question how and why in putting it together?
can it be different each time? why not?
how to achieve by not achieving? how to make by not making?
it's all in that.
it's not the new. it is what is yet not known,
thought, seen, touched but really what is not.
and that is.

Before installing the Finch piece, Hesse had spent eleven days in bed, and though she attended the opening, she was back in the hospital over Christmas. Between *Contingent* and her final entry into the hospital in March, she made her three last pieces.

 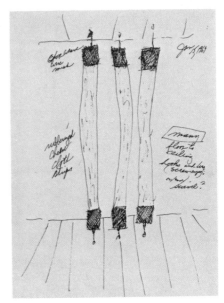

209. Contingent (see frontispiece for color plate), 1968–69, fiberglass and latex on cheesecloth, 8 units, each 9½–11′ x 3–4′.

212. Study for Contingent, 1969, pen and ink, 8¾ x 6″, whereabouts unknown.

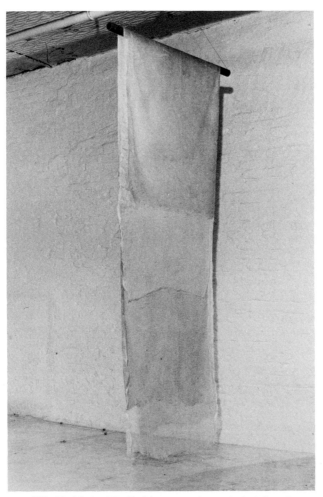

210. Untitled, 1968–69, latex over cheesecloth, 34″ x 12′.

211. Untitled, date unknown, pencil, ink wash, 17⅞ x 23⅞″, Fourcade, Droll, Inc. New York.

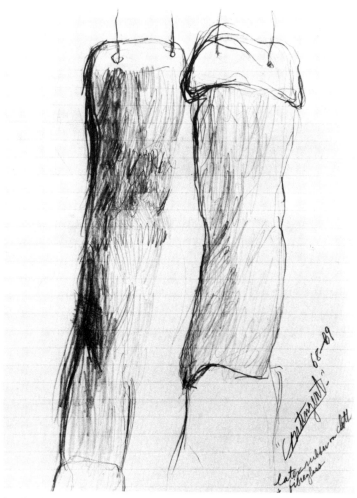

213. Study for Contingent, 1969, pencil on yellow lined paper, 8¼ x 11″, Fourcade, Droll, Inc., New York.

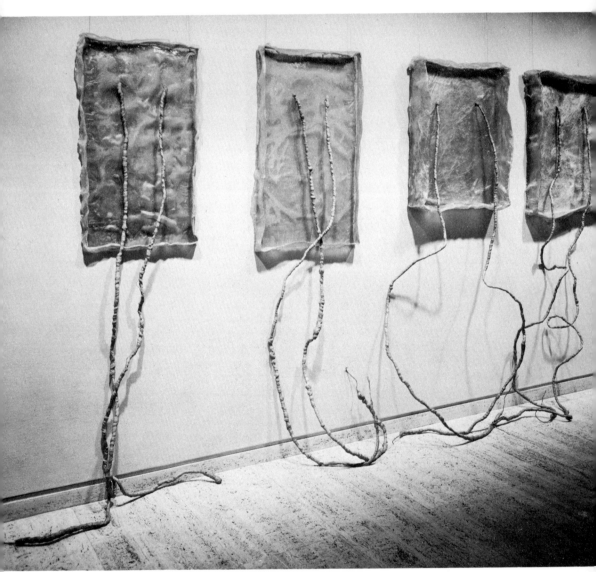

214. Untitled, 1970, fiberglass over wire mesh, latex over cloth and wire, 4 units, each 34– 42¾ x 23–34 x 2–6″.

Untitled: This piece, and its smaller prototype unit (fig. 215) refer back once more to the shallow boxes or trays that originated with the *Sans* sculptures. Enlarged this time, and hung as four separate reliefs, each is very different in size, shape (ranging from square to vertical) and contour. Each one had two gauze-wrapped and rubberized aluminum wires protruding from the upper middle and reaching the floor where, unlike similar elements in earlier pieces, they do not coil limply or elegantly, but bound back up toward the wall or leap and straddle each other. There is an early drawing in which two extra "streamers" irregularly connect the three boxes and the two protrusions from each one are placed differently (fig. 216); in another, a single tray sprouted many irregularly placed streamers; still another related sketch shows a much freer form for the backing, ("cheesecloth or rougher material as burlap") pierced by four lopsided holes from which the aluminum wires dangle; this was to be "uneven—irregular connect an unconnected hanging. . ." These are among many schemes for works connecting asymmetrically to each other or to other surfaces which would, it seems, have made more successful sculptures. There is a tight and strained, even forced feeling to the finished piece, which was the first one to be handled almost entirely by her two assistants, though Hesse oversaw all the work from her bed, and Johns also helped. It may be that, given the circumstances, she decided to work with an already familiar idea; certainly this piece is less inventive and harks back more to previous formal solutions than any of the other last works. "It was highly experimental—not in form or material but in working with other people," Barrette recalls. "The mechanical touch you see in it might be Jon and me. . . . We used to be pretty tough on her. We used to push her and she would push us. It made it a lot more fun—maybe that's partially responsible for the piece being as bizarre as I think it is." The suggestion that the obsessive quality of Hesse's work was dissipated when others were doing the handling is dispelled by Barrette: "In that piece she had us wrapping very soft lines made of ⅜" aluminum wire with gauze many many times wrapped and wrapped so they'd be lumpy in certain areas and unlumpy in others. She could be quite dogmatic. She got down on us when we felt some procedure was downright silly. The subtle distinctions between what's validly loose and what's invalidly loose—if you're working for someone else you maybe don't take them so seriously." These wrapped lines might also have been intended for another piece. "Things were getting very loose at that time. She wanted to expand. She was beginning to trust us—our esthetic judgment; maybe because we were students and divorced from any kind of art world reality."

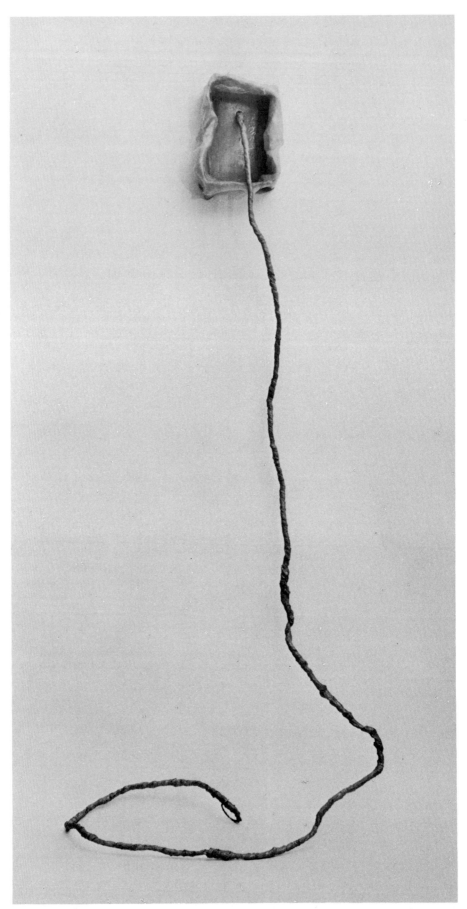

215. Untitled (prototype for fig. 214), 1970, fiberglass over wire mesh, latex over cloth over wire, 12 x 9 x 4½", cord 78".

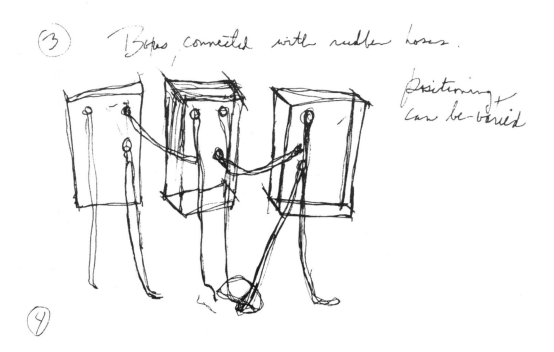

216. Two studies for Untitled (fig. 214), 1970, pen and ink, 7 x 7⅞″; pen and ink, 6¾ x 3¾″,
Fourcade, Droll, Inc., New York.

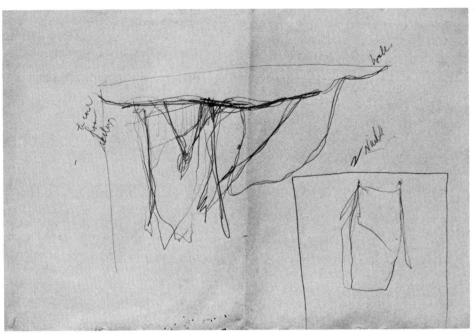

217. Study for Untitled (fig. 218) 1970, pencil, 12 x 18″, Fourcade, Droll, Inc., New York.

Untitled: This is the successor to *Right After,* its "ugly" counterpart. It was first made by Hesse directing David Magasis (a friend who had nothing to do with art): "It was something she'd had in mind. [She had made notes and drawings for it as early as November 1969.] *Life* magazine was coming to photograph in a couple of days. I went to my uncle's place and got cable cord of all sizes. I came back and she said ' Do something.' 'What?' 'Whatever you feel like doing. . . . Do you want to make a knot?' 'Yes.' So I made a knot." He dunked it in liquid rubber and strung it up; "She really had self-confidence at that time." Later Bill Barrette rubberized some more ropes with her and the piece got moved to the corner of the studio. Her notes indicate how free she wanted it to be: "hung irregularly tying knots as connections really letting it go as it will allowing it to determine more of the way it completes itself. Make it with at least 2 or 3 of us, connecting from wires from ceiling and nails from walls and other ways let it determine more itself how floppy or stiff it might be. Colors. how much rope/must be rope piece." From there she hoped to go, according to her notes, into pieces described as "non forms, non shapes non planned."

The piece has been called "unfinished"; its installation is half the work and must be done by someone extremely familiar with Hesse's ideas. LeWitt hung it at Documenta in 1972; it took two days and even then he felt he could have continued. It would look right from one angle and wrong from another. Nancy Graves, who installed it in Philadelphia the first time it was shown, remembers that Hesse was not happy with this piece, but was too sick to be sure about it. Its "unfinished" quality may, however, have been what Hesse wanted. Everything that the graceful *Right After* is not, this is—an apparently random tangle of lines which she once referred to as "the knot piece." The inevitable comparison to Jackson Pollock's painting is not unreasonable and she herself was quoted in *Life* as saying: "This piece is very ordered. Maybe I'll make it more structured, maybe I'll leave it changeable. When it's completed its order could be chaos. Chaos can be structured as non-chaos. That we know from Jackson Pollock." It does have the gestural intensity of Pollock's most passionately disturbed surfaces, and its sculptural suspension in mid-air, its central weight, deepens the sense of risk.

172

Untitled, 1970, latex over rope, string, wire, 3 strands: 12', 10½', 7½'.

219. Hesse's Bowery studio, upstairs, 1969–70.

220. Hesse's drawing table, 1970.

221. Untitled, 1970, fiberglass over polyethylene over aluminum wire, 7 units, each 7' 2"–
9' 3" x 10–16"

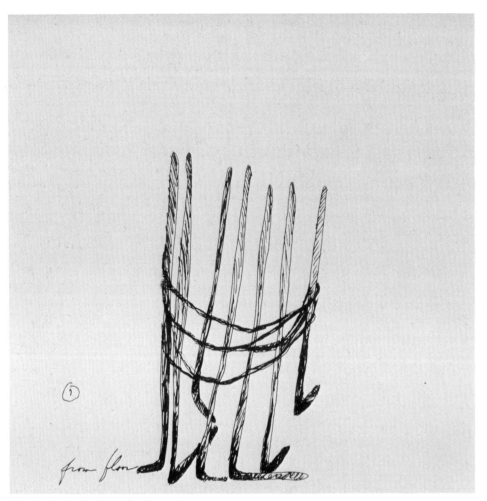

222. Study for Untitled (fig. 221), 1970, pen and ink, 8 x 10″, Lucy R. Lippard, New York.

Untitled: Hesse seems to have conceived this piece while in the hospital over Christmas 1969. Gioia Timpanelli remembers visiting her, and although Hesse was very sick she pulled out a pad of rough paper and showed Gioia a drawing made with thick pencil: ''I laughed and said it was the funniest piece I'd ever seen and she said she was glad because she thought so too. It was a drawing of this foot. She said she was going to make a piece for the Corning show from it.'' A second drawing (fig. 222) shows seven of these "feet" facing various ways but looped together in a semi-circle by rope or cord, originally intended to be a fiberglass web, like that in *Right After;* it would have supported the piece so it could stand freely on the floor. Before this drawing was made, sometime in the winter of 1969, Hesse visited Nancy Graves' studio, and saw, among other things, her *36 Legs: Variability + Repetition of Variable Forms.* Graves gave her a box of Johnson and Johnson casting bandage and from it Hesse made the model (fig. 223), which differs from the drawing primarily in the fact that the seven units stand on a small square mat and all face inwards, in a lopsided circle connected by frayed strands of wire, which give it a desolate air. (The Corning commission was made on the basis of this model, and although they showed the final version, they did not buy it because it was no longer in a circle.)

Johns remembers the model being done quite a bit before the piece was begun, which was in March 1970. It took about six weeks to do. ''She was very excited about it,'' Barrette remembers. '' wanted it big, but wasn't sure of the materials. We figured out a rough way of how to make these things. We wrapped this heavy aluminum wire loosely with sheets of polyethelene and tied them with thinner aluminum wire and that was the armature. Then we started to put on little pieces of fiberglass dipped in resin, just sticking them on. It was a terrible job.'' The poles were strung up in two rows in the studio while they were being constructed. Hesse could do nothing herself by this time. She and Doug Johns quarreled about whether the internal structure should show; she persisted and it finally did. About this time, by agreement with her student assistants, who did most of the work, the idea of the

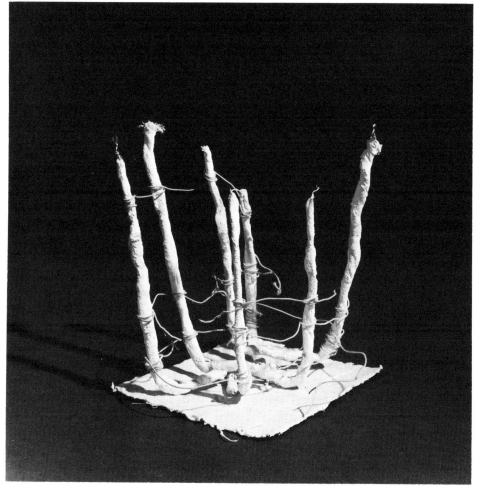

223. Model for Untitled (fig. 221), 1970, plaster over wire, cloth-covered wire, 7 units, each 4¾–6¾" h., base 5 x 5".

circle was abandoned. They were very excited about the piece and worked as much as three times a week on it. "It never dawned on me she was going to die," Barrette recalls. "We had all these wild plans about things we were going to do." When she went back into the hospital "we just kept on telling her how terrific the piece looked." But they did not want to finish it without her and the Corning opening was delayed. When it became apparent that they would have to finish it alone, there was some doubt as to how it should be arranged. They set it up and photographs were shown to Hesse. She liked it, although she was in no condition to make concentrated critical judgments.

Just before Hesse's death, the last piece (with *Vinculum I* and the untitled "tray and cord" piece) was hung by nylon threads from the ceiling at the Owens-Corning Fiberglass Center on Fifth Avenue in a show which also included the work of Tony DeLap and Frank Gallo. She never saw it. James Mellow wrote of it in the *New York Times* (July 5, 1970) that it was a piece "audacious in its awkwardness" and David Shapiro later remarked on its "primitivist, Stonehenge qualities" (*Craft Horizons*, February 1973). Rejection of the model's mat and connecting bonds had freed the big, bound, disembodied "legs" to wander randomly toward each other, lost, like the Giacometti figures or Beckett characters they suggest, in a vacant space. Because this sculpture was made by a dying woman, allusions have often been made to the "bandaged" and tragic quality of the seven units in their shiny swaddling. However, the artist's intention held no morbidity. Hesse loved surprises and felt this piece could be the ultimate in absurdity. The sense of isolation it imparts is a grander version of the pathos found in much of her earlier work, which it resembles more closely than the later sculpture. There is no evidence whatsoever that Pollock's (eight, not seven) *Blue Poles* is the source of these awkward creatures, which are far more Chaucerian than Jungian in their ponderous predicament (compounded, it should be said, by the problem of their support, which was never fully resolved). There is a fatalistic calm about them, and a humble look of waiting, without anticipation.

Before she left for the hospital for the last time on March 21, to have a third operation on March 30, Hesse asked Barrette to destroy three old works—the untitled spoke piece (fig. 64), *Long Life* (fig. 65), and *Total Zero* (fig. 76). The last gouache drawing she made abandoned the rectangular format of the others in that series and floated over the whole page, flowing up and slowly disintegrating toward the edges like smoke (fig. 225). Hesse died on May 29, 1970, alert and uncompromising until the last weeks.

Unfortunately, by the time the Guggenheim Museum's exhibition of Hesse's work opened in December 1972, she had beome a stereotype, or myth, the art world's answer to Sylvia Plath and Diane Arbus. That she did *not* commit suicide and had, on the contrary, an immensely strong will to live and to work, was ignored. The tragic facts of her life, which she herself admittedly had emphasized, came to submerge her work. The damage was reinforced by the substitution in *Artforum* (November 1972), at the time of the Guggenheim show, of Hesse's pathetic last diaries for a serious critical examination of the work; Robert Pincus-Witten's essay in the Guggenheim catalogue also contained inaccuracies about the work and overemphasized the life, ending in a flourish: "The voice no longer speaks to us, but beyond us. In her last year Eva Hesse discovered the sublime, another place and time at which the critic only guesses and which the historian maps only these superficial paths. She had left her Post-Minimalist colleagues and friends, and joined Newman, Still, Pollock, and Reinhardt." (She would have found the company irresistible, but not the context.)

24. Untitled, 1968–69, gouache, 30 x 22″, Mr. and Mrs. Norman S. Carr, Akron.

While a few voices were raised in protest or serious criticism against further exploitation of a major artist, they were drowned out by articles like Joyce Purnick's in the *New York Post* (December 13, 1972), subtitled "Tortured and Talented," which called the artist by her first name throughout, and misquoted, out of context, misled friends who had been under the illusion that background was being given for a sensible text on the art. The *National Review* (May 11, 1973) commented that the work was nihilist and "that this poor young woman was, like [the insane], exteriorizing her own internal chaos." The popular magazines consistently sounded this note, with Douglas Davis' sexist "Cockroach or Queen" piece in *Newsweek* (January 15, 1973) which called the sculpture "dainty" and "safe," ending patronizingly: "What is tragic about her early death is not the loss of a great artist. It is the loss of an intensely human person, cut off before finding—and completing herself." After all this soap opera, one had to agree with Kasha Linville Gula that "the American public finds it necessary to turn its great women artists into tragic figures and then to forget about their work—as if their deaths, with the emphasis on suicide, somehow explain their artistic output. . . . By implication, any woman who carries her art to heights that subordinate her personal life is bound to die tragically, probably by her own hand. It's a punishing sort of recognition, carrying with it the suggestion that without super-suffering the art couldn't have happened; that no woman artist can be truly great in a public sense unless she has so mucked up her personal life that she can't possibly be getting any satisfaction out of it" (*Ms. Magazine,* April 1973). One can't conceive of Gorky, whose life and death were still more catastrophic, being called "Arshile" in a newspaper article.

Nevertheless, the exhibition itself, installed by curator Linda Shearer, who also wrote a sensitive text in the catalogue, had a real impact, even in the anti-art atmosphere of Frank Lloyd Wright's dissected spaces, from which only *Sans II* and *Contingent* suffered visibly. The most recent generation of New York artists had never even seen Hesse's work, though her influence, direct and indirect, was widely acknowledged, and she had become a role model for many women artists. Hesse's art has survived these circumstances, which produced on the one hand a familiarity with certain ideas in the work which, when first seen, had been unfamiliar; and on the other hand a level of expectation hard to meet. Reactions to the exhibition were almost universally favorable. Hesse would have been elated by these, and by some of the adjectives used to describe her work: "significant," "important," "authoritative," "exceptional," even "great."

225. Untitled, 1969–70, gouache, 30¾ x 22½", Fourcade, Droll, Inc., New York.

SOME CRITICAL ISSUES

I

It is a curious characteristic of many of Hesse's works that once you have been touched by them you are caught between emotions. That they can be simultaneously experienced as humorous, impressive, whimsical, pathetic, calm, frantic, grand, or sad is a measure in some contradictory manner of the seriousness that lies at the core of her art. She compared her love of absurdity to *Waiting for Godot,* "where the main thing is waiting. Those people are there and they are doing nothing and yet they go on living. They go on waiting and pushing and they keep saying it and doing nothing. And it really is a key to understanding me. Only a few understand that my humor comes from there, my whole approach."[30]

The element Hesse called humorous might better be called human. Her sculptures are "funny" only in their unexpectedness. Absurdity takes the place of wit; the jokes have no punch line. There are a lot of loose ends. "She started in chaos and ended in paradox" (Gioia Timpanelli). In the same sense, the element called eroticism calls attention to the fearful attraction of contact, behind which lurks a dark survival humor, approaching what the Surrealists called "black humor"; and what Robert Smithson saw when he said that Hesse's humor coexisted with "a rather funereal quality—petrifaction, emptiness, paralysis." One of the Surrealists' primary vehicles was the iconography of the *personnage*—the composite figure-like, yet often abstract, form that has frequently emerged from a collage esthetic, from "the reconciliation of two distant realities" to create a new reality.[31] In an art concerned with delving into human consciousness or "unconsciously" tapping submerged elements within the artist, this form also reappears as a symbol for the self, or for the central esthetic focus. The image of the human figure in Hesse's art is a primitive or dreamlike incarnation, wholly disguised as abstraction in her sculpture, but responsible, by its very subversive existence, for still another level of the tension she wove so skillfully.

226. Untitled, 1960, charcoal and ink, 6 x 9″, Fourcade, Droll, Inc., New York.

It would, of course, be a mistake to see Hesse as consciously anthropomorphizing her work. She took great pains to erase such references. The plaintive aspect, or distant resemblances to a gawky child-like human figure in the early drawings or in pieces like *Laocoon, Sans I, Sans III, Vinculum I*, or her last piece, emerges from a profound identification between the artist and her materials, her forms. In this regard, I once used the term "body ego," which I understood to mean a strong, virtually visceral identification between the maker's and/or viewer's body and abstract or figurative form. I could also have used Gaston Bachelard's term "muscular consciousness."[32] Hesse's existential humor and her eroticism meet and merge not so much in the shapes themselves (which in the earlier pieces overtly resembled breasts, limp phalluses, etc.) but in the combination of shape and highly sensuous textures, the way forms swell or sag, lie or lean, the ways in which one can feel one's own body assuming those positions or relating to those shapes as to another body. The attraction between polarities is potentially erotic as well as potentially humorous. All readings of both elements are, however, highly personal. Take, for example, the following conversation between three people about Hesse's early work:

A: *Ishtar* was an extension of the breast into the penis—that dangling thing.

B: Or those dangling things could be the visualization of sucking, drawing out, desire for the mother. The threads look like umbilical cords, not penises, to me. Somebody said her cords were like "spilt milk."

C: But the bean-shaped things are phallic.

B: Or womb-like.

A: I'm talking about an undifferentiated sexuality . . . always two things in combination. Those buckets—buckled, punched in, they had a certain kind of stress factor, tension.

C: I thought of its organicness, coming out of an organic matrix inside her, a more psychological interpretation. I told her joking that she was sitting there making tumors—the organic growth principle, the external manifestation of internal manifestations.

A: Dessication of the organic. One can't exclude a psychoanalytical approach. Decisions are made through one's body needs. All perception is tainted with a psychoanalytical reading. If somebody's having Oedipal troubles it's going to come out in the perception. . . . It was as though she was trying to tie up these forces.

C: High-tension integration.

A: A subconscious bondage she seemed to exist in.

C: Women artists' fantasies. Acquiring a penis when you come into your own. A mystical penis.

B: Horrors.

A: You should go into the psychology of bondage. Having control, dominance of the object. It's so intensely in her work it could be an aspect of sublimation.[33]

C: The vulnerable side, the clinging side was totally counteracted by the more aggressive side. A lot of people looking at Eva's work don't realize how intellectual she was. They think of her as sensate, manipulative, tactile. . . . Those things are not just binding but placing in nets, imprisoning.

B: Holding something, bringing it *into* you, pulling it close. . . .

A: Tension between looseness and tightness. There's a need for liberation plus need for constraint ritualistically carried out. . . . There's an almost sadistic side.

C: Also a cradling, suspending in nets, building up forms like swaddled children. . . .

B: Making objects to be surrogate mothers? Soft, with cords, swaddled for protection.

Hesse admitted that "repetition feels obsessive," but it was so natural to her that she did not explore its ramifications. Repetition equals humor, much in the way that children can extract endless delight from the repetition of a phrase or joke. The continuing strain of the childlike (not childishness, although there was an element of immaturity) in Hesse's personality may have been responsible for some of the power of her art. Freud wrote that the artist sublimates less successfully than others, being more of a child, less willing to sacrifice those pleasures, and spoke of the connection between manual work and repressive sublimation, work as a "source of libidinal satisfaction when selected by free choice."[34] Norman O. Brown extended this in his theory that art activity is generated by want, by need, an "infantile sexuality," fundamentally auto-erotic.[35] In Hesse's case, she might be seen as thrown back into herself because the first object of her love—her mother —had "rejected her" by dying.

Whereas most expressionist artists with a nostalgia for the organic in either texture or image are ideologically unwilling to accept an ordered framework, or are unable to deal with its rigorous discipline, Hesse intuited early that this approach would allay her inclinations toward a private fetishism. Until 1965, her obsessive inner-directedness had lacked a method of commensurate intensity. The impact of the raw gesture, which had worked for de Kooning, the ambiguous atmosphere in which Gorky's formal tragedies took place, and the sheer momentum of Pollock's traceries, did not work for a painstaking and compulsive person. When she found her method—the then much-abused notion of a "system"—she saw it for something as simple as it was. More interested in adding than subtracting (see her titles), and in "the concrete and the abstract"[36] than illusion, she abandoned painting for sculpture, and "expressionism" for Minimal systems. These provided a mere context in which she could distract the modules from their expected norm. Often the fact that the units are at first glance identical or similar is the only "order" in a piece, its boundaries being infinitely alterable, as in *Repetition Nineteen*. Hesse introduced "humor" to an often deadpan and didactic art in the way her geometry was subject to curious alterations; the strangely flawed images seem to strive for a suggested perfection which they are destined not to meet. Asked if she was "satirizing Minimalism," she replied that she was only "punning her own vision, if anything."

II

The relationship between painting and sculpture became a major issue in the mid-1960's, when a great many painters turned to three-dimensional work. Sculpture was suddenly more "real" in its literalness and physicality, while painting and its illusionism were whispered to be dead. Hilton Kramer deplored this tendency in his review of "Eccentric Abstraction," where he compared Hesse to Pollock:

"Forms that were once part of the imagery of painting have now been set physically free to occupy real space—and lots of it. What was formerly part of the metaphorical and expressive fabric of painting is now offered as a literal *thing*. A kind of technological positivism triumphs, but at the expense, I think, of a genuine imaginative probity. Of course, much of the history of recent painting and sculpture is the history of such positivistic reduction. In this respect 'Eccentric Abstraction' only conforms to a general tendency to substitute the literal for the metaphorical, and to compensate with inflated physical scale for the diminution of imaginative energy. Here, as elsewhere, the prose of literal minds effectively displaces the old

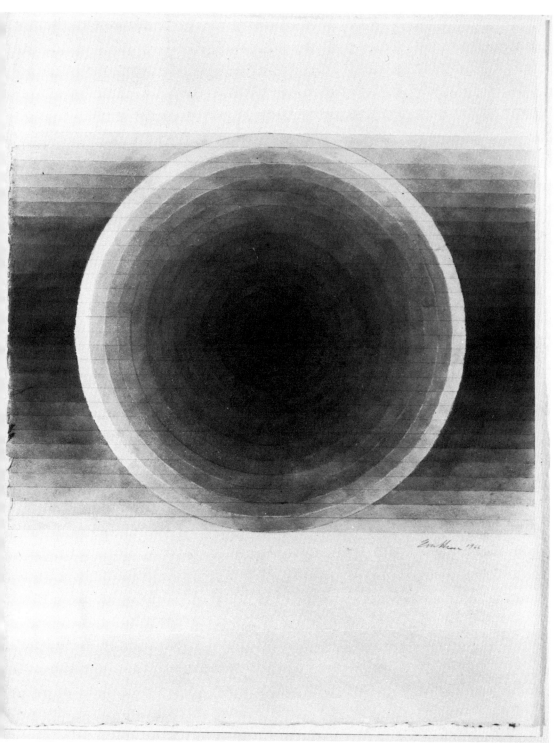

27. Untitled, 1966, ink wash, 12 x 9½", Marilyn Fischbach, New York.

poetry'' (*New York Times,* September 25, 1966). The next year I replied to Kramer that new materials had in fact liberated forms previously ''used up'' in painting. ''Three-dimensional objects can, I believe, return to the vocabulary of previous painting and sculpture, and by changing the syntax and the accents, more fully explore avenues exhausted in two dimensions or conventional materials and scale without risk of being unoriginal or reactionary'' (*Sculpture of the Sixties,* Los Angeles County Museum, 1967).

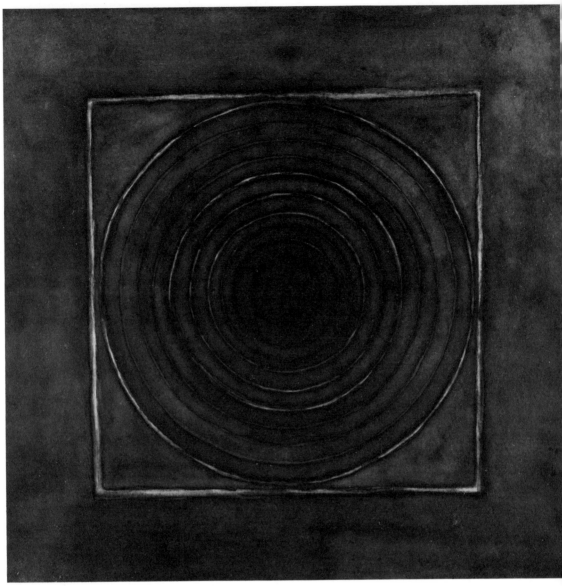

228. Untitled, 1967–68, ink wash, 9 x 9³/₁₀″, Fourcade, Droll, Inc., New York.

Soon afterward, the pictorial, or rather the linear aspect of sculpture took a turn toward the conceptual and the disintegrative, and it was no longer an issue whether pictorial effects in real space were essentially "dishonest" or "untrue" to the internal necessities of something called sculpture. (The "problem" has a way of defusing potential "solutions.") Although Hesse remained without doubt a sculptor, she had instinctively understood from the beginning how the cliché "drawing in space" could be reinvigorated with real linear materials—string, cord, wire, rope—instead of the unrealistically precarious "lines" of heavy materials used by the sculptors following David Smith. Since single and repeated forms and line, rather than composed interrelationships, had always been Hesse's strong point, she was able to bring them into sculpture in a unique way. From "letting her hair down" in *Ennead* to the last rubber rope "knot piece," she used line as a connector, a binder, its important function that of linking one "impossible space" with another.

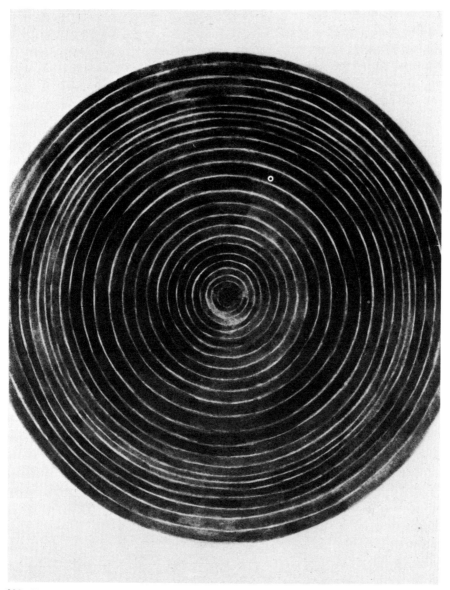

229. Untitled, 1967, ink wash, 12 x 9″, Fourcade, Droll, Inc., New York.

Kim Levin described her works as "unraveling" to become the "antithesis of Minimalism" (*Art News,* February 1973). It is the vitality of that line that caused Hesse's art to be compared often to primitive art; and it is the space that line defined that caused the "suggestion of homelessness—of forms that have abandoned the security of pictorial space, yet do not remain securely fixed in the 'real' space defined by sculptural objects." (Hilton Kramer, *New York Times,* December 17, 1972).[37]

The pictorial aspect of Hesse's art is not restricted to the fact that it can be related to Pollock or that some of it has been flat or rectangular, or hung on the wall, or even to her painterly surfaces which, as Amy Goldin noted, were related to a sculptural softness emphasizing the density of the plane (*Art News,* May 1969). Most of Hesse's work has the freedom of a very strong image, the kind that is easier to conceive in two dimensions. Her use of a single unit repeated is also a pictorial device which, used the way the "modular Minimalists" used it, could reduce three-dimensional facts to a planar or optical experience. Hesse, however, by making each of her modules unique, made them less a flat field and more sculptural. At the same time a large number of her works depend on the wall or the floor as the counterpart of a gridded or rectangular two-dimensional armature. (*Contingent*, although also made of quasi-rectangular panels, escapes from its armature and "hangs free.") Nevertheless, after first leaning on their given supports, they tend to depart into the unexpected. (*Ennead*, apparently hanging properly from wall to floor, suddenly picks up its skirts and reaches out to a perpendicular side wall; *Addendum*, still neater and better behaved, reaches the floor only to coil in luxuriously rubbery confusion, while *Hang-Up* loops an outrageous eight or ten feet into the viewer's space.) Smithson called Hesse's art "vertiginous," which would also describe the earlier drawings, in which gigantic scale changes and directional leaps over a fluctuating void were common occurrences. "Even as an Abstract Expressionist," she told Nemser, "I would do fantastically huge forms next to very small things. It would almost take on a kind or order within an order."

In a period when cleanliness and straight edges were close to the godliness of success, Hesse still associated concreteness with touch. She would mold the forms she sought by a personal tactile confrontation and by the accidents that happen in that realm, although these were allowed to operate only within a specified area, like the units of *Sequel, Schema, Repetition,* and *Accretion,* which are vulnerable to interruption but not, finally, to drastic change. And in a period when theory was so often called to the aid of the visual, she trusted her non-verbal instincts. "At times I've thought 'the more thought the greater the art,' " she said in 1970. "But I do have to admit there is a lot that I'll just as well let happen. . . . If I really believe in me, trust me to let some things happen without any calculated plan, let it come. . . ." She wanted to make art that could surprise, and she was canny enough to know that if it looks beautiful at first glance, a second glance may not be necessary. While Hesse's work may now look more "beautiful" (though equally powerful), at first sight it had a decided grotesquerie. The "ugly" turning "beautiful" in the public eye through a process of familiarity is a cliché of modern art appreciation which boils down to the unexpected (and therefore temporarily unacceptable) becoming acceptable. Once Baudelaire's *nouveau frisson* is gone, one is left with a work of art that sometimes turns out to be neither ugly nor beautiful, but merely pretty or pleasant. Hesse declared that for her "decorative is the only art sin. I can't stand gushy movies, pretty pictures and pretty sculptures, decorations on the wall." Getting away from the pretty had been a preoccupation of hers since she left art school. The eroticism, the humor, the new materials, were all means to that end.

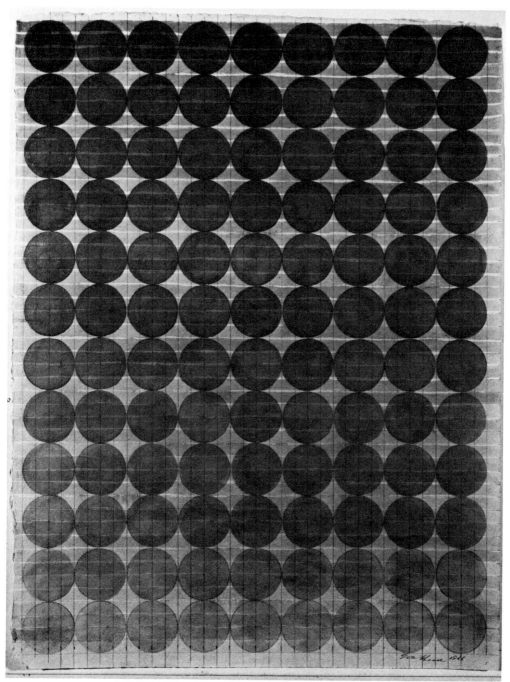

230. Untitled, 1966, ink wash, pencil 12 x 9½″, Marilyn Fischbach, New York.

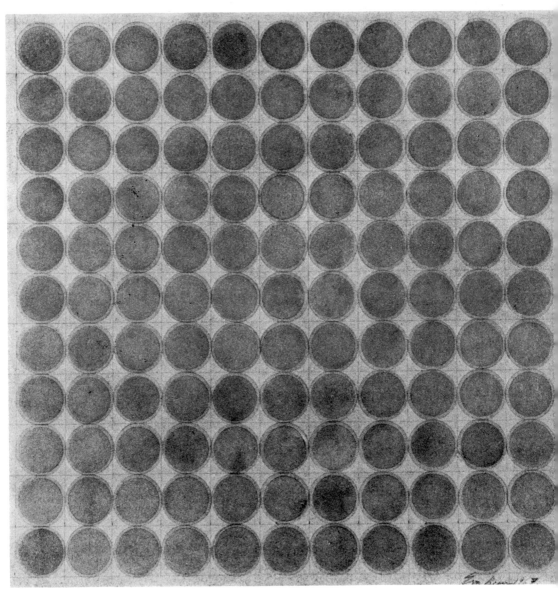

231. Untitled, 1967, ink wash, pencil, 11 x 11″, Fourcade, Droll, Inc., New York.

232. Untitled, 1966, ink wash, pencil, 9¾ x 7¾″, Walter Bareiss, New York.

III

I was charged by one friend of Hesse's to extricate her in this book from the "mere role of synthesizer—the traditional female role," as he put it. The fact remains that Hesse was a pivotal figure and a synthesizer, as have been most great loners.[38] She took exactly what she needed from the art around her, transformed it, and gave it back to the art world. The art around her tended to be pushed "forward" by avant-garde necessity, and, being a woman of her time, Hesse was not free of that necessity. But she was free to take contradictory elements and simply use them as vehicles for her own content ahead of her own time, rather than to continue or even initiate a specific "new trend." "I don't know if you can be completely out of the tradition, but I don't think I'm conservative," she told Nemser. "I know art history. I know what I believe in. I know where I come from or relate to or the work that I have looked at and am convinced by, but I feel so strongly that the only art is the art of the artist personally and found out as much as possible for himself and by himself. I don't mind being miles from everybody else. I think the best artists are those who have stood alone and who can be separated from what movements that have been made about them."

It is always tempting to settle upon specific "influences" among artists when similar images and techniques surface within a particular time and place span. But the more one experiences how "influence" really operates, the less one can depend on such superficial indices. To disentangle the network of relationships between any group of artists at any one time into a clear and pointed text inevitably leads to false conclusions. Most influences derive less from conscious imitation of or even unconscious absorption of exhibitions and reproductions seen or studios visited, than from "ideas in the air" which, at any single point in the history of contemporary art, are spawning parallel developments. Artists highly concerned with what other artists are doing (characteristic of the New York art world, for better or worse), are all subject to those possibilities which have been raised by their peers and have become general knowledge, possibilities which form an overall field within which everyone, no matter how dissimilar his or her style, is working. Thus "objective" accounts and presumptions about above-ground events and connections are in fact only fragmentary glimpses of an extraordinarily complex underground network, and are dependent as well upon conversations, friendships, rumors, rapports, quarrels, and interactions taking place in bars, studios, and beds, which can never be accurate or complete.

All her friends agree that Hesse was an intelligent artist with a highly developed critical sense, the very sense which for years kept her from full accomplishment. Since the content of her work is hers alone, it is only on the formal level that one can profitably compare it with that of other artists. When she returned from Germany in fall 1965, Hesse found in the art world a new climate of reduction, clarity, and intellectuality. Her immediate focus on monochrome, on gray and black, was a response to this climate, a means to make the work harder and clearer, as well as a result of her friendship with LeWitt, who stated categorically that black and white were the only "possible" choices for his own structures.[39]

In the literature on Hesse there has been an overemphasis upon the role of Jasper Johns in her decision for monochrome, which probably came from closer to home. Her own palette in 1960–61—previously her most personal and successful period of art-making—had been somber and monochromatic, based on the same grays, browns, and blacks of her mature work. Nevertheless, Johns' influence was pervasive by 1965. It was also a major factor in the development of the art of LeWitt, Bochner, Morris, and Frank Stella, among others. His numbers and letters —abstract "figures" enveloped in a sensuous wash—still find echoes in the work of innumerable younger artists. They are reflected in Hesse's dark washed circle drawings and sculpmetal washer reliefs. She may also have been generally affected by Johns' use of what Leo Steinberg called a "good modern picture plane that lets forms project out in space (always crossing the line between art and life!) . . . What you need is a solid protrusion that you can hang anything on—like a knob and an empty coat hanger; or a pair of hooks in the surface,"[40] an insight Hesse might have applied to *Hang-Up*. At the same time, Johns tends to be singled out because his works are so well-known. Again closer to home was Lee Bontecou, whose work had similar effects (see note 11).

Oldenburg also appealed to artists outside his pop and/or "realist" domain. "I absolutely respect Oldenburg, his writing, his person, his energy, his art, the whole thing, I do," Hesse said. "But I don't think I've studied it or taken or used those materials in any way. And I think he has humor. I never thought of it just as materials. He has his own thing, his intelligence, his statement, his depth. He interestingly enough is one of the few people in realism that I really like, if you are going to call that realism, which I don't. To me it is wholly abstract too, but you can recognize it." She had met Oldenburg through Irving Petlin as early as 1959, although she never knew him well. Unquestionably his art affected her—perhaps more viscerally than esthetically. Yet again closer to home, in regard to the use of soft materials for obsessively repeated and sexually suggestive forms, was Yayoi Kusama, also a friend of Hesse's.[41]

She liked Andy Warhol's work ("He is the most artist that you could be") and was drawn to Lucas Samaras' combination of eccentricity, eroticism, and humor; when others compared her work to his in 1966–67, she was pleased. She mentioned in her notebooks a show at the Whitney in 1967 which included: "1 beautiful Samaras (2 inferior ones) . . . a box covered with pins. Cover slightly ajar with bird's head forcing its way out from under cover. Old cords and ropes dropping out from front. The piece sits in a plexiglass case." It is not difficult to see why Hesse would like the contrasts between the box's jewel-like beauty and "old cords and ropes," between the implied warm flesh of the bird and cold sharp pins, the imprisonment motif overlaid with an obsessive pattern. Yet there is little formal resemblance in her own work, and Hesse's eroticism seems directly opposed to Samaras'; where his work is usually focused *in* upon himself, Hesse worked *out* from a body identification into a physical identification with the sculpture itself, as though creating a counterpart of herself and the absurdity of her life was a way to survive it.

233. Max Ernst, The Chinese Nightingale, 1920, pasted photographs and halftones, 4¾ x 3⅜″, formerly collection of Tristan Tzara, Paris.

235. Jackson Pollock, Free Form, 1946, oil on canvas, 19¼ x 14″, The Sidney and Harriet Janis Collection, Gift to the Museum of Modern Art, New York.

234. Arshile Gorky, Good Hope Road, II, 1945, oil on canvas, 25½ x 32⅝″, The Sidney and Harriet Janis Collection, Gift To The Museum of Modern Art, New York.

236. Willem de Kooning, Detour, 1958, oil on paper mounted on canvas, 59 x 42½″, Fourcade, Droll, Inc., New York.

If there are artists who concentrate on "singleness" and artists who concentrate on multiplicity, Hesse, with Oldenburg, Johns, and Samaras, must be put in the second category. Johns said in 1964 that he preferred work "that appears to come out of a changing focus—not just one relationship or even a number of them, but constantly changing and shifting relationships to things."[42] Alan Solomon wrote that Johns' work was a major point of departure for a new generation of artists because "before anything else [it has] to do with the avoidance of specific meanings, with the necessity for keeping the associational and even the physical meaning of the image ambiguous and unfixed."[43] Many of the artists Hesse was closest to, however, tried to outlaw ambiguity and double meanings in favor of a "single gestalt" or the unique identity of the object itself. Hesse's art balanced subjectivity with that longing for objectivity which exists most potently as a stretching of inner self-indulgence toward the outside; her work shows the strain of pursuing the unattainable "objective," without which it would have far less energy.

237. Jasper Johns, Scott Fagan Record, 1969, ink on plastic film, 12¼ x 12¼″, David Whitney, New York.

239. Claes Oldenburg, Giant Blue Men's Pants, 1962, canvas filled with shredded foam rubber, painted with liquitex and latex, 60 x 28 x 6¼″, private collection, Cambridge, Mass.

238. Andy Warhol, Coca Cola Bottles, 1962, oil on canvas, 82 x 105″, Harry N. Abrams Family, New York.

240. Yayoi Kusama, Chair, 1962 (on macaroni carpet, 1963), stuffed canvas, fringe over chair, Mr. and Mrs. Hart Perry, New York.

In that heyday of "rigor" and "structure," Hesse seemed "very radical or very eccentric," Bochner recalls. "She was never afraid of that. She wasn't afraid of being old-fashioned or of the work being about certain other issues, which right now looks very courageous, to be able to go up against public opinion like that." She kept her eyes and her ears open. She was willing to learn, which may have appeared to be lack of self confidence." Her isolation as a woman artist produced a certain internalization, and there were times when her artist friends' attitudes toward her seemed rather patronizing. She was a "beginner," and often, by choice, a "little girl." They admired her as much for working against the fashion as for the work she was actually making. Bochner, for instance, feels that until *Aught* and *Augment* in late 1968 she was making "discrete accumulations." LeWitt, Vollmer, and Bochner all told her that *Repetition Nineteen* didn't work when she insisted on denting and manipulating the forms, although later they acknowledged that it was an important piece. The preoccupations of her friends with aspects of art that were

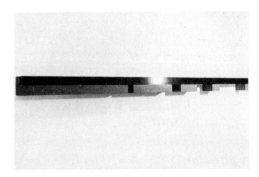

241. Carl Andre, installation of exhibition at Dwan Gallery, Los Angeles, March, 1967, concrete bricks.

243. Donald Judd, Untitled, 1965, painted aluminum, 8¼ x 161 x 8¼", Mickey Ruskin, New York.

242. Robert Ryman, Standard (detail; one panel of twelve), 1966–67, oil on steel, 48 x 48", Panza di Biumo, Varese, Italy.

244. Sol LeWitt, Open Modular Cube, 1966, painted aluminum 60 x 60 x 60", The Art Gallery of Ontario, Toronto, Canada.

foreign to her occasionally intensified her insecurity: "Sometimes I feel there is something wrong with me. I don't have that kind of precise mind or I just don't feel that way. I feel very very strongly in the way that I feel, but I don't stand on a kind of system. Maybe mine is another kind of system. . . . [My works are] much closer to soul or introspection, to inner feelings. They are not for architecture or sun, water or for the trees, and they have nothing to do with color or nature or making a nice sculpture garden. They are indoor things."

Hesse had something different in common with each of her friends; her art relationships tended to be as complex as her personal ones. Certainly ideas flowed in both directions. With Robert Ryman, she shared an intense involvement with "what went on in the studio" in a time when much was made of "post-studio art," and a genuine connection with the art of the 1950's. With Frank Viner, she shared an affinity for the bizarre combined with a respect for more geometrically rigorous work (they were both products, at different times, of the Yale art school). Certainly

245. Tom Doyle, Ripstaver, 1965, cast iron, steel, aluminum, 36 x 24 x 30″, F. Arnhard Scheidt, Kettwig, Germany.

247. Keith Sonnier, Untitled, 1968 (shown at Castelli Warehouse), latex, flocking, string, 12′ x 3′, Leo Castelli Gallery, New York.

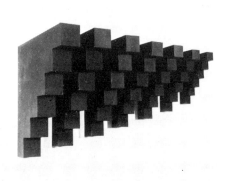

246. Robert Smithson, Alogon I, 1966, painted stainless steel, 35½ x 73½ x 35½″, The Whitney Museum of American Art (Gift of the Howard and Jean Lipman Foundation), New York.

248. Frank Lincoln Viner, Knox-Pattern #1, 1964, cloth and painted cloth, 114″ high, collection of the artist, New York.

her interest in serial arrangement was prompted by Sol LeWitt and by Donald Judd, although Hesse's attraction to the *absurdity* of repetition was personal. Bochner feels that the main thing Hesse got from LeWitt was "the same thing I got, which was a sense of ordered purposefulness. You did your work as clearly as you could; what you didn't know, you made apparent you didn't know. That's a lot more important than maybe it sounds." LeWitt's influence was particularly beneficial because of his openness to other kinds of ideas; it was never a stultifying element. With Carl Andre, it is not so easy to specify, although Hesse felt "very emotionally connected with his work. It does something to my insides." She thought of him as "really not a Minimalist . . . really more romantic," as she did Smithson, with whom she shared an unashamed belief in content, in the complicated "dialectic" of death, humor, sex; this sensibility was also familiar to Nancy Holt, not then an artist, but an acute participant in the art scene. With Keith Sonnier's work, Hesse shared a sensitivity to the ephemeral, to the emotive; they worked in similar forms

249. Richard Serra, Untitled, 1968, cast rubber, 144 x 192 x 6″, Mr. and Mrs. Joseph Helman, New York.

251. Robert Morris, Untitled, 1967–68, felt, 12″ thick, 264 pieces, National Gallery of Canada, Ottawa.

250. Bruce Nauman, Untitled, 1965–66, latex with cloth backing, 96 x 50 x 3½″, Panza di Biumo, Varese, Italy.

252. Lucas Samaras, Untitled Box Number 3, 1963, wood, pins, rope, stuffed bird, 24½ x 11½ x 10¼″, The Whitney Museum of American Art (Gift of the Howard and Jean Lipman Foundation), New York.

for a period around 1967–69. Sonnier has said that his use of cloth and membrane-like latex had to do with "himself as an adolescent" as well as with art (*Artforum*, October 1969) and he was among the few not to resist the subjective implications of his abstraction. Hesse knew Bruce Nauman and Robert Morris less well; the Dada inconsistencies in both their *oeuvres* eventually disenchanted her, though Nauman's "Eccentric Abstraction" work had certainly impressed her. The fundamental impersonality of Morris' art is the antithesis of Hesse's personalism, despite occasional formal resemblances between their work and her awe of Morris as an intellect. With Richard Serra, Hesse shared a respect for danger which in the 1950's had implied a determined mindlessness in the heat of creation but by 1968 had become an "act" not of the artist, but of the sculpture, almost independent of its creator. Serra has used gravity and weight as pure aggressive physicality, but not without an urge, similar to Hesse's, toward dramatic internal self-expression.

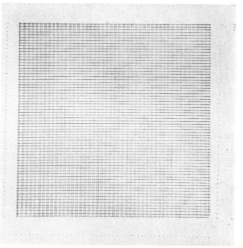

253. Lee Bontecou, Untitled, 1962, welded steel with canvas, 65 x 111 x 20″, Mr. and Mrs. Seymour Schweber, Great Neck, N. Y.

255. Agnes Martin, Untitled, pencil, ink, 9¼ x 9¼″, Robert Elkon Gallery, New York.

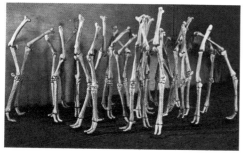

254. Nancy Graves, Variability of Similar Forms, 1970, steel, wax, marbledust, acrylic, 7 x 18 x 15′, private collection, New York.

256. Ruth Vollmer, Trigonal Volume, 1966, cast bronze, 9 x 9 x 12½″, formerly collection of Eva Hesse.

While he veered in the former direction she held a more poignant balance between the two. Agnes Martin's work has been mentioned in regard to Hesse's, and there are common elements in the way they approached structural elements like the grid. (Ruth Vollmer owns a Martin drawing, and Hesse admired it.) Mel Bochner correctly denies that Hesse "got anything" from him formally, but there is no question that for the two years they were close, his own admiration for Johns and his intellectual orientation affected her, due in part to her inordinate respect for the written word and those who dealt with it (from 1966–69, Bochner was known more as a writer than an artist): "This media of expression has always thrilled me," she wrote naively in her notebooks. "Because I think that if you write you must be intelligent! Then I thought one must know oneself to be able to write and that always thrilled me most of all—the idea of honesty is so challenging—much more so in words than pictures. It can be understood more clearly, be defined and comprehended.'' When Bochner gave her a portrait of herself made up of a spiral of words, she bought a huge thesaurus from which she subsequently chose her titles. She also bought some math books—a great fad at that time—though there were of course artists who dealt with the subject seriously, among them the sculptor Ruth Vollmer. As an artist and as a sensitive and loving older woman bearing her mother's name, also German by birth, also with some tragedy in her life, Vollmer was important to Hesse in a unique way. Toward the end of her life Hesse also saw a great deal of Nancy Graves, whom she admired particularly for a driving devotion to her work and an intellectual rigor imposed upon sensuous materials.

257. Mel Bochner, Portrait of Eva Hesse, 1966, pen and ink, 7½ x 7½", collection of the artist, New York.

IV

Early in 1965, Hesse wrote to Ethelyn Honig: "I wonder if we are unique, I mean the minority we exemplify. The female struggle, not in generalities, but our specific struggles. To me insurmountable to achieve an ultimate expression, requires the complete dedication seemingly only man can attain. A singleness of purpose no obstructions allowed seems a man's prerogative. His domain. A woman is side-tracked by all her feminine roles from menstrual periods to cleaning house to remaining pretty and 'young' and having babies. If she refuses to stop there she yet must cope with them. She's at disadvantage from the beginning. . . . She also lacks conviction that she has the 'right' to achievement. She also lacks the belief that her achievements are worthy. Therefore she has not the steadfastness necessary to carry ideas to the full developments. There are handfuls that succeeded, but less when one separates the women from the women that assumed the masculine role. A fantastic strength is necessary and courage. I dwell on this all the time. My determination and will is strong but I am lacking so in self esteem that I never seem to overcome. Also competing all the time with a man with self confidence in his work and who is successful also.

"I feel you have similar problems which is also evident in your work. Are we worthy of this struggle and will we surmount the obstacles. We are more than dilettantes so we can't even have their satisfactions of accomplishment. The making of a 'pretty dress' successful party pretty picture does not satisfy us. We want to achieve something meaningful and to feel our involvements make of us valuable thinking persons.

"Read 'The Second Sex.'

"I am finishing book now.

"I've always suffered with these thoughts but now I've temporarily found a spokesman. But naturally I don't feel a native ability that she or others has that have succeeded."

Hesse died just before the Women's Movement gained a broad impact on the art world and she considered herself one of the unique ones, almost a freak, since there were so few women artists at all visible at that time. She was very aware, however, of the injustices she herself had suffered and she expressed often to both male and female friends her conviction that she was not being taken as seriously as her male colleagues because she was a woman.[44] For the most part she kept her complaints private as did most women then, given the additional struggle implicit in making a public issue of them. In January 1969 she wrote across the bottom of a letter from a feminist: "The way to beat discrimination in art is by art. Excellence has no sex." Which is all very true, but there is a lot more to the question than that. Today it seems very clear that if a woman's experience in this society is entirely different from that of a man—biologically, socially, politically—and if "art is an essence, a center," as Hesse put it, coming from the inside of a person, then it would seem equally obvious that there are elements in women's art that are different from men's, not elements of quality but elements with esthetic results. One reason there is so much resistance to this idea is that men are still considered superior, therefore quality is unconsciously read into such a statement.

When Nemser asked her if she thought in terms of female and male forms, Hesse of course was adamant: "I don't see that at all. I'm not saying female/male when I work at it and even though I recognize that is going to be said, I cancel that." When asked if she felt there was any special feminine quality in her work, she replied in the most stereotyped terms: "If sensitivity means female, yes, it's female. I think my work is very strong and yet sensitive so there you have both so-called masculine and feminine." Within a more recent context she might have been able to feel that the strength too was feminine, and to see the work, and herself, as a female entity. At the time, however, her respect for and insistence on a personal content made superficial specificity seem irrelevant. The fact remains that Hesse, like many more women than men, used circles and a central focus (especially in her early work), distorted geometry, layers, veiled and hidden forms. While her hemispheres are usually non-assertive, her vessels usually empty, their very tangibility encourages a sensuous response; their evocativeness encourages a personal and associative response. Certainly she did not see her recurrent circle motif as anything but another "tight" or "regular" form, like the square or the rectangle, from which she was hoping to escape into forms as yet unknown—forms of her own making: "I think the circle was very abstract," she said in 1970, after she had stopped using it. "I could make up stories about what the circle means to man but I don't know if it was that conscious. I think it was a form, a vehicle. I don't think I had sexual, geometric. . . . It wasn't a circle representing life and eternity." She used perfection and imperfection to reconcile opposites, a gesture also "traditionally female." "I remember taking this perfect form and then putting a hole in the center and dropping out a very very flexible surgical hose, the most flexible rubber I could get, and I would make it very very long and then I would squiggle and wiggle. That was the extreme you could get from that perfect perfect circle."

Untitled, 1969, pencil, gouache, 20¼ x 14″, Fourcade, Droll, Inc., New York.

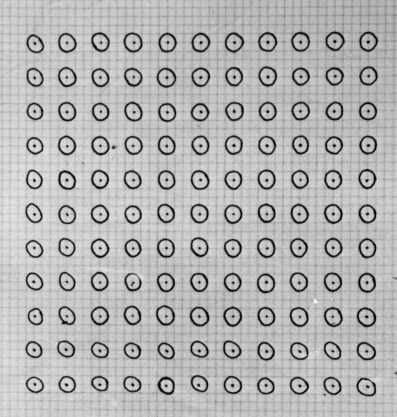

259. Untitled, 1967, ink on yellow graph paper, 8¼ x 10¾″, Fourcade, Droll, Inc., New York.

V

The most salient features of Hesse's art can be related to her fascination with repetition: "It's not just an esthetic choice," she said. "If something is absurd it's much more greatly exaggerated if it's repeated. Repetition does enlarge or increase or exaggerate an idea or purpose. I guess repetition feels obsessive." The wrapping and binding and layering process is also repetitive and makes the viewer relive the intensity of the making in a manner far from the abstract or didactic way in which process is used by most men. Women are always derogatorily associated with crafts, and have been conditioned towards such chores as tying, sewing, knotting, wrapping, binding, knitting, and so on. Hesse's art transcends the cliché of "detail as women's work" while at the same time incorporating these notions of ritual as antidote to isolation and despair. There is that ritual which allows scope to fantasy, compulsive use of the body accompanied by a freeing of the mind. The mythical Penelope is always being mentioned pejoratively in regard to art by women. Yet hers was a positive, not a negative action,despite its impermanence.[45] The act itself can be known, safe, but the result can be highly unexpected. Repetition can be a guard against vulnerability; a bullet-proof vest of closely knit activity can be woven against fate. Ritual and repetition are also ways of containing anger, and of fragmenting fearsome wholes.

Hesse used the grid as both a prison and a safeguard against letting an obsessive process or excessive sensitivity run away with her. Women frequently use rectilinear frameworks to contain organic shapes or mysterious rites of autobiographical content. An integral part of Hesse's work is that certain pleasure in proving oneself against perfection, or subverting the order that runs the outside world by action in one's inside world, in despoiling neat edges and angles with "home-made" or natural procedures that relate back to one's own body, one's own personal experience. Thus outwardly rational work can be saturated with a poetic and condensatory intensity that eventually amounts to the utmost in irrationality.[46] Repetition, and repetition of moveable units in particular, leads to fragmentation, the disintegration of one order in favor of a new one. At the end of her life Hesse was beginning to feel free and strong enough to follow repetition into that area.

Perhaps the most drastic way she allowed chance to prevail was in her use of latex. No other artist has invested so much time and major work in a medium known to be impermanent. At this writing at least three pieces have disintegrated. "I'm not sure where I stand on that," she said in 1970. "At this point I feel a little guilty about when people want to buy it. I think they know but I want to write them a letter and say it is not going to last. I'm conflicted. Because part of me feels that it is superfluous, that if I need rubber to use—that is more important. Life doesn't last, art doesn't last, it doesn't matter. But maybe that is a copout." It was a copout in a way—that surrender to the final absurdity. But it is also a rather touching and courageous statement reflecting Hesse's attitude about her imminent death. Her sense of time had always been a private one and certainly it had been stretched by the past year's experiences. What is surprising is that she did not separate her sculpture from her life with more clarity, did not seem at that point to think of her work as her memorial, did not attach her great drive and ambition to its permanent place in the world after she had left it. It is as though she had finally made her art for herself as a part of her life, that she had no picture of it after she was gone, that it made no difference whether or not it remained intact forever, if she herself could not survive to enjoy its triumphs; as though this were an acknowledgment of the ultimate tie between art and life.

60. Untitled, 1969, pencil, gouache, 21½ x 17″, Mr. and Mrs. Ernst Englander, New York.

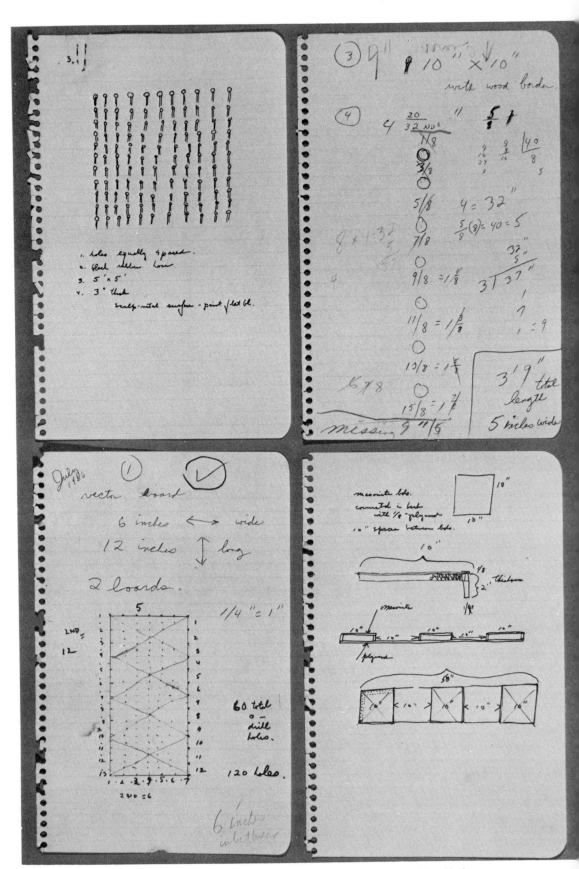

261. Four notebook pages, 1966, pencil, pen and ink, 7½ x 5″, Fourcade, Droll, Inc., New York.
The Museum of Modern Art, New York, Gift of Mr. & Mrs. Murray Charash.

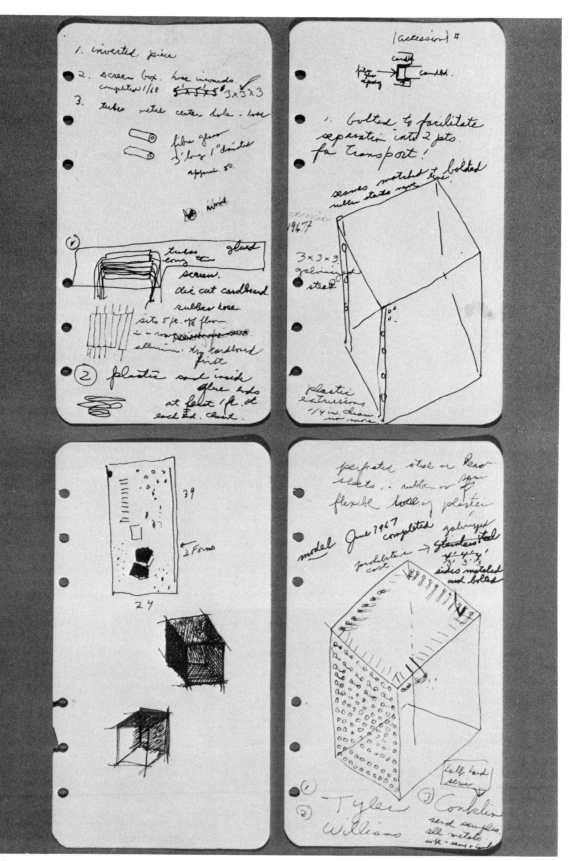

262. Four notebook pages, 1966, pencil, pen and ink, 7½ x 5", Fourcade, Droll, Inc., New York.
The Museum of Modern Art, New York, Gift of Mr. & Mrs. Murray Charash.

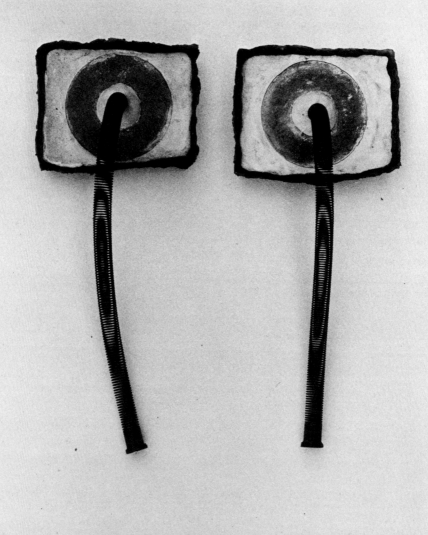

263. Untitled, 1967, foam rubber, pâpier-mâché, metal springs, 2 units, each 3x4x1″, springs 9½″.

NOTES TO THE TEXT

1. This and all other Hesse quotations cited either "from 1970" or "said to Cindy Nemser," as well as a few which are unspecified, come from the transcript of Nemser's interview with Hesse which was taped in three sessions early in 1970. Two sections were published in *Artforum* (May 1970) and *The Feminist Art Journal* (Winter 1973); the complete interview will appear in Nemser's book, *Art Talk: Conversations with Women Artists*, to be published by Scribners. Since I worked from the very rough transcript rather than from the published versions in most cases, there will be slight variations between the wording in my quotations and Nemser's. All other direct quotations are from Hesse's letters or from her diaries and notebooks, to which her family was kind enough to give me complete access.

2. Robert Smithson, in conversation with the author, June 5, 1973. Direct quotations in the text from friends and acquaintances of Hesse's have come from the (usually taped) conversations I had with them in preparation for this book in spring and fall 1973; or from letters written to me or to Hesse by the speakers. All quotations have been approved for publication by the speaker. Published sources are listed in parentheses in the text itself.

3. Victor Moscoso, painter, was probably Hesse's closest friend from Cooper Union and Yale.

4. These may have been notes from Albers' class, since he was the founder of a famous Bauhaus preliminary course involving what he called the "structure, fracture and texture" of materials.

5. This note is written across a dance program (c. 1967) and it is not entirely clear whether it refers to a "girl" being an object or a sculptor.

6. Hesse met Rosalind Goldman in the mid-1950's through Helene Papanek, and though their lives were very different, they remained close friends until Hesse's death. While in Germany she wrote: "I can trust Rosie and Sol, my real friends, and the only ones who really know and trust me. Mutual respect. They would *never* let me down."

7. Mark di Suvero was not involved in the festival, but was one of the most influential figures in this group, with which both Doyle and Hesse showed in May 1964 at the original gallery downtown on Park Place.

8. There was a good deal of talk in New York in the early 1960's about Fernand Léger's work as an alternative to expressionism; this may have been an indirect source for the machine images. Ethelyn Honig remembers Léger's coming up often in studio discussions with Doyle and Hesse, and Hesse mentioned seeing his work in Europe.

9. All fourteen of the relief-constructions made and shown at the Düsseldorf Kunsthalle in August 1965 were titled. Some of the same titles had been used previously for drawings in a group show at the same museum at Christmas, though they were not studies for those sculptures. The only two drawing titles *not* applied to sculptures were "See and Saw" and "Try to Fly"; presumably the former, like the latter (fig. 36), was sold.
   The Düsseldorf one-woman show brochure appears to list the works chronologically, but since the dimensions are similar and all the works were listed as *materialbilder* (mixed media), it is still difficult to tell which was which. Where the pieces themselves were unmarked or unavailable for perusal, the titles used here have been determined by Tom Doyle and me. Only two were not definitively titled—*Oomamaboomba* and *Tomorrow's Apples*, although there seems to be no associative rationale for the latter and it seems stylistically later than its place in the catalogue listing. To further confuse matters, this piece arrived from Germany with the title "Five in One," which Doyle does not remember as Hesse's title and does not appear in the catalogue or her own listings; it was shown under that title, however, at the Guggenheim exhibition.
   In addition, a postcard sent to the Honigs by Hesse three days before the Düsseldorf show opened says it consists of "twelve objects or reliefs or constructions," six drawings and sixteen small sketches, while the catalogue lists fourteen objects (the fourteen transparencies then taken still exist), twenty drawings and sixteen sketches. All the work is dated 1965.

10. None of the German reliefs were brought back to New York when they returned from Germany, but Hesse had 3"-square color transparencies of all of them.

215

11. Bontecou was also in Documenta in 1964, and her work was the only woman   represented by the Leo Castelli Gallery in the early 1960's; these facts alone would have impressed Hesse, but Bontecou's focus on gray and black, on rough "natural looking" materials, and, above all, her highly abstract yet sexual imagery, can surely be related to Hesse's own decisions.

12. The title "Not Yet" was not used for this piece, and in another notebook it is attached to the drawing for a different piece—a square with either holes or dots in a grid which may later have become *Stratum*. The nine-bag piece originally titled "Not Yet" consisted at one point of only seven plastic units hung separately on the wall with two shorter nets holding black balls (glass fishing floats); it was photographed by Dan Graham at this time and labeled "unfinished", leading to the mistaken adoption of this word as the title.

13. Hesse told Nemser she thought *Ennead* was done "in '65 when I first came back from Europe," but the notebook seems to be more concrete and contemporary evidence.

14. This was a small relief made in response to a plea to New York artists for work to place on the Los Angeles Peace Tower as part of a "Collage of Indignation" against the Vietnam War in 1965; one of the organizers was Hesse's old friend Irving Petlin. The piece was eventually removed from the tower, stored for several years, and raffled off for $25 in a benefit for the Valley Peace Center.

15. Hesse was also very impressed, as was I, with Gene Swenson's exhibition and book-length catalogue entitled *The Other Tradition*, held at the Institute of Contemporary Art in Philadelphia early in 1966. In it Swenson treated the kind of contradiction that Hesse dealt with. She was not in the show, probably because he did not know about her work when he organized it.

16. Also in the building at 29 West 57th Street at the time of "Eccentric Abstraction" were two similar group exhibitions which provided provocative comparative material: "Distillations" at Tibor de Nagy, organized by Eugene Goossen (Johansen, Castoro, Barry, Syverson, and Milkowski); and "Ten" at the Dwan Gallery, organized with the help of Ad Reinhardt (Morris, Judd, LeWitt, Smithson, Martin, Andre, Baer, Steiner, Flavin, and Reinhardt). The latter set in unmistakable terms the tenets of Minimalism at its best.

17. Bochner and LeWitt showed Hesse how to make a "working drawing," but difficulties with scaling led her to make the one for *Addendum* full scale.

18. This piece may be the one once called "Composition for Sylvia"; Sylvia Mangold had gone to Cooper Union and Yale right after Hesse.

19. *Repetition Nineteen II*—the one projected to have cords—was first called *Repetition Nineteen I*, according to one drawing; on another drawing it was inscribed as the "2nd of 3 versions," and on another, the "rubber (silicone) version" is listed as the "3rd of 3 versions," indicating that Hesse still intended to make it when the first two were complete.

20. This was suggested by Vollmer and Shearer in the Guggenheim catalogue.

21. The next to last line was to read: "In its simplistic stand, it achieves its own identity," but the line was omitted in the final version.

22. Artists included in the exhibition were: Anselmo, Bollinger, Hesse, Kaltenbach, Nauman, Saret, Serra, Sonnier, and Zorio; Rafael Ferrer contributed an uninvited piece by filling the stairwell with dead leaves. Morris' article reproduced the work of Pollock, Oldenburg, Bollinger, Paul, Saret, Serra, and two of his own felt pieces. The title was a word he had used in another context earlier in the 1960's and it was chosen by the magazine. If Morris was not consciously founding a "move-ment" in his own image, the implications were unavoidable; headlines about the warehouse show were: "In the Wake of Robert Morris," and "Under the Aegis of Robert Morris." By organizing the show but not participating in it, he put himself, probably unintentionally, in the position of a patriarchal figure introducing "younger artists," although many of them had actually been working in malleable materials and chance form for some time, as had others not included in the show. (The "Soft Sculpture" show I organized in 1968, in fact, introduced "anti-form" to Cedar Rapids, Iowa, among other places, before it was premiered in New York; included, along with Oldenburg, Kusama, and Bourgeois, were Hesse, Sonnier, Serra, Paul, Kaltenbach, Viner, Winsor, Nauman, Morris, etc.) The four artists omitted from the *Artforum* article were those who had in fact worked in this manner for the longest time—Barry Le Va, Josef Beuys, Nauman, and Hesse, not to mention several younger Europeans.

23. Though the Minimal esthetic of "order" was in fact "anti-order" as well; Don Judd, for example, was opposed to a rational or Cartesian "composed" order in favor of the "disorder" or lack of order involved in matter-of-fact repetition and progressions.

24. Clement Greenberg and his followers into what came to be called "formalism"; Anti-form might better have been called anti-formalism.

25. "My particles are sort of cuts across the mass spectrum in what I call a *clastic* way (plastic is flowing of form and clastic means broken or preexisting parts which can be put together or taken apart without joining or cementing). . . . My problem has been to find a set of particles, a set of units and then to combine them according to laws which are particular to each particle, rather than a law which is applied to the whole set like glue or riveting or welding. . . . My arrangements are essentially the simplest that I can arrive at, given a material and a place" (Carl Andre to Phyllis Tuchman, *Artforum*, June 1970).

26. This was suggested by Mel Bochner to Robert Pincus-Witten and included in the latter's Guggenheim catalogue essay.
27. Others in the Whitney show were Andre, Asher, Bollinger, Duff, Lobe, Morris, Nauman, Reich, Rohm, Ryman, Serra, Shapiro, Snow, Sonnier, and Tuttle. See bibliography for reviews.
28. According to Dr. Schapiro, Hesse had a primary tumor which exerted great pressure on the brain but affected neither her intelligence nor her personality until the terminal illness. Between operations, until the symptoms reappeared each time, she was completely "normal."
29. As stated in Pincus-Witten's Guggenheim catalogue text.
30. During this interview, it was Nemser who brought up Beckett, but Hesse had often previously identified with him in conversations with friends—myself and Smithson included.
31. Had Hesse thought about this consciously, she might also have connected it to her admiration for Gorky and Pollock, who, like the pre-abstract Rothko, Still, and Newman, had used the *personnage* as a central image in their early work; this goes back, of course, to Ernst, Miró, and de Chirico.
32. Gaston Bachelard, *The Poetics of Space,* Beacon Press, Boston, 1969, p. 11. In the Whitney catalogue Jim Monte described Hesse's work in terms of "human characteristics such as the softness of skin, the swell of a muscle or the indeterminate color of flesh fading under clothing after exposure to a summer sun." In the Pincus-Witten essay in the Guggenheim catalogue, a quotation from my article on erotic art (*Hudson Review,* Spring 1967, p. 95) is misattributed to Hesse because she copied a long passage into her notebooks; it referred to Oldenburg: ". . . as eroticism, his work is abstract. The stimuli arise from pure sensation rather than direct association with the objects depicted."
33. The relationship of binding and wrapping forms and a compulsive personality does not seem to have been specifically explored in psychological literature, but it does show up peculiarly often in art by women. One wonders whether Hesse's cord-bound shapes had their origins in an *activity* or in a projected *image* of the finished work. Another artist who works in a somewhat obsessive manner has suggested that there is a "frantic" aspect to his own actions, with erotic behavioral implications. There is also the possibility that such activity is connected to the judeo-puritan work ethic in which Hesse was raised; "if it isn't difficult, it isn't worth doing."
34. Quoted in Norman O. Brown, *Life Against Death,* Vintage Books, New York, 1959, p. 139.
35. *Ibid.* Carl Andre has spoken about his art in terms of desire: "I have some strong desires. . . . I want what is not yet in the world" (Lucy R. Lippard, *Six Years,* Praeger, New York, 1973, p. 157).
36. "The concrete and the abstract" was a criterion she used herself; at first Gorky and de Kooning best fulfilled this goal for her, and then in 1962 "in a more limited way, Dubuffet, Giacometti, Oliveira . . . Joan Brown."
37. The term "homelessness" refers back to Clement Greenberg's notion of certain Abstract Expressionist painting as "homeless representation," applicable to Hesse's work at times, in the sense of its precariousness.
38. Matisse, for example, "synthesized" Cubism and Fauvism (or Expressionism); Gorky and Pollock "synthesized" Surrealism and abstraction; Brancusi "synthesized" Cubism and Rumanian folk art, etc.
39. In "Paragraphs on Conceptual Art" (*Artforum,* Summer 1967) LeWitt wrote: "In conceptual art the idea or concept is the most important aspect of the work. . . . The idea becomes a machine that makes the art. . . . Conceptual art is not necessarily logical. . . . The ideas need not be complex. Most ideas that are successful are ludicrously simple . . . ideas are discovered by intuition." His ideas and Hesse's thus diverge and also cross.
40. Leo Steinberg, *Jasper Johns,* Wittenborn, New York, 1963, p. 27.
41. Earlier, Kusama had painted tiny white circles all over white canvases the size of the walls of the Brata Gallery; at the Green Gallery her phallic extrusions of stuffed canvas bristling from the surfaces of chairs, couches, ladders, and so forth constituted some of the most memorable art shown in New York in the early 1960's.
42. Jasper Johns, (*Art News,* February 1964), p. 43.
43. Alan R. Solomon, *Jasper Johns,* Whitechapel Gallery, London, 1964, p. 8.
44. I can attest to this myself, as I don't think I ever took her as seriously as she deserved either, due to my own conditioning in this area. She complained to me, LeWitt, Droll, Honig, Wapner, Graves, and Smithson, among others.
45. Hanne Darboven, whose work can be compared on certain levels of obsession with Hesse's, said in reply to a critic's query as to whether she would turn out to be "pioneer or Penelope": "I *prefer* Penelope. What an accomplishment!" (*Artforum,* October 1973.) Looking at this type of work from a different point of view, it can be seen as avoidance behavior, a means of controlling the energy of strong emotional content instead of dealing with it at gut level, and producing thereby an effect of something "having been done" instead of "being."
46. This sentence is taken almost verbatum from an article written by John Chandler and myself, "The Dematerialization of Art" (*Art International,* February 1968) in regard to the work of Darboven, Hesse, and Andre.

CHRONOLOGY: THE ARTIST'S LIFE

1936 Eva Hesse born January 11, Israelite Hospital, Hamburg, Germany, a Capricorn, with Scorpio rising; father: Wilhelm Hesse; mother: Ruth Marcus Hesse.

1939 Flees Germany after Nazi pogrom; to Amsterdam on a children's train with sister Helen; taken by parents to London and New York, where they settle at 630 West 170th Street.

1945 Receives U.S. citizenship; parents divorced, father remarries.

1946 January: mother commits suicide; attends P.S. 173, then Humboldt Junior High (P.S. 115) and wins honor awards.

1952 June: graduates from the School of Industrial Arts.
September: enters Pratt Institute of Design for advertising design course.

1953 December: leaves Pratt, gets a job at *Seventeen Magazine*, takes classes at the Art Students League.

1954 June: Helen Hesse marries Murray Charash.
Summer: begins to see Dr. Helene Papanek; works at Camp Lebanon, Whitehouse Station, N.J.; meets Rosie Goldman.
September: receives $100 for article published in *Seventeen;* enrolls at Cooper Union, lives on East 6th Street; meets Camille Reubin, Victor Moscoso, Ellen Leelike.

1955–57 At Cooper Union. Studies under Marsicano, Welliver, Barnet, Gwathmey, Candell; lives at Judson Student House; meets Ellis Haizlip.
Summer 1955: Camp Lebanon.

1956 Receives scholarship from Educational Foundation for Jewish Girls.
Summer: works for Educational Alliance Playschool and in a boutique on West 4th Street; father has heart attack.

1957 Graduates from Cooper Union; receives Yale-Norfolk scholarship for summer.
Fall: enters Yale School of Art and Architecture; rooms with Ellen Leelike and Kitty Don; studies with Albers, LeBrun, Chait; begins to see Dr. Samuel Dunkell.

1959 Receives scholarship; sells painting to Leif Sjöberg, visiting professor from Columbia; takes drawings to Museum of Modern Art, New York, where she receives encouragement and $2.00 cab fare; graduates from Yale with B.F.A.
Summer: counselor at Camp Laurel Wood, North Madison, Conn.; applies to UCLA graduate school and is rejected; moves to New York (82 Jane Street); meets Claes and Patty Oldenburg through mutual friend Irving Petlin.

1960 Rents studio space from Phyllis Yampolsky on Ninth Avenue; meets Peter Forakis, David Weinrib, Sol LeWitt.
November: has gynecological operation; begins to sell her work.

1961 February: moves to 238 Park Avenue South, sharing loft with Eila Kokkinen.
April: in watercolor exhibition at the Brooklyn Museum and in "Drawings: Three Young Americans" at the John Heller Gallery; meets Tom Doyle; spends summer with him in Woodstock and meets Grace Bakst Wapner there.
November 21: marries Tom Doyle; moves to Fifth Avenue and 15th Street.

1962 Summer spent in Woodstock where she makes her first sculpture, for the Ergo Suits Travelling Carnival.

1963 March: first one-woman exhibition of drawings at Allan Stone Gallery; Doyles move to the Bowery between Broome and Grand Streets; meets Robert Ryman, Lucy Lippard, Frank Viner, Robert and Sylvia Mangold.

1964 June: Doyles leave for a year in Kettwig-am-Ruhr, Germany, under the patronage of F. Arnhard Scheidt; travels to Switzerland (July), Mallorca (August) alone to see Ethelyn Honig, Paris (September) to meet Doyle and go to Rome, Florence, Zurich, returning to Kettwig October 4.
October: to Düsseldorf for Robert Morris exhibition, Essen for Gorky exhibition, and Amsterdam for Dubuffet exhibition.
December: to Berlin, East Germany; three drawings in Christmas exhibition at Kunsthalle in Düsseldorf; reads Simone de Beauvoir's *The Second Sex;* begins first three-dimensional construction.

1965 January: father contracts pneumonia.
February: private showing of Doyle's and Hesse's work at Scheidt's; makes last paintings.
Spring: meets Meret Oppenheim in Switzerland.
May: informal exhibition of Doyle's and Hesse's work outdoors at Scheidts' home.
August: One-artist shows for Doyle and Hesse at Düsseldorf Kunsthalle; Werner Nekes makes undistributed film of show;
travel to London and Ireland.
September: returns to New York; begins to make freestanding monochrome sculpture.

1966 Separation from Doyle; marriage ends. Meets Robert Smithson, Nancy Holt, Mel Bochner, Ruth Vollmer, Dan Graham, Ann Wilson, Gene Swenson, Michael Todd.
May: *Hang-Up, Ishtar, Long Life* in "Abstract Inflationism and Stuffed Expressionism" show at the Graham Gallery with Viner, Linder, Morrell and Orenstein.
Summer: to Easthampton to visit Don and Franca Vlack. August: father dies in Switzerland.
October: *Metronomic Irregularity II, Several, Ingeminate* in "Eccentric Abstraction" at Fischbach Gallery with Viner, Nauman, Potts, Bourgeois, Adams, Kuehn, and Sonnier;
Teaches children in Riverdale. Meets Carl Andre and Rosemarie Castoro.

1967 February: on "Erotic Symbolist" panel at the School of Visual Arts with Hasen, Bourgeois, Thek, Wines and Decker.
March: Eva Hesse, the artist's stepmother, enters hospital for successful surgery on brain tumor. Joins Fischbach Gallery.
Summer: to Maine to visit Droll, Leaf, Lippard; to Southhold, L.I. to visit Vollmer; works with Dorothy James.
Fall: discovers latex; *Addendum* in Finch College Museum "Art in Series" show.

1968 January 4–15: to Mexico City with Vollmer; 17–18 visiting artist at Oberlin College. Dorothy Beskind makes film *Eva Hesse* in studio (winter 1967–68).
First piece fabricated: *Accession II* at Arco Metals; visits Aegis Reinforced Plastics on Staten Island and makes plans for fiberglass fabrication; meets Douglas Johns there.
March: exchanges studio visits with Richard Serra and Keith Sonnier.

Summer: begins fabrication of *Repetition Nineteen* at Aegis.

September: begins teaching at the School of Visual Arts.

October: *Seam* in "Antiform" show at John Gibson Gallery; *Sans II* completed at Aegis. Robert Morris visits her studio to select work for "Warehouse show"; Doug Johns devotes himself to Hesse's work.

November 16: one-woman show opens at Fischbach Gallery; first symptoms of illness appear; meets Gioia Timpanelli.

December: *Aught* and *Augment* in "Nine at Leo Castelli" warehouse show; *Sans II* shown in Whitney Annual and a section sold to Whitney Museum; spends Christmas with the Wapners in Woodstock.

1969: January 26: lecture at Boston Museum School.

February: begins to work with Martha Schieve as assistant.

March: *Aught, Augment, Vinculum II* in "When Attitudes Become Form," Bern.

April 6: collapses; April 18: first operation for brain tumor at New York Hospital.

May: recuperates at the Charash home in Fair Lawn, N.J.; attends opening of "Anti-Illusion" show at the Whitney Museum in a wheelchair.

Summer: in Woodstock with Wapners and Gioia Timpanelli; begins "Woodstock series" of drawings. August 18: second operation for brain tumor.

Fall: begins to work with Bill Barrette and Jon Singer as assistants on *Contingent,* which is shown at the Finch College Museum's "Art in Process IV" in December; radiation and chemotherapy treatments; *Repetition Nineteen III* sold to Museum of Modern Art.

Christmas and New Year's spent in hospital.

1970: Interview with Cindy Nemser; begins working on last two pieces.

March 21: reenters hospital; March 30: third operation for brain tumor.

May: last piece shown at Owens-Corning Fiberglass Center; she cannot attend. Nemser interview published in *Artforum* with *Contingent* on the cover.

May 29: dies at New York Hospital.

National Endowment grant announced posthumously.

1. RINGAROUND AROSIE   fig. 46
   1965
   pencil, acetone, varnish, enamel, ink, glued cloth-covered
   electrical wire on papier-mâché and masonite
   26⅜ x 16½"
   Fourcade, Droll, Inc., New York

2. TWO HANDLED ORANGEKEYED UTENSIL   fig. 48
   1965
   paint, papier-mâché and varnish on masonite
   16½ x 26⅜"
   Collection Mr. and Mrs. F. Arnhard Scheidt, Kettwig, Germany

3. AN EAR IN A POND   fig. 49
   1965
   paint, cord, and papier-mâché on masonite
   26⅜ x 17¾"
   Fourcade, Droll, Inc., New York

4. LEGS OF A WALKING BALL   fig. 51
   1965
   paint, cord, papier-mâché, and metal on masonite
   17¾ x 26⅜"
   Fourcade, Droll, Inc., New York

5. OOMAMABOOMBA   fig. 52
   1965
   paint, cord, cord-wrapped metal, and plaster on masonite
   21¼ x 25⅝"
   Fourcade, Droll, Inc., New York

6. TOMORROW'S APPLES (5 IN WHITE)   fig. 53
   1965
   painted concretion, enamel, gouache, varnish, cord-wrapped wire,
   and papier-mâché on masonite
   25⅝ x 21⅝"
   Fourcade, Droll, Inc., New York

7. 2 IN 1   fig. 54
   1965
   cord, glue, paint, and wooden ball on masonite
   21¼ x 27⅛"
   Collection Mr. and Mrs. F. Arnhard Scheidt, Kettwig, Germany

8. H + H   fig. 55
   1965
   enamel, gouache, alcohol-varnish, and ink on masonite
   21¼ x 27⅛"
   Collection Mr. and Mrs. F. Arnhard Scheidt, Kettwig, Germany

9. COOL ZONE   fig. 56
1965
aluminum and painted cloth-bound cord on masonite
15 x 15", cord 45"
Fourcade, Droll, Inc., New York

10. PINK   fig. 57
1965
painted cord, papier-mâché, and button on masonite
21⅝ x 25⅝"
Collection Mr. and Mrs. F. Arnhard Scheidt, Kettwig, Germany

11. C-CLAMP BLUES   fig. 58
1965
painted concretion, metal wire, bolt, and painted plastic
ball on masonite
25⅝ x 21⅝"
Collection Mr. and Mrs. F. Arnhard Scheidt, Kettwig, Germany

12. UP THE DOWN ROAD   fig. 59
1965
aluminum paint on styrofoam and cloth-bound cord on masonite
27¼ x 21¼"
Collection Mr. and Mrs. F. Arnhard Scheidt, Kettwig, Germany

13. EIGHTER FROM DECATUR   fig. 60
1965
paint, cord, and metal on masonite
27⅛ x 21¼"
Fourcade, Droll, Inc., New York

14. TOP SPOT   fig. 61
1965
flexible metal cord, electrical cord, metal hardware, paint,
plastic ball, and porcelain socket on masonite
27⅛ x 21¼"
Collection Mr. and Mrs. F. Arnhard Scheidt, Kettwig, Germany

15. UNTITLED   fig. 64
1965
painted wood and iron
c. 10'6" high
Destroyed in 1970 at the request of the artist

16. UNTITLED   fig. 66
1965
acrylic paint on wood
45 x 22 x 2½"
Fourcade, Droll, Inc., New York

17. LONG LIFE   fig. 65
1965
cord, papier-mâché, epoxy and enamel over beach ball and hose
20" diameter, hose 7'
Destroyed in 1970 at the request of the artist

18. INGEMINATE   fig. 67
    1965
    papier-mâché, surgical hose, cord, and sprayed enamel over balloons
    22″ long, 4½″ diameter, hose 12′
    Fourcade, Droll, Inc., New York

19. SEVERAL   fig. 68
    1965
    painted papier-mâché over rubber hose
    7′ x 11″ x 7′
    Fourcade, Droll, Inc., New York

20. UNTITLED   fig. 69
    1965
    enamel painted cord over wood or metal and hose
    32″ diameter, hose 12′4″
    Fourcade, Droll, Inc., New York

21. ISHTAR   fig. 70
    1965
    wood, plastic, cord and rubber
    36 x 7½ x 2½″
    Collection Mr. and Mrs. Ronald B. Lynn and family, Teaneck, New Jersey

22. HANG UP   fig. 71
    1966
    acrylic on cloth, wood and steel
    72 x 84 x 78″
    Collection Mr. and Mrs. Victor W. Ganz, New York

23. TOTAL ZERO   fig. 76
    1966
    rubber, plastic epoxy, acrylic, polyurethane, papier-mâché
    over inner tube and metal
    2′3″ x 2′3″ x 3′
    Destroyed in 1970 at the request of the artist

24. UNTITLED   fig. 83
    1966
    acrylic paint, cord over papier-mâché and masonite
    9 x 9 x 2″
    Collection Mel Bochner, New York

25. LAOCOON   fig. 75
    1966
    acrylic paint, cloth-covered cord, wire, papier-mâché over plastic plumbers'
    pipe
    10′ x 24″ x 24″
    Allen Memorial Art Museum, Oberlin College, Ohio
    This is the second version of Laocoon. The first version
    is beneath it. See fig. 74.

26. VERTIGINOUS DETOUR   fig. 78
    1966
    enamel, rope, net and plaster
    net 23″ long, ball 40″ circumference
    Collection Mr. and Mrs. Victor W. Ganz, New York

27. UNTITLED   fig. 77
    1966
    painted rope, net, papier-mâché, weights.
    42½ x 11½ x 6″
    Ex-collection John Coplans, New York
    Collection The Mayor Gallery, Ltd., London

28. UNFINISHED, UNTITLED or NOT YET   fig. 79
    1966
    painted rope, net and plaster with weights
    72 x 24 x 14″
    Collection Mr. and Mrs. Victor W. Ganz, New York

29. COMPART   fig. 81
    1966
    acrylic paint, cord over papier-mâché and masonite
    48 x 9 x 12″, 4 panels, each 9–12 x 1–2½″
    Collection Mr. and Mrs. Henry Y. S. Tang, New York

30. UNTITLED   fig. 82
    1966
    acrylic paint, cord and papier-mâché over masonite
    33 x 10–12 x ½–2¼″
    Fourcade, Droll, Inc., New York

31. ENNEAD   fig. 80
    1966
    dyed string and painted papier-mâché
    36 x 22 x 1½″
    Collection Mr. and Mrs. Victor W. Ganz, New York

32. UNTITLED   fig. 84
    1966
    acrylic paint, cord over papier-mâché on wood
    7½ x 7½ x 4″
    Private collection, New York

33. UNTITLED   fig. 85
    1966
    enamel paint, cord over papier-mâché and balloon, string
    31 x 26″, string 77″
    Collection Ruth Vollmer, New York

34. UNTITLED   fig. 86
    1966
    enamel paint, cord over papier-mâché and balloon
    46½ x 11½ x 2½″
    Private collection, New York

35. UNTITLED   fig. 87
1966
enamel paint, cord over papier-mâché and balloon
Collection Mr. and Mrs. Thomas Lenk, Stuttgart, Germany

36. UNTITLED
1966
papier-mâché over balloon
23 x 20″
Ex-collection Robert Ryman, New York
Fourcade, Droll, Inc., New York
Unfinished. See text p. 66.

37. METRONOMIC IRREGULARITY I   fig. 107
1966
painted wood, sculpmetal, and cotton-covered wire
12 x 18 x 1″
Collection the Estate of Robert Smithson

38. METRONOMIC IRREGULARITY II   fig. 108
1966
painted wood, sculpmetal and cotton-covered wire
3 panels, each 48 x 48″; installed 4 x 20′
Fourcade, Droll, Inc., New York
This piece was made for the "Eccentric Abstraction" exhibition and was
dismantled after it; the elements are in original condition.

39. METRONOMIC IRREGULARITY III   fig. 109
1966
painted wood, sculpmetal and cotton-covered wire
10 x 50 x 2¼″
Collection Mr. and Mrs. Victor W. Ganz, New York

40. ITERATE   fig. 118
1966
woodshavings, glue on board, string and acrylic
20 x 20″
Collection Robert Pincus-Witten, New York

41. STUDY FOR SCULPTURE   fig. 119
1967
sculpmetal, cord, Elmer's glue, Liquitex paint, varnish on masonite
10 x 10 x 1″
Fourcade, Droll, Inc., New York

42. UNTITLED   fig. 115
1966
woodshavings, glue, rubber tubing
9 x 9 x 1″, cord 7½″
Private collection, New York

43. ONE MORE THAN ONE   fig. 116
1967
acrylic, papier-mâché, plastic cord, wood
15½ x 8½ x 5½″
Collection Stephen Antonakos and Naomi Spector, New York

44. DITTO   fig. 114
     1967
     sculpmetal on plexiglass and wire cords
     15 x 14½", height with cords 70"
     Collection Mr. and Mrs. John Lloyd Taylor, Milwaukee

45. UNTITLED   fig. 124
     1967
     sculpmetal over steel washers on wood
     36 x 36 x 1"
     Fourcade, Droll, Inc., New York

46. UNTITLED (COMPOSITION FOR SYLVIA?)   fig. 117
     1967
     woodshavings, glue on board, acrylic and rubber tubing
     12 x 10"
     Collection Robert and Sylvia Mangold, Calicoon Center, New York

47. CONSTANT   fig. 120
     1967
     woodshavings, glue on board, acrylic and rubber tubing
     60 x 60 x 5¾"
     Collection Mr. and Mrs. Victor W. Ganz, New York

48. COMPASS   fig. 121
     1967
     sculpmetal over steel washers and wood
     10 x 10 x 1¼"
     Collection Marilyn Fischbach, New York

49. RANGE   fig. 122
     1967
     aluminum grommets, sculpmetal on cardboard
     12 x 12 x ¼"
     Collection Marilyn Fischbach, New York

50. CINCTURE   fig. 123
     1967
     sculpmetal over steel washers and wood
     10 x 10 x 2"
     Collection Marilyn Fischbach, New York

51. WASHER TABLE   fig. 126
     1967
     rubber washers on wood
     49½ x 49½ x 8½"
     Private collection, New York

52. UNTITLED   fig. 127
     1967
     sculpmetal over steel washers on wood
     8 x 8"
     Collection Dr. Helene Papanek, New York

53. UNTITLED   fig. 263
    1967
    foam rubber, papier-mâché, and metal springs
    two units, each 3 x 4 x 1″, spring 9½″ high
    Collection Robert J. Berenson, New York

54. FOR JOSEPH   fig. 135
    1967
    painted plaster over paperboard box, and hair in plastic
    3½ x 2½ x 4″
    Collection Mr. and Mrs. Norman Goldman, New York

55. INSIDE I   fig. 134
    1967
    paint, wood, papier-mâché, wire and acrylic
    12 x 12 x 12″
    Fourcade, Droll, Inc., New York

56. INSIDE II   fig. 134
    1967
    paint, wood, papier-mâché, cord, weights, acrylic
    5 x 7 x 7″
    Fourcade, Droll, Inc., New York

57. ACCESSION I   fig. 145
    1967
    aluminum and rubber tubing
    14½ x 14½ x 9⅛″, each rubber tube 5″
    Ex-collection Ethelyn and Lester Honig, New York
    Fourcade, Droll, Inc., New York
    Model for Nos. 70, 71.

58. MAGNET BOARDS   fig. 130
    1967
    sculpmetal on wood and magnets
    24 x 24 x 2″, 4 units, each 12 x 12 x 2″
    Collection Mr. and Mrs. Henry Feiwel, New York

59. ADDENDUM   fig. 129
    1967
    painted papier-mâché, wood and rubber tubing
    5 x 119 x 6″, total height with cords, 84″
    Collection Mr. and Mrs. Victor W. Ganz, New York

60. REPETITION NINETEEN I   fig. 152
    1967
    aluminum screening, papier-mâché, Elmer's glue, polyester resin,
    Dutch Boy Diamond Gloss Paint
    19 units, each approximately 10 x 8″, irregular
    Study Collection, The Museum of Modern Art, New York.
    Gift of Mr. and Mrs. Murray Charash

61. Test units for REPETITION NINETEEN II   fig. 150
    1967
    latex and rubber tubing
    3 x 3½ x 3½", cords 22–40"
    There are 4 of these test pieces; "Repetition Nineteen II"
    does not exist.
    Collections: Dr. and Mrs. Aaron Esman, New York
                  Private collection, New York (included in No. 62)
                  Fourcade, Droll, Inc., New York, 2 units

62. UNTITLED   fig. 132
    1967
    latex test pieces in glass and metal case
    14⅝ x 10¼ x 10¼"
    Private collection, New York

63. UNTITLED   fig. 177
    1967
    rubberized cheesecloth
    4 units, each 7 x 6 x 2"
    Collection Grace and Gerald Wapner, Woodstock, New York

64. Model for SCHEMA   fig. 162
    1967
    latex
    9½ x 9½"; 9 hemispheres, each 2½" diameter
    Private collection, New York

65. SCHEMA   fig. 157
    1967
    latex
    42 x 42", 144 hemispheres, each 2½" diameter
    Fourcade, Droll, Inc., New York

66. SEQUEL   fig. 158
    1967
    latex
    30 x 32", 92 spheres, each 2½" diameter
    Fourcade, Droll, Inc., New York

67. SANS I   fig. 163
    1967–1968
    latex and metal grommets
    6' x 7" x 1"
    Collection Mrs. Sidney Gerber, Seattle
    No longer exists.

68. STRATUM   fig. 164
    1967–1968
    latex (white), string, metal grommets
    42 x 42"
    Collection Mrs. Sidney Gerber, Seattle
    No longer exists.

69. Test pieces for REPETITION NINETEEN II   fig. 151
     1967–1968
     latex and rubber tubing
     4 units, very irregular, 5½–8″ x 10¼–11″, cords 18–62″
     Collections: Dr. and Mrs. Aaron Esman, New York, 1 unit
                  Fourcade, Droll, Inc., New York, 3 units

70. ACCESSION II   fig. 143, detail fig. 142
     1967–1968
     galvanized steel, plastic tubing
     30¾ x 30¾″ x 30¾″
     Collection The Aldrich Museum of Contemporary Art, Ridgefield, Connecticut

71. ACCESSION III   see fig. 177
     1968
     fiberglass and plastic tubing
     30″ x 30″ x 30″
     Collection Dr. Peter Ludwig, Wallraf-Richartz-Museum, Cologne

72. ACCESSION IV
     1968
     galvanized steel and rubber tubing
     8 x 8 x 8½″
     Collection Ethelyn and Lester Honig, New York

73. ACCESSION V   fig. 146
     1968
     galvanized steel and rubber tubing
     10 x 10 x 10″
     Private collection, New York

74. REPETITION NINETEEN III   fig. 153
     1968
     fiberglass
     19 units, each 19–20″ x 11–12¾″ diameter
     Collection The Museum of Modern Art, New York
     Gift of Anita and Charles Blatt

75. SANS II   fig. 176, 178
     1968
     fiberglass
     5 units, each 38 x 86 x 6⅛″
     entire piece 38 x 258 x 6⅛″
     Collections: Whitney Museum of American Art, New York, 2 units,
                  Gift of the Albert List Family and Dr. and Mrs. Lester J. Honig
                  Dr. and Mrs. Norman Messite, New York, 1 unit
                  Jared Sable, Toronto, 1 unit
                  Mr. and Mrs. Burt Amel, New York, 1 unit

76. UNTITLED   fig. 170
     1968
     rubberized cheesecloth with plastic clothespin added
     by artist for display purposes.
     c. 9 x 30″
     Fourcade, Droll, Inc., New York

77. UNTITLED   fig. 131
1968
test pieces in mixed media in glass and metal case
14⅝ x 10¼ x 10¼"
Collection Mr. and Mrs. Robert Kardon, Marion Station, Pennsylvania

78. UNTITLED   fig. 133
1968
test pieces in mixed media on latex and washers in glass and
metal case
14⅝ x 10¼ x 10¼"
Collection Stephen Antonakos and Naomi Spector, New York

79. AREA   fig. 171
1968
latex on wire mesh, metal wire
20' x 3', 10 sections, each 24 x 36"
Ex-collection Jan Runnquist, Geneva, Switzerland
Fourcade, Droll, Inc., New York

80. SEAM   fig. 172
1968
latex on wire mesh, metal wire
9' x 4'
Kaiser Wilhelm Museum, Krefeld, Germany

81. Model for ACCRETION   fig. 173
1968
painted wooden tubes, plastic tubing
19 tubes, each 20½" long x 1" diameter; 6 tubes have 120" plastic extrusions
Fourcade, Droll, Inc., New York

82. ACCRETION   fig. 175
1968
fiberglass
50 tubes, each 58 x 2½" diameter
Fourcade, Droll, Inc., New York

83. AUGMENT   fig. 179
1968
latex over canvas
19 units, each 78 x 40"
Collection Kaiser Wilhelm Museum, Krefeld, Germany

84. AUGHT   fig. 179
1968
double sheets of latex stuffed with polyethylene sheets, metal grommets
4 units, each 78 x 40"
Fourcade, Droll, Inc., New York

85. Model for AUGMENT   fig. 180
1968
latex on cotton fabric
29 units, each 8½ x 4½ x 2¾"
Collection Stephen Antonakos and Naomi Spector, New York

86. UNTITLED   fig. 168
    1968
    unfired clay on painted cardboard
    13½ x 1¼ x ⅞"
    Collection Ruth Vollmer, New York

87. UNTITLED   fig. 140
    1968
    epoxy paint and string on stuffed canvas
    11 x 13 x 13 x 6"
    Collection Ruth Vollmer, New York

88. UNTITLED (2 pieces) fig. 137
    1968
    string on stuffed canvas
    each 11 x 13 x 13 x 6"
    Fourcade, Droll, Inc., New York
    Same as no. 87 without epoxy paint

89. UNTITLED   fig. 136
    1968–1969
    latex on wire mesh, staples, wire, and rubber bands
    6⅞ x 3½"
    Collection Gioia Timpanelli, New York

90. SANS III   fig. 183
    1969
    latex and metal grommets
    13' x 3" x 1½"
    Fourcade, Droll, Inc., New York

91. CONNECTION   fig. 182
    1969
    fiberglass on wire
    20 units, each 16–65½ x 3"
    Collection Mr. and Mrs. Victor W. Ganz, New York

92. UNTITLED   fig. 181
    1969
    latex over cloth tape and balloon
    7 x 2½ x 2½"
    Published as a multiple in an edition of 100 for Tanglewood
    Press, New York, as part of 7 *Objects/69.*

93. VINCULUM II   fig. 194
    1969
    latex on wire mesh, wire, staples, and string
    3" x 16' (192")
    Fourcade, Droll, Inc., New York

94. VINCULUM I   fig. 195
    1969
    fiberglass, rubber tubing and metal screen
    8'8" x 2', 2 parts, each 104 x 8½"
    Collection Mr. and Mrs. Victor W. Ganz, New York

95. EXPANDED EXPANSION   fig. 196
    1969
    fiberglass and latex on cheesecloth
    10 x 15 x 20', 3 units of 3, 5, and 7 poles each
    Fourcade, Droll, Inc., New York

96. UNTITLED   fig. 197
    1969
    fiberglass on wire
    62' (744") x 1"
    Collection Helmut Klinker, Bochum, Germany

97. TORI   fig. 199
    1969
    fiberglass on wire mesh
    9 units, each 30–47" x 12½–17" x 10¼–15"
    Collection Karalyn and Steven Robinson, Miami, Florida

98. RIGHT AFTER   fig. 208
    1969
    fiberglass over string
    6½ x 15 x 10'
    Collection Milwaukee Art Center, Gift of the Friends

99. Test piece for CONTINGENT   fig. 210
    1969
    rubberized cheesecloth
    12' x 34"
    Collection Stephen Antonakos and Naomi Spector, New York

100. Prototype for one unit of CONTINGENT
     1969
     fiberglass and rubberized cheesecloth
     10' x 36"
     Collection Donna Schneier, New York

101. CONTINGENT   fig. 209 and frontispiece
     1969
     fiberglass and latex on cheesecloth
     8 units, each 114–168" x 36–48"
     The National Gallery of Australia, Canberra

102. UNTITLED   fig. 218
     1969–1970
     latex over rope, wire, and string
     3 units, (1) 12', (2) 10½', (3) 7½'
     Collection Mr. and Mrs. Victor W. Ganz, New York

103. Model for one unit of UNTITLED (no. 104)   fig. 215
     1970
     fiberglass over wire mesh, latex over cloth over wire
     12 x 9 x 4½", cord 78"
     Fourcade, Droll, Inc., New York

104. UNTITLED   fig. 214
     1970
     fiberglass over wire mesh, latex over cloth over wire
     4 units, each 34–42¾″ x 23–34″ x 2–6″
     Collection Mr. and Mrs. Victor W. Ganz, New York

105. Model for UNTITLED (no. 106)   fig. 223
     1970
     plaster over wire and cloth-covered wire
     7 units, each 4¾ x 6¾″, base 5 x 5″
     Collection Mr. and Mrs. Victor W. Ganz, New York

106. UNTITLED   fig. 221
     1970
     fiberglass over polyethylene over aluminum wire
     7 units, each 74–111″ high x 10–16″ circumference
     Collection Mr. and Mrs. Victor W. Ganz, New York

BIBLIOGRAPHY

I. *By the Artist (entries arranged chronologically)*

1. [Letter protesting Mayor Daley], 1968, *Art News,* vol. 76, no. 7, November 1968, p. 29 (Hesse one of several signatories).
2. [Unpublished tape of lecture], Boston Museum School, January 26, 1969.
3. [Statement on *Contingent*], *Art in Process IV,* Finch College Museum of Art, December 1969, n.p.; see also bibl. 95.
4. "Fling, Dribble, and Dip", *Life,* vol. 68, no. 7, February 27, 1970, p. 66.
5. "An Interview with Eva Hesse", *Artforum,* vol. 7, no. 9, May 1970, p. 59–63; by Cindy Nemser; see also bibl. 6.
6. "Eva Hesse: Her Life", *Feminist Art Journal,* vol. 2, no. 1, Winter 1973, p. 13–14; by Cindy Nemser, part 2 of bibl. 5.
7. [Letter to Sol LeWitt], *Sol LeWitt,* Haags Gemeentemuseum, The Hague, July 25–August 30, 1970, p. 27.
8. "Eva Hesse: Last Words", *Artforum,* vol. 11, no. 3, November, 1972, p. 74–76; introduced and edited by Robert Pincus-Witten.

See also bibls. 10, 13, 33, 49, 67, 117.

II. *On the Artist (entries arranged alphabetically by author, or title when no author cited)*

9. Davis, Douglas, "Cockroach or Queen", *Newsweek,* January 15, 1973, p. 73.
10. "Eva Hesse", *Art Press* (Paris), no. 3, March–April, 1973, p. 20–21; includes statements by the artist.
11. "Eva Hesse Dies: Sculptor was 34", *The New York Times,* May 30, 1970, p. 23.
12. Gula, Kasha Linville, "Eva Hesse: No Explanation", *Ms. Magazine,* April 1973, p. 39–42.
13. "It's All Yours", *Seventeen,* September 1954, p. 140–41, 161; includes statements by the artist.
14. Kramer, Hilton, "A Career Cut Short by Death", *The New York Times,* December 17, 1972.
15. Levin, Kim, "Eva Hesse: Notes on New Beginnings", *Art News,* vol. 72, no. 10; February 1973, p. 71–73.
16. Lippard, Lucy R., "Eva Hesse—The Circle", *Art in America,* vol. 59, no. 3, May–June 1971, p. 68–73.
17. Nemser, Cindy, "My Memories of Eva Hesse", *Feminist Art Journal,* vol. 2, no. 1, Winter 1973, p. 12–13.
18. Pincus-Witten, Robert, "Eva Hesse: Post Minimalism Into Sublime", *Artforum,* vol. 10, no. 3, November 1971, p. 32–44.
19. Purnick, Joyce, "A Portrait of the Artist, Tortured and Talented", *The New York Post,* December 13, 1972.
20. Rose, Barbara, "A Special Woman, Her Surprise Art," *Vogue,* March 1973, p. 50.
21. "Sculptures: Eva Hesse", *Aphra,* vol. 3, no. 1, Winter 1972–72, p. 42–45; photographs of work.
22. Shapiro, David, "The Random Forms in Soft Materials and String by the Late Young Innovator Eva Hesse", *Craft Horizons,* February 1973, p. 40–45, 77.

See also reviews of one-woman exhibitions, section III.

III. *One-Woman Exhibitions and Reviews (entries arranged chronologically).*

23. Allan Stone Gallery, New York, *Eva Hesse, Recent Drawings,* opened March 12, 1963. Announcement.
    P(etersen), V(alerie), *Art News,* vol. 62, no. 3, May 1963, p. 19.
24. Kunstverein für die Rheinlande und Westfalen, Kunsthalle, Düsseldorf, *Eva Hesse: Materialbilder und Zeichnungen,* August 6–October 17, 1965. 4 p. checklist, illus.
25. Fischbach Gallery, *Eva Hesse: Chain Polymers,* November 16–December 5, 1968. Announcement.
    L(ast), M(artin), *Art News,* vol. 67, no. 7, November 1968, p. 14.
    Kramer, Hilton, *The New York Times,* November 23, 1968, p. 54.
    "Eva Hesse," *Arts,* Vol. 42, No. 3, November 1968, p. 58.

Perreault, John, "The Materiality of Matter", *The Village Voice*, November 28, 1968, p. 19.

Taped review, WNCN, New York, December 3, 1968.

Frank, Peter, *The Columbia Owl*, December 4, 1968, p. 6.

Mellow, James R., "New York Letter", *Art International*, vol. 8, no. 1, January 1969, p. 53–54.

Wasserman, Emily, *Artforum*, vol. 7, no. 5, January 1969, p. 60.

26. Fischbach Gallery, New York, *Eva Hesse, New Drawings*, April 3–23, 1970. Announcement.

Kramer, Hilton, *The New York Times*, April 18, 1970.

R(osenstein), H(arris), "Review and Previews", *Art News*, vol. 69, no. 4, Summer 1970, p. 62.

27. School of Visual Arts Gallery, New York, *Eva Hesse*, October 4–November 1, 1971; organized by Linda Shearer. Poster announcement.

B(aker), E(lizabeth) C., *Art News*, vol. 70, no. 8, December 1971, p. 16.

Perreault, John, "Art", *The Village Voice*, October 21, 1971, p. 35.

28. The Detroit Institute of Arts, *Eva Hesse*, September 27–November 5, 1972. Brochure with text by organizer Frank Kolbert.

29. Solomon R. Guggenheim Museum, New York, *Eva Hesse: A Memorial Exhibition*, December 7, 1972–February 11, 1973; organized by Linda Shearer. Catalogue (including bibliography); texts by Shearer and Robert Pincus-Witten. Exhibition traveled to: Albright-Knox Art Gallery, Buffalo (March 6–April 22, 1973); Museum of Contemporary Art, Chicago (May 19–July 1, 1973); Pasadena Museum of Modern Art, Pasadena (September 18–November 11, 1973); University Art Museum, Berkeley, California (December 12, 1973–February 3, 1974).

Kramer, Hilton, "Memorial For an Admired Art Talent", *The New York Times*, December 18, 1972; see also bibl. 14.

Genauer, Emily, "Art and the Artist", *The New York Post*, December 16, 1972.

Perreault, John, "Knotted and Split at the Seams", *The Village Voice*, December 21, 1972, p. 31–32.

Hughes, Robert, "Vulnerable Ugliness", *Time*, January 1, 1973, p. 37.

Rose, Barbara, "The Real Thing", *New York Magazine*, January 1, 1973, p. 60.

Trini, Tommaso, "Tregua fra tendenze negli USA," *Corriere della sera* (Milan), January 7, 1973.

Helfer, Judith, "Eva Hesse: wirkungs-und gehaltvolle Retrospektive", *Aufbau*, January 12, 1973, p. 19.

"Szene: Kunstlerinnen", *Der Spiegel*, January 15, 1973.

Picard, Lil, "Aus dem Nachlass der Avantgarde", *Die Welt*, January 25, 1973.

Baker, Elizabeth C., "Eva Hesse", *Saturday Review*, February, 1973, p. 57–58.

Sheridan, Lee, "Eva Hesse: Memorial Exhibition, Art Show of Astonishing Beauty", *Springfield* (Mass.) *Daily News*, February 7, 1973.

Baker, Kenneth, "Memorial Exhibition", *The Christian Science Monitor*, February 16, 1973.

Boice, Bruce, "Reviews", *Artforum*, vol. 12, no. 7, March 1973, p. 89–91.

Crimp, Douglas, "New York Letter," *Art International*, Vol. 17, No. 3, March 1973, pp. 40–42, 69.

Reeves, Jean, "Eva Hesse Sculpture Exhibits Wide Range of Materials", *Buffalo Evening News*, March 6, 1973.

Willig, Nancy Tobin, "Eva Hesse: Cries and Whispers Live in Sculpture", *Buffalo Courier-Express*, March 11, 1973, p. 5.

Schjeldahl, Peter, "Eva Hesse at the Guggenheim", *Art in America*, March–April, 1973, p. 99.

Berenson, Ruth, "Art", *National Review*, May 11, 1973, p. 53.

Danieli, Fidel, "L.A. Art Sight Lines", *Los Angeles Weekly News*, September 28, 1973.

Terbell, Melinda, "Eva Hesse Retrospective", *Artweek*, vol. 4, no. 33, October 6, 1973, p. 1, 16.

Wilson, William, "Eva Hesse's Memorial to a Life of Pain", *The Los Angeles Times* October 7, 1973, p. 52.

Smith, Barbara, "Eva Hesse Retrospective", *Los Angeles Weekly News,* November 2, 1973, p. 24.

Albright, Thomas, "A Moving Experience", *The San Francisco Chronicle,* November 13, 1973.

Shere, Charles, "U.C. Retrospective Explores the Work of Eva Hesse", *The Oakland Tribune,* December 23, 1973.

"Announcement", *Art Week,* vol. 5, no. 2, January 12, 1974, p. 1.

Markell, Jon, "The Tragic Life and Forceful Sculpture of Eva Hesse", *U.C. Berkeley Daily California Arts Magazine,* January 18, 1974.

IV. *Selected General Books and articles (entries arranged alphabetically by author)*

30. Bochner, Mel, "Serial Art, Systems, Solipsism", *Arts,* vol. 41, no. 8, Summer 1967, p. 39–42; reprinted in Gregory Battcock, ed., *Minimal Art,* E. P. Dutton, New York, 1968.

31. Bochner, Mel. "The Serial Attitude," *Artforum,* vol. 6, no. 4, December 1967, p. 28–33.

32. Bonito Oliva, Achille, *El Territorio Magico: Comportamenti alternativi dell'arte,* Centro Di/Edizioni, Florence, 1972, p. 67, 111.

33. Celant, Germano, *Arte Povera,* Gabriele Mazzotta Editore, Milan, 1969, p. 56–60; includes statement by the artist. (Also published as *Art Povera: Earthworks—Impossible Art—Actual Art—Conceptual Art* by Praeger, New York, 1969.)

34. Chandler, John, "Art in the Electric Age", *Art International,* vol. 13, no. 2, February 1969, p. 24.

35. Chandler, John, "Tony Smith and Sol LeWitt; Mutations and Permutations", *Art International,* vol. 12, no. 7, September 1968, p. 16–19.

36. "Conceptual art Arte povera Land art Body art 1966–1969", *Bolaffiarte,* (Turin), vol. 4, no. 31, June–July 1973, p. 74.

37. Davis, Douglas, "The Invisible Woman is Visible", *Newsweek,* November 15, 1971, p. 130–131.

38. Goldin, Amy, "Sweet Mystery of Life", *Art News,* vol. 68, no. 3, May 1969, p. 46–51, 62.

39. Gordon, Leah, "Myths of Sensibility", *Time,* March 20, 1972, p. 72–77.

40. Johnston, Jill, "As Anybody Lay Dying", *The Village Voice,* January 25, 1973, p. 23, 26.

41. Lee, David, "Serial Rights", *Art News,* vol. 66, no. 8, December 1967, p. 42–45, 68.

42. LeWitt, Sol, "Paragraphs on Conceptual Art", *Artforum,* vol. 15, no. 10, Summer 1967, p. 70–83, illus. only.

43. Lippard, Lucy R., *Changing: Essays in Art Criticism,* E.P. Dutton; New York, 1971.

44. Lippard, Lucy R., "Eccentric Abstraction", *Art International,* vol. 10, no. 9, November 20, 1966, p. 28, 34–40; reprinted in bibl. 43.

45. Lippard, Lucy R., "Eros Presumptive", *The Hudson Review,* Spring 1967, p. 91–99; reprinted in Gregory Battcock, ed., *Minimal Art,* E.P. Dutton, New York, 1968.

46. Lippard, Lucy R., *Six Years: The Dematerialization of the Art Object . . . . ,*Praeger, New York, 1973.

47. Lippard, Lucy R. and Chandler, John, "The Dematerialization of Art", *Art International,* vol. 12, no. 2, February 1968, p. 31–32; reprinted in bibl. 43.

48. Monte, James, " 'Making It' With Funk", *Artforum,* vol. 5, no. 10, Summer 1967, p. 56–59.

49. Nemser, Cindy, *Art Talk: Conversations With 12 Women Artists,* Charles Scribner's Sons, New York, 1975. Includes bibls. 5 and 6.

50. Pincus-Witten, Robert, "Rosenquist and Samaras: The Obsessive Image and Post Minimalism", *Artforum,* vol. 11, no. 1, September 1972, p. 64–69.

51. Rose, Barbara, "Problems of Criticism VI: The Politics of Art, Part III", *Artforum,* vol. 7, no. 9, May 1969, p. 46–51.

52. Rosenberg, Harold, "The Art World: Deaestheticization", *The New Yorker,* January 24, 1970, p. 62–67.

53. Smithson, Robert, "Quasi-Infinities and the Waning of Space", *Arts,* vol. 41, no. 1, November 1966, p. 28–31.

54. "The New Season: Mostly Minimal", *The Village Voice,* September 19, 1968, p. 18–19; photographs.

See also bibl. 4 and reviews of group exhibitions.

V. *Selected Group Exhibitions and Reviews (entries arranged chronologically)*

55. The Brooklyn Museum, New York, *21st International Watercolor Biennial*, April 10–May 28, 1961. Catalogue with essay by Hertha Wegener.

55a. Wadsworth Atheneum, Hartford, *Drawings*, 1961; organized by Samuel Wagstaff, dates unknown.

56. John Heller Gallery, New York, *Drawings: Three Young Americans*, April 11–May 2, 1961. Illustrated brochure.

    J(udd), D(onald), *Arts,* vol. 35, no. 7, April 1961, p. 60.

    R(oskill), M(ark), *Art News,* vol. 60, no. 2, p. 64.

    O'Doherty, Brian, *The New York Times,* April 18, 1961, p. 34.

57. Amel Gallery, New York, *First Showing of Gallery Group,* December 19, 1963–January 6, 1964. Announcement.

58. Park Place Gallery, New York, *Invitational Show,* opened March 16, 1964. Poster announcement.

59. Kunstverein für die Rheinlande und Westfalen, Kunsthalle, Düsseldorf, [Christmas drawing exhibition], November–December, 1964.

59a. Home of Isabel and F. Arnhard Scheidt, Kettwig am Ruhr, *Tom Doyle and Eva Hesse,* May 15, 1965. Invitation.

60. Graham Gallery, New York, *Abstract Inflationism and Stuffed Expressionism,* March 1–26, 1966; organized by Joan Washburn. Illustrated brochure.

    Gruen, John, "Art: Young Americans", *New York Herald Tribune,* (New York Magazine Section), March 13, 1966, p. 32.

    Lippard, Lucy R., "An Impure Situation", *Art International,* vol. 10, no. 5, May 1966, p. 60–65.

    Pincus-Witten, Robert, *Artforum,* vol. 4, no. 9, May 1966, p. 54.

61. Fischbach Gallery, New York, *Eccentric Abstraction,* September 20–October 8, 1966; organized and text by Lucy R. Lippard (not same as bibl. 44).

    Glueck, Grace, "New York Gallery Notes: ABC to Erotic", *Art In America,* vol. 54, no. 5, September–October, 1966, p. 105–108.

    Kramer, Hilton, "It's Art, But Does It Matter?" *The New York Times,* September 25, 1966. Section 2, p. 27, 29.

    Antin, David, "Another Category: 'Eccentric Abstraction' ", *Artforum,* vol. 5, no. 3, November 1966, p. 56–57.

    B(ochner), M(el), *Arts,* vol. 41, no. 1, November 1966, p. 57–58.

62. Riverside Museum, New York, *30th Annual Exhibition: 'Yesterday and Today' 1936–1966,* American Abstract Artists, September 25–November 27, 1966. Announcement.

63. School of Visual Arts Gallery, New York, *Working Drawings and Other Visible Things on Paper Not Necessarily Meant to be Viewed as Art,* December 2–23, 1966; organized by Mel Bochner. Poster announcement.

64. Ithaca College Museum of Art, Ithaca, New York, *Drawings 1967,* January 17–February 25, 1967; texts by Daniel Gorski and Gretel Leed.

65. The Weatherspoon Gallery, University of North Carolina, Greensboro, *Art on Paper Invitational 1967,* October 15–November 22, 1967; organized by Gilbert H. Carpenter. Catalogue.

66. The Lannis Museum of Normal Art, New York, *Normal Art,* opened November 12, 1967; organized by Joseph Kosuth. Announcement.

67. Finch College Museum of Art, Contemporary Wing, New York, *Art In Series,* November 22, 1967–January 6, 1968. Exhibition organized by Elayne H. Varian with Mel Bochner. Acoustiguide recording by participating artists including Eva Hesse.

    Willard, Charlotte, "Primary Forms", *The New York Post,* December 9, 1967, p. 46.

    Perreault, John, "Repeating Absurdity", *The Village Voice,* December 14, 1967, p. 18. See also bibls. 30, 31, 41.

68. The New York State Fair, Syracuse, *Art Today 1967,* August 29–September 4, 1967; organized in cooperation with the New York State Council on the Arts.

69. Moore College of Art, Philadelphia, *American Drawings, 1968,* January 13–February 16, 1968; selected by Richard Anuskiewicz, Brian O'Doherty, Stephen Prokopoff. Poster announcement.

70. Galerie Rickc, Cologne, *Programm I,* May 29–September 15, 1968. Announcement.

71. Milwaukee Art Center, Milwaukee, *Directions 1: Options,* June–August 18, 1968. Catalogue with essay by Lawrence Alloway; traveled to the Museum of Contemporary Art, Chicago, September 14–October 20, 1968.

72. John Gibson Gallery, Projects for Commissions, New York, *Anti-Form,* October 5–November 7, 1968. Announcement.

73. Kunsthalle, Cologne, *Kunstmarkt 1968,* October 15–20, 1968. Poster announcement.

74. American Federation of Arts, *Soft and Apparently Soft Sculpture,* October 6, 1968–October 12, 1969; circulating exhibition organized by Lucy R. Lippard. Description in A.F.A. catalogue.

75. Flint Institute of Arts, Flint, Michigan, *Made of Plastic,* October 18–December 1, 1968; catalogue forward by G. Stuart Hodge.

76. Whitney Museum of American Art, New York, *Annual Exhibition,* December 17, 1968–February 9, 1969; organized by Robert Doty and John Gordon. Catalogue.
      Perreault, John, "Illusions of Reality", *The Village Voice,* December 26, 1968, p. 22–23.
      "Floating Wit," *Time,* January 3, 1969, p. 44.

77. Leo Castelli (Warehouse), New York, *Nine at Leo Castelli,* December 4–28, 1968; organized by Robert Morris. Poster announcement.
      Perreault, John, "Art: A Test", *The Village Voice,* December 19, 1968, p. 19.
      Kozloff, Max, "Nine in a Warehouse", *Artforum,* vol. 7, no. 6, February 1969, pp. 38–42.
      Müller, Gregoire, "Robert Morris Presents Anti-Form", *Arts,* vol. 43, no. 4, February 1969, pp. 29–30.
      Smith, Larry, "Flexible Constructions: Floppy and Wonderful", *The Village Voice,* February 6, 1969, pp. 13, 34, 38.

78. Institute of Contemporary Art, University of Pennsylvania, Philadelphia, *Plastics and New Art,* January 15–February 25, 1969; traveled to the Marion Koogler McNay Art Institute, San Antonio, Texas, March 16–April 13, 1969. Catalogue with essay by Stephan S. Prokopoff.

79. Wilcox Gallery, Swarthmore College, Swarthmore, Pennsylvania, *Hard, Soft, and Plastic,* February 7–March 3, 1969. Announcement.

80. Finch College Museum of Art, New York, *Drawing: Some Recent Trends,* March 1969; organized by the Art History Seminar under the supervision of Diane Kelder and Susi Bloch. Catalogue with paragraph on Hesse by A(nne) R. S(mith).

81. New Jersey State Museum, Trenton, *Soft Art,* March 1–April 27, 1969; organized and catalogue essay by Ralph Pomeroy.
      Pomeroy, Ralph, "Soft Objects: At the New Jersey State Museum", *Arts,* vol. 43, no. 5, March 1969, pp. 46–48.

82. New York Shakespeare Festival Public Theatre, New York, *Art/Peace Event,* March 5–May 4, 1969. Announcement.

83. The Museum of Modern Art, New York, *New Media, New Methods,* March 16, 1969–August 16, 1970; circulating exhibition organized by Kynaston McShine.

84. University Gallery, University of Minnesota, Minneapolis, *The Artist and the Factory,* March 19–April 16, 1969. Catalogue with essay by Charles S. Savage.

85. Galerie Heiner Friedrich, Munich, *Drawings,* March 20–April 14, 1969. Poster Announcement.

86. Kunsthalle, Bern, *When Attitudes Become Form/Works-Concepts-Processes-Situations-Information,* March 22–April 27, 1969; organized by Harald Szeemann. Catalogue with essays by Scott Burton, Gregoire Müller and Tommaso Trini; traveled to Museum Haus Lange, Krefeld, May 10–June 15, 1969 and to the Institute of Contemporary Art, London, September 28–October 27, 1969, where it was revised with a new catalogue by Charles Harrison.

87. Whitney Museum of American Art, New York, *Anti-Illusion: Procedures/Materials,* May 19–July 6, 1969; organized and with catalogue essays by Marcia Tucker and James Monte.
      Perreault, John, "Art", *The Village Voice,* May 29, 1969, p. 16.
      Aach, Herb, "The Materials of Art Versus the Art of Materials", *Craft Horizons,* July–August 1969, p. 37–38.
      Wasserman, Emily, *Artforum,* vol. 8, no. 1, September 1969, p. 56–57.

88. The New Gallery, Cleveland, *Seven Objects,* May 24–June 30, 1969; also shown at Galerie Ricke, Cologne, Summer 1969. Announcement.

89. The Westmoreland County Museum of Art, Greensburg, Pennsylvania, *Recent Trends in American Art,* May 25–July 6, 1969. Checklist.

90. The Aldrich Museum of Contemporary Art, Ridgefield, Connecticut, *Highlights of the 1968–1969 Season,* June 22–September 14, 1969; organized by Dorothy Mayhall. Catalogue with introduction by Larry Aldrich.

91. Seattle Art Museum, Seattle, *557,087,* September 5–October 5, 1969; traveled to Vancouver Art Gallery, Vancouver, as *955,000,* January 13–February 8, 1970; organized by Lucy R. Lippard. Catalogue on loose index cards.

> Plagens, Peter, "557, 087", *Artforum,* vol. 8, no. 3, November, 1969, p. 64–67.

92. Fort Worth Art Museum, *American Drawings,* October 28–December 6, 1969; organized by Peter Plagens and Henry Hopkins. Catalogue with essay by Peter Plagens.

> Plagens, Peter, "The Possibilities of Drawing", *Artforum,* vol. 8, no. 2, October 1969, p. 50–55 (slightly revised version of catalogue essay).

93. The Jewish Museum, New York, *Plastic in Editions,* November 19, 1969–January 4, 1970; organized by Susan Tumarkin Goodman. Checklist.

94. Galerie Ricke, Cologne, *Profile,* December 3, 1969–January 5, 1970.

95. Finch College Museum of Art, Contemporary Wing, New York, *Art in Process IV,* December 11, 1969–January 26, 1970; organized and with catalogue foreword by Elayne H. Varian.

> Müller, Gregoire, "Art in Process IV", *Arts,* vol. 44, no. 3, December/January 1970, p. 54–55.
>
> Leider, Philip, *Artforum,* vol. 8, no. 6, February 1970, p. 70.

96. Heckscher Museum, Huntington, New York, *The Expressive Line,* December 21, 1969–January 25, 1970. Catalogue.

97. Skidmore College, Saratoga Springs, N.Y., *Group,* January 6–30, 1970.

98. Sidney Janis Gallery, New York, *String and Rope,* January 7–31, 1970.

99. Reese Palley Gallery, San Francisco, *Multiples and Graphics,* January 13–31. Poster announcement.

100. Milwaukee Art Center, Milwaukee, *A Plastic Presence,* January 30–March 8, 1970; in coordination with the Jewish Museum, New York, November 19, 1969–January 4, 1970, and the San Francisco Museum of Art, April 24–May 24, 1970. Catalogue with introduction by Tracy Atkinson.

> Müller, Gregoire, *Arts,* vol. 44, no. 2, November 1969, p. 36–37.
>
> Gruen, John, "A Sticky Hodgepodge", *New York Magazine,* November 17, 1969, p. 58.
>
> Perreault, John, "Plastic, Very Present", *The Village Voice,* December 4, 1969, p. 28, 63.
>
> Glueck, Grace, "Art Notes: Building the Plastic Image", *The New York Times,* Section D, December 7, 1969, p. 28.
>
> Pincus-Witten, Robert, *Artforum,* vol. 8, no. 5, January 1970, p. 69.

101. The Emily Lowe Gallery, Hofstra University, Hempstead, New York, *Hanging/ Leaning,* February 2–27, 1970; organized and catalogue introduction by Robert R. Littman.

102. Cooper-Hewitt Museum of Decorative Arts and Design, Smithsonian Institution, New York, *The Drawing Society of New York Regional Exhibition: 1970,* March 9–May 9, 1970; selected by Eila Kokkinen, Marcia Tucker, Diane Waldman, Elaine Dee. Catalogue introduction by James Biddle; essay by Robert Motherwell. Circulated nationally, fall 1970–fall 1971, by the American Federation of Arts.

103. The Art Museum, Princeton University, *American Art Since 1960,* May 5–27, 1970; organized by the graduate students of the Department of Art and Archeology for Professor Sam Hunter's Seminar on Contemporary Art. Announcement.

104. Owens-Corning Fiberglass Center, New York, *Tony Delap/Frank Gallo/ Eva Hesse: Trio,* May 14–September 5, 1970. Traveled to Owens-Corning Fiberglass Center, Detroit, as *Art in Automobile,* October 1970.

> Mellow, James R., "Three Sculptors in a Plastic Mode", *The New York Times,* July 5, 1970, section 2, p. 17.

105. Galerie Ricke, Cologne, *Zeichnungen Amerikanischer Künstler,* May 15–June 25, 1970. Catalogue.

106. Foundation Maeght, St. Paul-de-Vence, France, *L'art vivant aux Etats-Unis*, July 16–September 30, 1970.
107. The Museum of Modern Art, New York, *Recent Acquisitions*, July 31–October 18, 1970. Checklist.
108. Galerie Yvon Lambert, Paris, *American Drawings*, September 1970. Announcement.
109. Institute of Contemporary Art, Boston, *Works Mostly on Paper*, October 20–November 14, 1970. Announcement.
110. Institute of Contemporary Art, University of Pennsylvania, Philadelphia, *Against Order: Chance and Art*, November 14–December 22, 1970. Catalogue with essay by Robert Pincus-Witten.
111. Trinity College Art Gallery, Hartford, Connecticut, *Works in Plastic*, 1970; organized by Mitchell Pappas.
112. Museum of Modern Art, Art Lending Service, New York, *Paperworks*, November 24, 1970–January 10, 1971; organized by Pierre Apraxine. Checklist.
113. Janie C. Lee Gallery, Dallas, *Drawings*, December 1970–January 1971. Announcement.
114. University of Maryland Art Gallery, College Park, *Editions in Plastic*, December 3, 1970–January 23, 1971. Catalogue with introduction by Marchal E. Landgren.
115. Whitney Museum of American Art, New York, *The Permanent Collection—Women Artists*, December 16, 1970–January 19, 1971; organized by Elke Solomon.
116. Paula Cooper Gallery, New York, *Drawings*, December 19, 1970–January 13, 1971. Announcement.
117. *1971 Triennale of India*, New Delhi, January 31–March 31, 1971; organized by Waldo Rasmussen, International Council of the Museum of Modern Art, New York. Brochure includes statement.
118. Finch College Museum of Art, Contemporary Wing, New York, *Projected Art: Artists at Work*, March 13–May 2, 1971; organized by Elayne H. Varian. Checklist.
119. Katonah Gallery, Katonah, New York, *Materials and Methods: A New View*, March 21–May 2, 1971. Catalogue with essay by Robert Pincus-Witten.
120. The Corcoran Gallery of Art, Washington D.C., *Depth and Presence*, May 3–30, 1971. Catalogue introduction by Stephen S. Prokopoff.
121. Museum of Modern Art, Art Lending Service, New York, *Summer Show*, July 8–September 30, 1971. Checklist.
122. M. Knoedler & Co., New York, *Selections of Work by Gallery Artists*, September 14–October 15, 1971. Announcement.
123. The Aldrich Museum of Contemporary Art, Ridgefield, Connecticut, *Sculpture and Shapes of the Last Decade*, October 3–December 12, 1971.
124. Museum of Contemporary Art, Chicago, *Six Sculptors: Extended Structures*, October 30–December 12, 1971. Catalogue with introduction by Stephen S. Prokopoff.
125. Bykert Gallery, New York, *Drawings and Prints*, November 6–December 2, 1971. Announcement.
126. School of the Museum of Fine Arts, Boston, *Changing Terms*, December 3, 1971–January 14, 1971. Catalogue.
127. Institute of Contemporary Art, University of Pennsylvania, *Grids*, January 26–March 1, 1971. Catalogue with essay by Lucy R. Lippard; Organized by Suzanne Delehanty.
128. Salem Fine Arts Center, Winston-Salem, North Carolina, *Women*, February 27–March 19, 1972; organized in conjunction with the North Carolina Museum of Art, Raleigh, March 25–April 20, 1972. Catalogue with introduction by M. Brawley Hill.
129. Kunsthaus, Hamburg, *American Woman Artist Show*, April 14–May 14, 1972. Catalogue with essays by Lil Picard and Sibylle Niester.
130. The High Museum of Art, Atlanta, *The Modern Image*, April 15–June 11.
131. Philadelphia Museum of Art, *Friends Purchase Party*, opened April 20, 1972; organized by Anne d'Harnoncourt.
132. The Art Institute of Chicago, Chicago, *Seventieth American Exhibition*, June 24–August 21, 1972.
    Canaday, John, "Win, Draw, or Lose at Chicago's All-American Show" *The New York Times*, June 25, 1972, p. 19.

133. Museum Fridericianum and Neue Galerie, Kassel, *Documenta 5,* June 30–October 8, 1972. Catalogue with essay on Hesse by Lucy R. Lippard, p. 16, 143–144.
    Borden, Lizzie, "Cosmologies", *Artforum,* vol. XI, no. 2, October 1972, p. 35–40.
134. The New York Cultural Center, *3D Into 2D: Drawing for Sculpture,* January 18–March 10, 1973; organized and catalogue introduction by Susan Ginsburg; traveled to Vancouver Art Gallery, Vancouver; National Gallery of Canada, Ottawa; Allen Memorial Art Museum, Oberlin College, Oberlin, Ohio; University Art Museum, University of California, Santa Barbara; University Art Museum, University of California, Berkeley.
    Borden, Lizzie, "3D Into 2D", *Artforum,* Vol. XI, No. 8, April 1973, p. 74.
135. The Whitney Museum of American Art, New York, *American Drawings: 1963–1973,* May 25–July 22, 1973; organized and catalogue introduction by Elke M. Solomon.
    Borden, Lizzie, "Art Economics and the Whitney Drawing Show", *Artforum,* Vol. XII, No. 2, October 1973, p. 87.
136. Seattle Art Museum Pavilion, Seattle, *American Art: Third Quarter Century,* August 22–October 14, 1973; organized by Jan van der Marck. Catalogue.

INDEX TO THE TEXT

PHOTO CREDITS

DUE